Marta Benenti
Expressiveness

Epistemic Studies

Philosophy of Science, Cognition and Mind

Edited by
Michael Esfeld, Stephan Hartmann and Albert Newen

Editorial Advisory Board:
Katalin Balog, Claus Beisbart, Craig Callender, Tim Crane, Katja Crone,
Ophelia Deroy, Mauro Dorato, Alison Fernandes, Jens Harbecke,
Vera Hoffmann-Kolss, Max Kistler, Beate Krickel, Anna Marmodoro, Alyssa Ney,
Hans Rott, Wolfgang Spohn and Gottfried Vosgerau

Volume 45

Marta Benenti
Expressiveness

Perception and Emotions in the Experience
of Expressive Objects

DE GRUYTER

ISBN 978-3-11-099675-3
e-ISBN (PDF) 978-3-11-067001-1
e-ISBN (EPUB) 978-3-11-067014-1
ISSN 2512-5168

Library of Congress Control Number: 2020941662

Bibliographic information published by the Deutsche Nationalbibliothek
The Deutsche Nationalbibliothek lists this publication in the Deutsche Nationalbibliografie;
detailed bibliographic data are available in the Internet at http://dnb.dnb.de.

© 2022 Walter de Gruyter GmbH, Berlin/Boston
This volume is text- and page-identical with the hardback published in 2020.
Typesetting: Integra Software Services Pvt. Ltd.
Printing and binding: CPI books GmbH, Leck

www.degruyter.com

Acknowledgments

The core of this work is the result of my Ph.D. training at the North West Philosophy Consortium (F.I.N.O.), to which I would like to express my sincere gratitude. I am particularly grateful to the members of the philosophy departments of the University of Turin, the University of Eastern Piedmont, the University of Genoa and the University of Pavia for their stimulating activities and for their tireless efforts that make this doctoral program possible.

I am personally thankful to Alberto Voltolini and Cristina Meini for their unceasing support and thoughtful feedback on my work. And I owe my heartfelt gratitude to Paolo Spinicci, whose encouraging support never faded in the last ten years.

I had the opportunity to conduct my research at many philosophy and psychology departments and research centres in Europe, and I would like to thank all those scholars with whom I fruitfully discussed my ideas, especially Fiona Macpherson, Albert Newen, Bence Nanay, and Joerg Fingerhut, who supervised my work abroad.

Conversations with Lisa Giombini, Matteo Ravasio and Alessandro Bertinetto challenged my views on music in particular and on aesthetics in general, while Giovanna Fazzuoli's analytic approach to contemporary art challenged my views on painting. Needless to say, all faults and *naïvetés* still present in my reasoning are mine.

Turning this research into a proper book would have not been possible without the support of the Italian Academy for Advanced Studies in America at Columbia University, whose members, fellows and staff provided me with the perfect environment to cast doubts on most of my writing. Many thanks shall go, finally, to my extremely patient editors Aaron Sanborn-Overby and James Martin for their meticulous work.

The Italian section of *Doctors Without Borders* is the addressee of my deep gratitude as well. The people that I was lucky enough to know there showed me a meaningful way of being in this world that I shall always keep in mind.

Staying human is not always easy in academia, so I need to thank all those people who remind me of this priority on a daily basis: my colleagues, friends, family, and Tommaso. But I am particularly grateful to Marta Caravà, Cristina Nencha, Fabiana Ambrosi, Giovanna Fazzuoli, Camilla Parisi, Lisa Giombini, Martina Rosola, Anna Ichino and Özden Merçan, who struggle everyday as young women researchers to make this a gentler place.

Contents

Acknowledgments —— V

Introduction —— 1

Chapter 1
Theories of Expressiveness: Some Desiderata and an Overview —— 7
1.1 The Apparent Paradox of Expressive Objects —— 7
1.2 The "Pathetic Fallacy" and Expressiveness as Illusion —— 9
1.3 Expression and Expressiveness —— 16
1.4 Desiderata for a Theory of Expressiveness —— 20
1.5 Projectivism: Sartre and Wollheim —— 23
1.6 Arousalism: Matravers, Ridley, and Robinson on Art and Emotions —— 31
1.7 Resemblances and the Contour Theory: Kivy and Davies —— 38
1.8 Imaginative Theories: Levinson and Noordhof —— 44

Chapter 2
The Phenomenology of Expressive Experience —— 55
2.1 Some Agreement: The Perceptual Character of Expressive Experience —— 55
2.2 Some Ambiguity: The Imaginative Character of Expressive Experience —— 58
2.3 Some Disagreement: The Affective Load of Expressive Experience —— 62
2.3.1 The Phenomenal Character of Felt Emotions —— 67
2.4 The Phenomenal Character of Expressive Experience —— 73
2.4.1 Time —— 74
2.4.2 Movement —— 76
2.4.3 Expressive Experience of Simple and Complex Features —— 81

Chapter 3
The Content of Expressive Experience —— 85
3.1 The Problem of Content —— 85
3.2 Response-Dependence —— 87
3.2.1 Imaginative Responses —— 88
3.2.2 Cognitive and Affective Requirements —— 91
3.3 Causal Triggers —— 95
3.4 The Heresy of the Separable Experience —— 97

3.5   Dealing with the Heresy —— 100
3.5.1   The Weeping Willow —— 101
3.5.2   The Musical Gesture —— 103
3.5.3   The Minor Chord —— 111
3.6   Dynamic Properties —— 112

Chapter 4
Metaphors and Resemblances —— 119
4.1   An Important Distinction —— 119
4.2   Metaphorical Descriptions —— 122
4.3   Metaphorical Use of Concepts in Aesthetic Ascriptions —— 127
4.4   Cognitive Penetration and Expression Recognition —— 132
4.5   Recognitional Expressive Experiences Shaped by Metaphorical Concepts —— 137

Chapter 5
Secondary Meaning and Core Affect —— 141
5.1   What if Resemblances Lack? —— 141
5.2   Cluster-Concepts and Emotions as Patterns —— 144
5.3   Metaphorical, Quasi-Metaphorical, and Secondary Meaning —— 150
5.4   Emotions as Core Affect and Meta-Emotions as Conceptual Recognition —— 156
5.5   Recognitional Experiences of Chords and Colours —— 162
5.6   Expressive Experience Without Concepts? —— 167

Conclusions —— 171

References —— 173

Index —— 185

Introduction

When we talk about *expressiveness*, we refer to a number of phenomena and experiences. People can be expressive; gestures can be expressive; words and speeches, as well as paintings, statues, faces; but poems, songs, and pieces of music can also be expressive. So what does expressiveness consist in? What do the listed items have in common that makes them expressive? Do we talk about the same properties when we refer to the expressiveness of an artwork and the expressiveness of a human face? Moreover, all these things can be expressive of emotions, intentions, and even concepts. Does expressiveness amount to the same phenomenon in all these cases?

There is no need to bring up philosophy in order to realise how common and widespread expressive attributions are, both in everyday speech and experience, and in the artistic and aesthetic field. It is therefore not surprising that the philosophical interest in expressiveness is far from recent. Moreover, it arose in very different philosophical traditions and in relation to several disciplines, from psychology to musicology, to art history, art criticism and artistic practices.

This volume focuses in particular on the expressiveness of inanimate objects. How is it possible that we hear music or see paintings as expressive of affective states? How is it that this experience extends to that of natural landscapes, atmospheres, and even of simple colours, sounds, shapes? These questions have not been addressed systematically so far. There exists a long tradition of research about musical expressiveness that, however, tends to neglect visual experiences. Furthermore, many philosophers have dealt with the problem of expression in the arts, that is, the possibility that affective states are expressed *through* or *by means of* artworks. Yet – as we will see – expressiveness cannot be reduced to expression. Firstly, because not only artworks are expressive and, secondly, because a theoretical but clear distinction can be drawn between something being *the expression* of an emotion (also independently of its appearance) and it being *expressive of* an emotion (therefore characterising its way of appearing). In addition, aesthetic research tends to list expressiveness among the aesthetic properties, but such an aesthetic status does not seem to exhaust the phenomenon of expressiveness.

What is especially intriguing about expressiveness is that it tackles many issues concerning the nature of perception and that of affective experiences. Indeed, questions about the possibility that states such as anxiety, melancholy, sadness, solemnity, liveliness are ascribed to non-sentient beings such as artworks, represents a challenge for theories of perception on the one hand and for theories of emotions on the other. Moreover, most of these questions lie at the crossroads of aesthetics and the philosophy of mind, linking the domains of developmental psychology and cognitive sciences more generally.

In short, the philosophical discussion about expressiveness shows a captivating complexity. It is worth making an effort to clarify it. As often is the case in analytic philosophy, the contemporary debate has inherited arguments and problems already existing in past traditions conveying them in an apparently clearer fashion. For this reason, the main arena of this research is the analytic debate of the last fifty years. However, accounts elaborated within the phenomenological tradition and Gestalt psychology will also play a relevant role.

Taking a snapshot of the history of philosophy, much of what has been written about this topic is actually the result of studies in Gestalt psychology that relate to visual and auditory perception and their application to the arts and aesthetic experience. Besides the classical works by Christian von Ehrenfels, Kurt Koffka, Max Wertheimer, Wolfgang Köhler, and Rudolf Arnheim,[1] I shall mention the studies conducted by Paolo Bozzi and his students,[2] which I will not explicitly refer to – but, whose imprint originally inspired my research and will appear as a watermark in the text.[3]

In the aesthetic domain, Wassily Kandinsky (1912) famously put forward a theory of synaesthesia and expression in painting based on the arousal power of colours and shapes, which I will mention only in passing, focusing instead on more recent outcomes of this approach. Theodor Lipps' (1903) work on empathy can instead be taken as a model for projectivist theories of expressiveness that philosophers such as Gregory Currie and Kendall Walton recently reconsidered. Moreover, another stream of research that I will not address, but that bears relevant connections to the topic of expressiveness is James J. Gibson theory of affordances.[4]

As to the variety of styles and disciplines in which the phenomenon of expressiveness has been discussed, further areas of inquiry that deserve to be mentioned include studies on physiognomy and atmospheres, whose origins trace back to Georg Simmel's notion of *stimmung*.[5] A phenomenological approach to atmospheres understood as affective qualities of environments and

---

[1] In particular, references to this topic can be found in Von Ehrenfels (1890), Koffka (1935), Köhler (1938). Arnheim's work will be directly addressed, especially in Chapter 3.
[2] Bozzi (1990).
[3] I am especially indebted to Parovel (2012) for her in-depth review and insightful analysis of psychological studies about expressiveness and Gestalt psychology.
[4] Gibson (1979).
[5] Simmel (1913).

situations has been developed above all by German philosophers Gernot Böhme and Hermann Schmitz,[6] and the Italian philosopher Tonino Griffero.[7]

Importantly, the present volume does not intend to exhaust the debate about expressiveness, neither from a historical nor from a conceptual point of view. Its goal is far more limited and is two-fold. Firstly, it consists in the clarification of one of the fundamental issues concerning expressiveness, namely the *experience* one can have of this phenomenon. Secondly, it aims at introducing an account of expressiveness that strives to avoid some of the problems of the already existing theories. As to the first purpose, it can be condensed in the question: what does the *experience* of expressive inanimate objects amount to? As I will show, several attempts have been made to reply to this question. However, they entail numerous misunderstandings about – among other things – the kind of experience that is at stake; how (and whether) to distinguish its "content" from its "phenomenal character"; which cognitive functions are involved in such an experience, and precisely what role is played by emotions. As to the second purpose, I will put forward a proposal that tries to preserve many of the central claims derived from previous theories. Bearing in mind their weaknesses, my proposal will draw together these key insights into a reassessment of what I will be calling *expressive experience*.

Here is, in a nutshell, what the reader will encounter in this book. In order to pave the way for a thorough discussion, the first chapter introduces, describes, and highlights the main claims of some of the paradigmatic accounts of expressive experience. The problem of expressiveness is unpacked as a contradiction that most philosophical theories assume more or less explicitly: the capacity of objects to express emotions contradicts their inability to feel emotions. One of the outcomes of such an assumption are theories of so-called "pathetic fallacy" according to which expressive experience is but an illusion. As a preliminary step, I introduce the distinction between *expression* and expressiveness. Whereas the former (technical) term refers to the manifestation of emotions, the latter points to those perceptual features whose relation to emotions (in a way that every theory struggles to clarify) does not require that any emotion is actually felt by anyone. The distinction was formerly drawn by Alan Tormey (1971) and formally has been taken on by most theorists, but it often goes neglected. The assumption – whether overt or covert – that dealing with expressive experience

---

6 E.g. Böhme (1995); Schmitz (2014).
7 Griffero (2010) and (2013). I would like to take the opportunity to thank Tonino Griffero for the numerous chances he gave me to discuss both his work and my own. His phenomenological and metaphysical approach to atmospheres represented a continuous challenge to my views, forcing me to avoid generalisations and to enlarge my perspective.

consists in dealing with a somehow contradictory phenomenon attests that, in many cases, this distinction is not fully understood. By acknowledging this assumption, I reassess the contradiction of expressive experience and insist that the experience of expressiveness should be accounted for as a perceptual experience of properties that – despite being connected with emotions broadly conceived, and in a way that deserves convincing explanations – do not bear a necessary relation to actually felt emotions.

Following this preliminary discussion, the focus shifts to the *desiderata* that a satisfactory theory of expressive experience should fulfil. With the aim of providing a conceptual grid to navigate the available views on the matter, I assume that a theory of expressive experience should account for (i) its phenomenal character, (ii) its representational content, (iii) its relation to emotions and (iv) its compatibility with empirical results. Once the ground has been prepared, the critical overview can be carried out. To begin with, Sartre's projectivist theory of emotions introduces a distinction between felt emotions and what we ascribe to the mere appearance of objects. Following Richard Wollheim, I contend that the fundamental and most mysterious case of expressive experience is the one in which we are not feeling the emotion that we ascribe to the object. The connection between felt emotions and those ascribed to objects is instead emphasised by so-called *arousalism*. Despite acknowledging that expressive experience is phenomenally perceptual, supporters of arousalism explain this phenomenon on the basis of the capacity of music to elicit emotions and feelings. After discussing some of the problems of this approach, Contour theory is introduced as a view that better accounts for the mentioned distinction between expression and expressiveness. Although, upon closer scrutiny, contour theory also presents problematic aspects, I endorse its perceptualist approach as the one that most adequately captures the perceptual nature of expressive experience.

The overview section is completed by those philosophers who consider imagination responsible for expressive experience. Their theories share a fundamental concern: they deny that expressive properties are worldly features. Rather, they consider expressive properties as depending on the imaginative response of subjects.

The second chapter is concerned with the way in which the various theories deal with the listed *desiderata*. I first show that most theories allow for a perceptual phenomenal character of expressive experience, while the crucial disagreement emerges when it comes to assessing the emotional side of this phenomenal character. Once one acknowledges that expressive experience is phenomenally perceptual, the question arises about what role is played by emotions in making this experience *sui generis*. Notably, some arousal theorists claim that felt emotions are part of the phenomenal character, whereas most other theories deny that this is the case. Some clarity on this aspect of expressive experience is provided by studies addressing the phenomenology of emotions. Available explanations of its phenomenal peculiarity appeal to the temporal development of expressive experience, its capacity to elicit bodily movements, and its complexity. I introduce and discuss these options, arguing that none of them is well suited to distinguish expressive experience from other phenomenally perceptual experiences.

The next task is to examine the content of expressive experience. After briefly framing the problem of content within representationalism broadly conceived, the third chapter is meant to clarify the role of response-dependence in accounts of expressive properties. For this purpose, I mainly exploit Paul Noordhof's theory that appeals to sensuous imagination. While trying to do justice to the subtleties of his view, I cast doubts on his scepticism about the possibility that expressive properties are "properties of the world". More specifically, I question the sub-personal simulation mechanism introduced by the theory as well as the implications of a cognitive intervention that seems to be required by such an account. I conclude that this theory ultimately appeals to a causal explanation. Importantly, I do not deny that this move is legitimate, but I suggest that it is not necessary at the explanatory level that concerns the experience's content. This criticism relies on Malcolm Budd's argument regarding the "heresy of the separable experience", which proves to be an extremely helpful tool for the development of an alternative account.

The second half of the third chapter offers a way to escape the heresy. I suggest a distinction between three kinds of expressive experience based on the role played by resemblances. Firstly, there is the case of the *weeping willow*, which is meant to exemplify the perception of something as expressive of emotions in virtue of its being perceived as similar to emotional expressions. Secondly, there is the expressive *musical gesture*. In order to deal with this sort of experience, Christopher Peacocke put forward his account based on metaphors. Although his theory is appealing, it remains vague with regard to the exact role played by the perception of resemblances. For this reason, I investigate plausible ways to complete this account, by examining theories of so-called *seeing-as*. Thirdly and lastly, I examine the case of the *minor chord*. The fact that a minor chord sounds sad is admittedly problematic for theories of expressiveness in general and for contour theory in particular. The problem is that minor chords do not resemble human expressions – the same holding for colours and for very elementary shapes. After arguing against conventionalist solutions, I postpone an examination of a positive account for this case to the last chapter. The rest of the chapter is devoted to examining the sort of properties that might constitute the content of expressive experiences. Adopting a phenomenological perspective and relying on a gestaltic approach, I claim that expressive properties are inherently dynamic, low-level properties whose specificity is well captured by the evocative notion of *rythmos*.

The fourth chapter analyses the relation between the phenomenal character and the content of expressive experience by assessing the role played by concepts. I assume that *experiencing* a property differs from *recognising* it as being such a property. Whereas the former can occur without conceptual interventions, the latter requires the application of concepts. The aim of the chapter is to explain the case of the musical gestures doing justice to Peacocke's claim that it involves concepts. At the same time, I try to preserve the idea that the content of the experience is constituted by low-level dynamic properties. The envisaged solution appeals to weak cognitive penetration.

The fifth and last chapter is an attempt to extend this view to the more mysterious case of the minor chord. In order to clarify the kind of knowledge of emotions that is plausibly required for the self-ascription of affective states, emotions are defined as multi-componential items captured by cluster-concepts. Relying once again on the debate that has developed in aesthetics in recent years, I argue that emotion concepts can modify the phenomenal character of expressive experience if they apply with their secondary meaning. Another pivotal notion is introduced at this stage, that is *core affect*. The hypothesis is that, in the case of expressive experience of simple expressive properties, concepts seem suitable in virtue of those properties sharing the same dimensional space of core affect. Shades of colours and sounds do not *resemble* emotional expression; rather, they are perceived as located along the same vectors that structure core affect, namely arousal (dynamism) and valence (potential pleasantness or harm to the organism's wellbeing). Finally, I suggest and find support in empirical evidence that, being the content of (at least) simple expressive experiences already inherently connected with our emotions in the basic form of core affect, conceptual intervention might not be needed. Although this is still treated as an open issue, it promises to account for the connection between expressiveness and emotions.

Chapter 1
Theories of Expressiveness: Some Desiderata and an Overview

An intuitive way to present expressiveness as a philosophical problem consists in noticing that we consider both animated beings and inanimate objects to be expressive. Our linguistic practices seem to bear witness to this trend, as the same, similar or analogous attributions are used to describe both human beings – or animals – and objects – or arrays of objects. We may contemplate a sad landscape, choose a colour because it is lively, a certain outfit because it is cheerful, find a sunset melancholy, and a piece of music joyful. Our descriptions make use of adjectives that belong to the semantic field of psychological and especially affective states, such as *happy, cheerful, gay, lively, agitated, nervous, sad, melancholy, mournful, quiet, serene, peaceful*, etc., regardless of whether the objects of these attributions are animated or not. Yet most of the time we seem to be aware of the difference between animated and inanimate objects. Thus, philosophy should try to to clarify in which sense both sorts of objects can express psychological and especially affective states.

In § 1.1 the problem of expressive objects will be introduced in terms of a contradiction, that is, in the way in which most of the literature seems to deal with it. § 1.2 serves to present and discuss theories that make such a contradiction particularly evident, to the extent that they consider expressive experience illusory. In § 1.3 the fundamental distinction between expression and expressiveness is drawn, while in § 1.4 the *desiderata* for a theory of expressiveness are listed. Projectivist approaches and arousalism are presented and discussed in § 1.5 and in § 1.6 respectively. In § 1.7, contour theory for musical expressiveness is introduced and extended to visual experiences. Finally, § 1.8 offers a discussion of imagination-based approaches to expressive experience.

1.1 The Apparent Paradox of Expressive Objects

Historically, as well as in most of the contemporary literature, the expressiveness of inanimate objects has been regarded as a contradiction. On the one hand, indeed, emotional expression paradigmatically involves some psychological agent capable of feeling and manifesting affective states. On the other hand, we accept that inanimate objects can not only trigger affective reactions, but also express emotions. This is particularly evident for music, but applies also to visual artworks like paintings and sculptures and to objects that are not necessarily related to arts, such as pieces of furniture, interiors and natural landscapes. Behind this way of conceiving the problem there is an intuition that is worth trying to articulate. Let me call this intuition the Thesis of the Inanimate Objects' Expressiveness and split it into two arguments.

Thesis of the Inanimate Objects' Expressiveness (IOE): Inanimate objects express emotions.

Argument (1):
P1 Emotions are psychological states
P2 Only animate beings possess psychological states
C1 Only animate beings can feel emotions

So far, so good, since P1 and P2 sound as quite uncontroversial premises. In particular, they seem to be consistent both with how emotions are understood in folk psychology and with a more technical notion of "emotion".[8] The conclusion C1 introduces the notion of *feeling* as the way in which emotions are *possessed* by sentient beings: emotions are *felt*, and this is *prima facie* acceptable.

The second part of the argument can be given the following structure:

Argument (2):
C1 Only animate beings can feel emotions
P3 To express an emotion implies that one feels that emotion
C2 Only animate beings can express emotions

Clearly, if one is disposed to accept P3 as a matter of fact, then one will also take C2 to be true. As a consequence, one will deny that inanimate objects can express emotions. So articulated, the intuition that only animate beings can feel emotions leads to the conclusion that, when we describe inanimate objects as being expressive of emotional states, we somehow fall prey to a contradiction. But how can this be the case? Is it plausible that we make a systematic

---

[8] For the moment, let us simply consider "folk conceptions" as intuitive and widespread conceptions of emotions that do not mobilise any specific knowledge of the mind's functioning, while "technical conceptions" as models that are adopted by cognitive scientists and neuroscientists. I will directly deal with the distinction between folk and technical conceptions of emotions in the last chapter. Moreover, I will discuss phenomenological aspects of emotions in Chapter 2, section 2.4. Most of the authors that are called into question in the present and next chapters do not endorse any specific theory of emotions (an important exception is Robinson 2005). Therefore, it seems fair to treat their theories as relying on a folk notion.

error in describing objects like this? Are we aware of this gross mistake when we commit it? Although IOE proceeds smoothly, there is something counterintuitive about its outcome, the oddity plausibly residing in P3. Can we assume as a platitude that to express an emotion implies that one feels it? A first step towards the clarification of this oddity calls into question a rather old-fashioned theory, which explicitly addresses the phenomenon of expressiveness as the result of a fallacy.

1.2 The "Pathetic Fallacy" and Expressiveness as Illusion

The history of the term "pathetic fallacy" dates back to John Ruskin's vast treatise *Modern Painters* (1843–1860), and has been endorsed and developed by George Santayana in the early twentieth century. *Modern Painters* is a milestone in art criticism, aiming to prove the superiority of William Turner's painting to all previous landscape painters. Yet, despite Ruskin's endeavour (lasting for seventeen years and culminating in a five-volume work), which strenuously argues for a renewal of art criticism, it cannot be said that his theory of expressiveness is philosophically compelling. It is nonetheless worth introducing as it provides a well-defined target for our discussion.

According to Ruskin, when people – artists and especially poets – apply psychological traits to objects such as landscapes or inanimate pieces of nature, they are making *erroneous evaluations* and producing *wrong judgements*. As the adoption of the word "fallacy" suggests, Ruskin believes that the experience of something as expressive, and the subsequent attribution of an affective character, is just a mistake. And such a mistake is explained by the fact that the subject of the experience (and utterer of the judgement) is under the influence of an emotion. In the light of this risk, artists should be well aware of the difference "between the ordinary, proper and true appearances of things to us; and the extraordinary, or false appearances, when we are under the influence of emotion" (Ruskin 1843, p. 147). In the latter case, that is, when emotions interfere with a clear apprehension of the world, appearances are deceptive and artists who engage in a creative work ought to carefully avoid such an illusion.

According to Ruskin's normative view, being so influenced by affective states has negative aesthetic implications. Faithful to his overall perspective that art must perform an accurate documentation of nature, he argues that the artist who does not keep his or her eyes "firmly on the pure fact" and instead "views all the universe in a new light through his tears" fails to provide an aesthetically valuable work (Ruskin 1843, p. 152–153). An expressive world is a misleading world, distorted by overwhelming, irrational affects. So conceived, theorizing the pathetic fallacy can be understood as a first attempt to solve the contradiction of expressiveness that results from IOE: as stated by P3, only animate beings can express emotions, hence expressive inanimate objects are the result of a misattribution.

In *The Life of Reason* (2011 [1905]), philosopher George Santayana puts forward an analogous solution to the same problem, claiming that attributions of affective qualities to objects – what he defines "tertiary qualities" – result from an uncritical, chaotic attitude towards the world, typical of primitive societies, infants, magicians, lovers, and poets. Underdeveloped, naïve mentalities as well as attitudes that are not responsive to reasons tend to be victims of the pathetic fallacy. In Santayana's words: "The pathetic fallacy is [...] what originally peoples the imagined world" (Santayana 2011, p. 91). The evolution and development of human societies emerged in such a way so as to move beyond this irrational attitude in favour of a progressive introduction of critical thinking. Traces of this ancient, illusory attitude can still be found in dead metaphors and in fairy tales. As he writes: "A complete illusion this sense remains in mythology, in animism, in the poetic forms of love and religion" (Santayana 2011, p. 91).[9] Accordingly, our ancestors – as well as we ourselves as infants or in the grip of love – were capable of experiencing the world as expressive, whilst nowadays we have mostly lost this capacity. For this reason, Santayana deems the pathetic fallacy as being "normal yet ordinarily fallacious", say, something inherently part of the human way of experiencing the world that nevertheless should be – and actually has been – defeated by *true* descriptions of the world. Analogously to Ruskin, Santayana believes that the pathetic fallacy is to be avoided by artists and that also poets "will soon prefer to describe nature in natural terms and to represent human emotions in their pathetic humility" (Santayana 2011, p. 91).

So, even though he maintains that attributions of psychological traits to objects is a response to a natural attitude of human ontogenetic and phylogenetic evolution, Santayana considers the corresponding experience as *deceptive*, explicable on the basis of a lack of rationality. When experiences are not under the guidance of reason, we are doomed to face a misleading reality and to produce ultimately mistaken judgements about it. Once more, the contradiction is resolved by maintaining that inanimate objects do not *actually* express emotions.

---

[9] Interestingly, Santayana believes that sciences can also commit pathetic fallacies by transposing in nature what actually belongs to human behaviours and feelings. With regard to the scientific notion of 'force' he observes that it is "a transposed sensation of effort [...] we think of our own pulling, we say the object itself pulls" and then "this intermittent effort is made potential or slumbering in what we call strength or force" (Santayana 2011, p. 89).

1.2 The "Pathetic Fallacy" and Expressiveness as Illusion

In certain conditions and especially when rationality wavers, subjects may be led to experience these objects as expressive. But appearances can be – and in this case *are* – deceiving.[10] Explaining objects' expressiveness in terms of a pathetic fallacy amounts to considering such expressiveness as a case of *illusion*. On this view, the experience of expressive objects consists in the experience of an object looking different from the way it actually is, owing to the affective state of the subject.

If this interpretation of the pathetic fallacy is sound, then a quick glance at the contemporary debate on illusions can be helpful. Even if the definition is controversial, it is standardly maintained that illusion consists in the perception of a (worldly) object paired with a misperception of one or more of its properties. Moreover, beliefs about illusory experiences are such that they prove to be wrong when tested by means of testimony, other tools or senses (Macpherson & Batty 2016). Optical illusions are the most common example. When we are confronted with (1) the Müller-Lyer illusion or (2) the Hering illusion, our experience is such that we form the beliefs that (1) the two horizontal lines have different lengths and that (2) the two vertical lines are curved, respectively. However, the application of a ruler to the figures is sufficient to provide evidence that changes our beliefs, in spite of the configurations remaining unaltered. Namely: we will come to think that (1) the two lines of the Müller-Lyer are of equal length and that (2) the two lines of the Hering illusion are straight and parallel – although their appearance will remain unchanged.

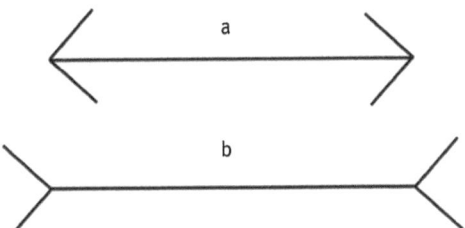

Figure 1: The Müller-Lyer illusion. Reproduced by the author.

---

10 It is worth mentioning that Santayana introduces the pathetic fallacy when accounting for mindreading. Not by chance, the paragraphs devoted to the pathetic fallacy are included in chapter VI of the first volume of his study, which is dedicated to the "discovery of fellow-minds".

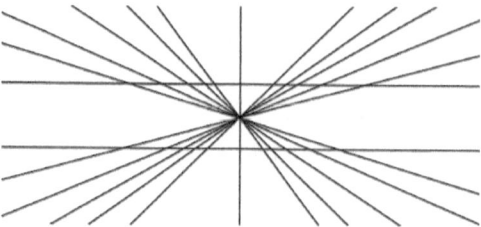

Figure 2: The Hering Illusion. Reproduced by the author.

We may also consider the common example of the stick that looks bent when immersed in water. We see it as bent and form the consistent belief that it must be bent, or broken. But if we take the stick out of the water, we realise that we were wrong in thinking that it was bent: it is actually straight and its bent appearance is determined by some environmental conditions, namely, refraction that occurs in water.

Given these paradigmatic examples, let us ask whether the case of expressive objects could be described in an analogous way. According to those accounts that rely on the pathetic fallacy, we happen to perceive (see or hear) objects – such as certain portions of nature or artworks – as expressive, but this experience is a case of misperception in that we see or hear features that those objects do not actually have. However, such an experience can in principle be corrected using rationality as a tool. Indeed, what both Ruskin and Santayana have in mind is that if one removed the affective condition impairing a correct experience, one would be able to change one's belief about, say, the landscape looking sad or the funeral march sounding sombre. On such a comparison, the adoption of a rational stance in the case of expressive objects parallels the application of a ruler for the case of the Müller-Lyer or the use of touch to test the real shape of the apparently bent stick in the water. So conceived, the analogy between perceptual illusions and the pathetic fallacy holds. Hence, it is worth trying to take this idea one step further.

As already pointed out, illusions are such that we form wrong judgements on the basis of an experience: when we see the Müller-Lyer, we form the belief that "the two segments are of the same length" and when we see the bent stick we form the belief that "it is broken". Consistently, supporters of the pathetic fallacy view argue that we form wrong judgements about nature and artworks as long as we attribute psychological states to them. Therefore, if the analogy were sound, we should say that when we are under the influence of negative feelings and we contemplate a sad landscape, we form the belief that "the landscape is sad". As said, in order for something to be an illusory experience, it must be possible, in principle, to correct our beliefs about it on the basis of further evidence: a measuring ruler applied to the segments of the Müller-Lyer will reveal that "They are of the same length", and the use of touch will reveal that the bent stick "is intact and straight". Thus, according to the analogy, by applying the ruler of rationality (so to speak) to the misleading experience of a sad landscape we obtain the correction of the previous belief: "the landscape is not sad (I was only being deceived by my own emotions)".

Now, a judgement of the kind "the landscape is sad" may be amended in two alternative ways based on the experience we have of the qualities involved, and in one further way based on the belief we form. At least one of these three senses should do justice to the intuition from which the idea of a pathetic fallacy stems: either (a) the landscape is not sad but cheerful, and we just misperceived its expressive quality; or (b) the landscape is not sad but affectively neutral, and we ascribed to it a quality that, by definition, it cannot instantiate, which might be the result of our phantasy or projection; or (c) we wrongly entertain the belief that objects such as a landscape can be literally sad and therefore express such an affective state.

Starting from (a), we interpret the negative sentence "the landscape is not sad" as meaning that "the landscape is, instead, cheerful". In which case, the misleading expressive quality would be replaced by the attribution of the correct expressive quality. The deceptive experience so interpreted would be similar to the case of a person who mistakenly took a wall to be painted in pink instead of white. We would not conclude from this misattribution that the colour pink does not apply to painted walls, but rather that something went wrong with the person's experience – either something in the environmental conditions or in her visual system. Clearly, this interpretation is inconsistent with the notion of pathetic fallacy and the theory it supports. In point of fact, if the experience of a sad landscape and the resulting belief were wrong in this sense, the supporter of the pathetic fallacy would implicitly acknowledge the possibility that a landscape instantiates one of these expressive looks. However, supporters of the pathetic fallacy view reject precisely the possibility that a landscape instantiates *any* expressive features, ruling them out as illusory.

Let us therefore consider (b), namely the interpretation according to which our illusory belief that the landscape is sad can be corrected by the belief that the landscape is affectively neutral. When Ruskin and Santayana argue that we can – and ought to – correct our expressive experience and subsequent beliefs by getting rid of our emotions, they are claiming that the resulting amended experience is neutral with regard to its affective character. Accordingly, the choice would not be between the landscape being sad or cheerful, but rather between the landscape being sad or devoid of any affective character. Also according to this interpretation, in order to establish whether a landscape is sad or affectively neutral, one has to be able to point at certain features that the landscape is seen as instantiating, taking them as evidence for choosing one of the two alternatives (sad or neutral). But if one allows for the possibility to identify these features, then one allows for the possibility that a landscape instantiates a sad look, whatever the environmental or psychological conditions of the experiencing subject may be. In short, one should be able to say: "Well, now that I am no more in the grip of my sorrow, the landscape does not have that sad look that it used to have when I was depressed", this sentence implying that the landscape used to have a definite appearance at that time. Looking sad, despite being a misleading appearance for a landscape, must amount to some describable features which can be corrected (or even completely wiped out) by a more critical or more "rational" observation. Even in such cases, it seems that the pathetic fallacy view should accept that landscapes described as sad by sensitive poets or within primitive cultures, are *sad-looking*, although this might depend on certain psychological conditions of the beholders. And accepting this point means that one should be able to say something about such a (misleading) sad appearance, in the same way that one is able to say how the stick immersed in the water appears (bent).

If the supporters of the pathetic fallacy view allowed for the possibility of giving such a description, even in its more general terms, they should also accept that there is at least a sense in which an inanimate landscape can *be sad* – namely the sense in which it *looks sad*. However, given that neither Ruskin nor Santayana say how something expressive of an emotion should look in order to deceive us, it seems that the burden of the illusion is entirely on the wrong judgement that follows from this illusory experience. In other words, the error that characterises the attribution of affective qualities to objects lies at the level of the belief one forms, rather than in the experience it is supposed to stem from.

Let us now focus on (c), according to which the phrase "the landscape is not sad" amounts to saying that "a landscape cannot be literally sad". If the pathetic fallacy view cannot allow for the possibility that *being sad* refers to the appearance of the landscape, then it must refer to some further property, namely the psychological state of sadness that in principle, within the framework of a non-animistic thought, landscapes cannot entertain. On this interpretation, the belief that "the landscape is sad" is wrong, as long as it is taken to mean that "the landscape possesses the affective state of sadness". Thus, the deceptive character of expressive qualities of objects consists in the idea that we form a belief that cannot be true by definition. The subsequent negation of this belief would then be that "the landscape does not possess the affective state of sadness". As the supporters of the pathetic fallacy do not say how a landscape should look in order to be mistakenly experienced as sad, they must be saying that, rather than undergoing a misleading perceptual experience, we produce a misguided belief. So, when we see a landscape and judge that it is sad, we are actually experiencing a neutral landscape with its colours, lights, shades and shapes, but given that we are under the influence of our emotions, we erroneously believe that it entertains the emotional state of sadness.

Although this latter interpretation is plausibly the most consistent with the basic intuition of the pathetic fallacy, it is questionable at least in one important respect. Needless to say, we undergo all sorts of delusional experiences involving perceptions and emotions and produce related misjudgements. However, when this happens, one of the consequences is that we behave in accordance with what we believe to be the case. To stick to mere perception, the well-known Looney Tunes character Wile E. Coyote is famous for crashing into fake scenery artfully painted on mountain faces by the Road Runner. Or, to extend to illusions caused or influenced by emotions, fear of darkness can erroneously lead us to think that a squeak of the door in the next room is produced by someone who is about to assault us, and therefore make us run away. But this general feature of illusions does not seem to apply to experiences of expressive objects. If the belief we form when confronted with a sad landscape were "that it is sad", in the sense that it possesses the affective state of sadness, we would be inclined to behave in accordance with such a belief. However, this does not happen: we usually do not attempt to comfort it, nor do we pity melancholy pieces of music. At best, we can be influenced by the sadness expressed by the landscape or by the piece of music, but in a way that is distinct from our behavioural and affective response to animate beings that we believe to possess and express their sadness.

This remark allows us to introduce the idea that the belief we form about certain objects being sad, melancholy or lively is to be understood in a different way from that of a delusional judgement concerning affective experiences. Namely, our experiences attest that the sort of belief we form when experiencing a sad piece of music or a lugubrious painting, is different from – though somehow related to – the belief that the object in question expresses an emotion as a result of its possessing the corresponding affective state. It seems that, whenever we ascribe affective features to inanimate objects, we do so on the basis of a sensory experience of objects *having a certain look*.

In summary, interpretations (a) and (b) of the pathetic fallacy-based approach show that the belief "the landscape is sad" can be understood as meaning "the landscape looks sad", whereas in interpretation (c) – the one the pathetic fallacy approach is committed to – this translation does not apply. However, taking expressive ascriptions to imply the attribution of psychological affective states does not do justice to our experiences and related behaviours. Explanatory efforts must therefore concentrate on the best way to account for such ascriptions as entailing the attribution of specific appearances to objects.

1.3 Expression and Expressiveness

Once it is acknowledged that attributions of expressiveness to objects are not *ipso facto* attributions of felt affective states, philosophers need to establish a satisfactory link between affective states (emotions, feelings, moods) and the appearances of inanimate things. Historically, the need to distinguish between expressive appearance on one side and emotions on the other has been particularly pressing within the aesthetic debate in analytic philosophy of the Thirties and Forties. In this debate, philosophers were particularly concerned about the possibility that artworks express the affective (or, more broadly, the intentional) states of their creators by, so to speak, embodying them.

In his seminal work *The Concept of Expression*, Alan Tormey questions what he calls the expression theory. According to Tormey's interpretation, expression theory endorsed by John Dewey (1934), Robin George Collingwood (1938), and Curt Ducasse (1944), among others,[11] addressed the problem of how emotions may result in artworks through creative processes – creative processes themselves being a form of expression. Overtly overlooking the specificities of each of their theories, Tormey introduces a synthetic formulation of their approach:

> (E-T) [Expression T] If art object O has expressive quality Q, then there was a prior activity C of the artist A such that in doing C, A expressed his F for X by imparting Q to O (where F is a feeling state and Q is the qualitative analogue of F). (Tormey 1971, p. 103)

In short, Tormey takes the core of expression theory to be that expressive qualities of objects are necessarily the result of the corresponding (intentional, since it is directed to an X) affective state, manifested by the creator in creating that object. On this view, the expression of a feeling or intentional state more generally and the expressive qualities of artworks are necessarily linked.

More recently, Dominic Lopes has re-examined the plausibility of such an account. Let us take the pictorial example he vividly introduces and discusses.

---

[11] Tormey's list include also E.F. Carritt, D.W. Gotshalk, George Santayana, Leo Tolstoy, and Eugene Véron.

He names the view that expressiveness implies the attribution of expression to creators "personalism" and writes:

> If van Gogh's *Wheatfield with Crows* is not expressive, then what is? The sky blazes so blue that it is almost black, while the grain, intensely yellow, pushes vigorously against the horizon. Overhanging this determined, even forced, joy is a flock of crows, expressing foreboding. [...] According to one version of personalism, we are to understand the picture as expressing van Gogh's emotions. [...] He externalizes his emotions by painting a scene expressing them. (Lopes 2005, p. 59)

As Lopes admits, the intuition behind personalism is not preposterous. Indeed, pictures and drawings are often used in clinical settings to diagnose the emotional state of people who have difficulties in articulating their emotions. Similarly, a creator may well expose her feelings and psychological states. Nonetheless, Lopes observes, the states of mind that are involved in creative activities may well conflict with the emotions expressed by the resulting artworks, so that there seems to be no necessary connection between what a work expresses and what a creator feels.

Targeting this same problem, Tormey argues that attributions of expressive qualities to artworks concern the works themselves and cannot, for instance, be denied or supported by references to the emotional state of the artist.

> If it turned out that Mahler had experienced no state of mind remotely resembling despair or resignation during the period of composition of *Das Lied von der Erde*, the expression theorist would be obliged to conclude that we were mistaken in saying that the final movement (*Der Abschied*) of that work was expressive of despair or resignation; and this seems hardly plausible. (Tormey 1971, p. 104–105)

Against the expression theory, Tormey insists that any theory of expressive qualities of artworks must acknowledge that expressive ascriptions are about properties of the objects, rather than properties of their creators (Tormey 1971, p. 104). The most relevant consequence of accepting this point is that judgements about expressive features of artistic objects can be endorsed or falsified only on the basis of their aspect, say, of their perceivable qualities, rather than on the basis of biographical considerations about the affective life of their creators. Tormey is once more very clear on this:

> 'That's a sad piece of music' is countered not by objections such as, 'No, he wasn't' or 'He was just pretending' (referring to the composer), but by remarking 'You haven't listened carefully' or 'You must listen again; there are almost no minor progressions and the tempo is *allegro moderato*'. (Tormey 1971, p. 105)

The explanation that Tormey provides for the confusion at the basis of the expression theory introduces the distinction between expression and expressiveness. He claims that expression theorists wrongly assume that "express" and "being expressive of" an emotion are always synonyms. But if this were the case, then we would think that somebody's expressive face is always expressing some actually felt emotional state, whereas "the equivalence is not guaranteed" (Tormey 1971, p. 107). In point of fact, we use the term "expressive" in relation to facial patterns, in at least three different fashions: firstly, we can use it *intransitively*, i.e. in such a way that the question "expressive of what?" would not be legitimate. In this case, "expressive" only means the particular disposition of a face to display a wide range of facial expressions. Secondly, "expressive" can be followed by the specific emotion that a face may seem to express, such as "expressive of rage", "expressive of joy", in which case it can refer to the way the face looks, without necessarily implying that the expressed emotion is actually felt by the person. Thirdly, the term may be used as a synonym of "to express", so that the statement "her gesture was expressive of anguish" could be translated as "she was expressing her anguish through that gesture". Far from being a merely speculative consideration about common linguistic uses, these remarks grasp an important point of the discussion, namely the fact that expressive qualities of artworks do not bear a necessary relation to actual expressions of felt emotions. And this is both because, especially in the case of artworks, being "expressive" does not automatically mean to express some specific emotion (one can be told to play a piece *espressivo* without expressing any particular emotion), and because being expressive of an emotion does not necessarily imply that one feels that emotion.

In more recent times, this distinction has been taken on by Peter Kivy (1980), who rephrased it in terms of "express" and "being expressive of". According to Kivy, the former label applies to actual expressions caused by affective states, whereas the latter can be predicated both of animated and inanimate objects that display certain perceivable features – namely, expressive features. So, the attempt to vindicate the independence of expressive features of artworks from the emotional life and intentions of their creators results in a clearer notion of expressiveness that may be applied both to artworks and to persons.

Elaborating on this distinction, Jenefer Robinson writes: "[...] although they can go together with marvelous effect, [expression and expressiveness] are related but conceptually distinct phenomena" (Robinson 2007, p. 39). In her view, the term "expression" refers to the external manifestation of an internal state. Therefore, both a face and a painting can be "expressions" insofar as they are means to manifest felt emotions. On this count, artworks *can* be expressions of emotions and there are cases in which it is correct to interpret them in this way (Robinson refers in particular to Romantic painters and composers who explicitly conceived of their works as emotional expressions). Thus: "Expression is fundamentally something that agents or imagined agents (implied artists, narrators or characters) *do* (or are imagined as doing)" (Robinson 2007, p. 21). "Expressiveness", instead, refers to the capacity of behaviours and works of art to convey some affective character to the audience, regardless of their being the outputs of felt emotions. As Tormey had already noticed, there is no necessary link between expressiveness and expression, as long as for something to be expressive does not imply for it to be the expression of some felt emotion. And this is true, according to Robinson, for both human and artistic expressions. In point of fact, she observes, facial and behavioural expressions can be judged to be more or less expressive. Let us think about a very common expression of joy, such as a smile: both a stereotyped smile displayed by an emoticon and the one displayed by a human face do express joy, so they both are *expressions* of joy; but we would probably judge the latter to be *more expressive* than the former. The same could be said about two smiles displayed by two persons: one might be more expressive than the other although they both are expressions of joy.

The same conceptual distinction can be rephrased for the case of inanimate objects and artworks in which, as suggested, the difference between expression and expressiveness is even sharper. Robinson writes:

> *Jingle Bells* is arguably an expression of cheerfulness, but it is not very expressive music: it is monotonous and banal, even annoying. A more expressive piece of cheerful music would be the culmination of Beethoven's *Egmont* with its expressive expression of triumphant joy. Similarly, a piece of music can be sad in a boring mindless inexpressive way (plod plod plod in the base, moan moan moan in the treble) or in a more revealing and expressive way as in Purcell's funeral music for the death of Queen Mary or the Beethoven funeral march from the *Eroica* symphony. (Robinson 2007, p. 32)

One could be sceptical about this distinction being so clear and argue that it may be a matter of degree rather than a conceptual difference. On this perspective, *Jingle Bells* would only express "less joy" than Beethoven's *Egmont*. However, this is not very convincing: in principle, indeed, not all artworks that we know to be the expression of an artist's despair, are necessarily expressive of desperation. On the contrary, an artist can express her anguish by realising finely balanced works that the audience may experience as expressive of peace and serenity. Expressiveness is therefore independent of its being attributable to expressions which, in turn, can be more or less expressive, depending on their recognisable features. Robinson explicitly writes that: "expression is neither necessary nor sufficient for expressiveness" (Robinson 2007, p. 36), as there can be expressions of emotions that are completely inexpressive.

It is now worth recalling *Argument (2)* of IOE:

C1 Only animate beings can feel emotions
P3 To express an emotion implies that one feels that emotion
C2 Only animate beings can express emotions

The aforementioned conceptual distinction between expression and expressiveness questions P3 by means of a conceptual clarification: P3 is true as long as one takes into account only one way in which the verb "to express" can be intended, namely what we have called "expression". But, as seen in Robinson's analysis above, P3 reveals some ambiguity when one focuses on objects and their expressive qualities. Firstly, it is reasonable to think that objects themselves can be ways to express the emotions of their creators, as the expression theory criticised by Tormey maintains. Secondly, there is a way to distinguish between "expression" and "expressiveness" (or, according to Kivy's terminology, between "to express" and "to be expressive of") that challenges the allegedly necessary relation between expression and felt emotions. So, the contradiction may be domesticated through the reformulation of:

P3 To express an emotion implies that one feels that emotion
as:
P3* To express an emotion implies that one feels that emotion, but to be expressive of an emotion does not imply that one feels that emotion.

The consequence of this reconsideration will be that:
C2* Only animated beings can express emotions, but both animate and inanimate beings can be expressive of emotions.

Note that this is just a step towards a more complete reconsideration of the paradoxical approach to the problem of expressiveness. By avoiding the reduction of expressiveness to the actual expression of felt affective states, the paradox of expressive objects ceases to appear paradoxical. When dealing with expressive objects, one should take into account the distinction between various ways to understand the verb "to express". This more nuanced approach helps to refine the concept of expressiveness as something that has to do with the appearance of things and that in principle does not need to be explained by the presence of psychological states.

1.4 Desiderata for a Theory of Expressiveness

While keeping the conceptual distinction between expression and expressiveness firm, philosophers interested in accounting for expressive objects must find a theoretically satisfying balance between various components of this phenomenon. Before introducing and discussing the main positions animating the debate nowadays, it is important to have in mind the requirements that such a theory should fulfil. For reasons that will become clearer below, most existing accounts are interested in explaining what I will hereafter refer to as "expressive experience",[12] that is the experience of objects – natural objects as well as artefacts – as instantiating expressive qualities. The nature of these qualities is accordingly defined on the basis of the sort of experience that mobilises them. Instead of asking "what are expressive qualities (or properties)?", the question "how do we experience expressive qualities (or properties)?" will be the main point of contention in the debate that is about to follow. The desiderata to be satisfied will therefore concern a theory of expressive experience rather than a metaphysical assessment of expressive properties. The relationship between these complementary sides of the phenomenon is beyond the scope of this study.

Most philosophers tend to agree on that expressive experience of objects is oddly two-faced. On the one hand, the experience of expressive objects looks like a perceptual experience, this being attested by our common linguistic appeal to sense modalities: we *see* expressive landscapes and we *hear* expressive music. On the other hand, expressive experience has a peculiarly affective component, as attested in turn by our language games: we see *melancholy* landscapes and hear *cheerful* pieces of music. The puzzle of objects' expressiveness has been treated as a sort of contradiction precisely on the basis of this duplicity. Because affective states are mental states, the fact that objects *look expressive of emotions* must be explained by resorting to felt emotions. However, as we have already said, such an intervention cannot entail the attribution of mental states to objects. Indeed, it must account for the distinction between the expression of actual emotions and the expressiveness that can be recognised in objects without taking it to be the outcome of some actually felt and subsequently expressed emotion. Unlike what is maintained by the pathetic fallacy view, there is no illusion going on, as long as expressive features are experienced as belonging to objects, rather than as the outcome of felt emotional states. Given this premise, four main requirements can be listed that theories of expressive experience must meet.

i. Phenomenal Character or What-it-is-Like

The first requirement for a theory of expressive experience is that it accounts adequately for the corresponding phenomenology, that is, the way it is like for a

---

[12] This term comes from Noordhof (2008). The phrase is patterned after terminology relating to "perceptual experience", "imaginative experience", "emotional experience" and so on. It has been noticed that this term might create some confusion, as it gives the idea that *the way in which the experience is undergone* is expressive rather than being an experience *of* expressive features (I am grateful to Diego Marconi for expressing his perplexity on this point). Nevertheless, the label has the virtue of brevity, so that I will adopt it from now on, taking its meaning to be "whatever experience of expressive features".

subject to experience an inanimate object as being expressive of an emotion. Such an account should in particular cast light on what – if anything – is special about expressive experience if compared to other, paradigmatic experiences, such as perceptual, imaginative or mnemonic ones. The notion of *phenomenal character* has been debated extensively in the philosophy of mind, so – for the sake of generality – the following definition can be adopted: the phenomenal character of an experience is the "distinctive way it is like – from the inside, as it were – to undergo experiences of its type" and therefore amounts to "how the experience presents itself to introspection" (Kriegel 2002, p. 175). As we will see, this task is usually dealt with by philosophers interested in expressiveness by referring both to introspection and to psychological results based on subjective reports.

ii. Content or What the Experience is About
The second requirement that a theory of expressive experience has to meet is an account of what expressive experience *is about* and how the content of the experience relates to the phenomenal character. A satisfactory theory of expressiveness should be able to say what sort of properties – if any – are represented in the content of expressive experience and whether they cause, are determined by or entertain a supervenience relation with the phenomenal properties of expressive experience.

iii. Role of Emotions
A good theory of expressive experience should clearly account for the role played by emotions. As we have already seen, expressive experience is taken to be relevantly connected to emotions, but it must neither be confused in principle with the attribution of mental states, nor with provoked arousal. That is, expressive experience must not be confused with the experience of actual *expression* and should be accounted for as being relatively independent of it (Robinson 2005). However, although the view that we are necessarily aroused when we undergo expressive experiences has been strongly criticised – as will become clearer later on – emotions cannot be jettisoned as merely being contingently related to that experience. Rather, a theory of expressiveness should find a way to account for emotions that does justice both to phenomenology and to the strong intuition that emotions somehow partake in expressive experience.

iv. Empirical results
Last but not least, theorists of expressive experience must be aware that their theories should accommodate most empirical data that are relevant for the

matter. This implies both using such data when it comes to the analysis of the experience's character and content as well as providing a theory with some heuristic value to be fruitfully employed by the empirical sciences.

Keeping these desiderata in mind, the most relevant and influential theories of expressiveness and expressive experience can be introduced and their capacity to fulfil these requirements can be tested.

1.5 Projectivism: Sartre and Wollheim

To deny that the experience of expressiveness is misleading in the sense implied by the pathetic fallacy is not yet to exclude that emotions we feel can play a role in shaping perceptual experiences. This is indeed the case exemplified in the second interpretation of pathetic fallacy proposed above. We may happen to undergo an emotion, for example we could feel sad or in a depressive mood due to whatever reason and "about" whatever object or event (if any). There is widespread agreement both throughout the history of philosophy and in psychology that when we find ourselves in such conditions we tend to experience objects in different ways. Emotional states can for example affect the way we perceive space, slant, distances, and sizes (for an overview, see Stefanucci, Gagnon, and Lessard 2011). Thus, it is also reasonable to think that the affective states we are in can make us perceive objects around us as being charged with those same affective states or similar ones. An inexhaustible source of examples can be found in literary fiction. The "hyperoptimist" protagonist of Philip Roth's *American Pastoral*, for instance, after discovering the unbearable truth about his daughter's disappearance and his wife's betrayal, finds what used to be a friendly environment absolutely hopeless:

> At dinner – outdoors, on the back terrace, with darkness coming on so gradually that the evening seemed to the Swede stalled, stopped, suspended, provoking in him a distressing sense of nothing more to follow, of nothing ever to happen again, of having entered a coffin carved out of time from which he would never be extricated [...]. (Roth 1997 [2016], p. 337)

Everyday experiences are rich in similar cases that are compatible with the sort of experience described by the supporters of pathetic fallacy view. However, as we have shown, their explanation neglects the possibility that those experiences amount to the attribution of affective properties to the way those objects *look*, rather than to a misattribution of affective states. Let us consider one way to explain the case in which we are in the grip of our emotional states that does not appeal to mistaken attributions. Instead, it allows for the possibility that objects have a specific appearance when we see or hear them under the influence of affective states. It consists in the claim that the emotional states we undergo can be projected upon and "dye" the objects we are surrounded by, providing them with a particular look.

In his book *The Emotions. Outline of a Theory* (1939 [1993]), French phenomenologist Jean-Paul Sartre put forward an instructive theory that is worth considering. In this essay, Sartre defines emotion as "a certain way of apprehending the world" (Sartre 1993, p. 52).[13]

> What is constitutive of the emotion is that it perceives upon the object something which exceeds it beyond measure. There is, in effect, a world of emotion. All emotions have this in common, that they make a same world appear, a world which is cruel, terrible, gloomy, joyful, etc. [...] a world of individual syntheses maintaining connections among themselves and possessing qualities.   (Sartre 1993, p. 79–80)

The peculiar character of emotions consists in our assuming a specific attitude so as to "constitute" a specific world, namely, the world of emotions, whose qualities are nevertheless perceived as qualities of the world itself. Analogously to what happens when we see colours, distances or shapes, we experience the qualities of the world disclosed by emotions "passively". According to this phenomenological approach it is possible to distinguish between situations in which we focus on the affective state we are in, so that the state itself becomes the object of our experience, and those cases in which – independently of the awareness we have of our affective states – our emotions make the world acquire a certain look. Sartre claims that, when we are in the grip of an emotion, we experience the world in a specific way. The objects of our experience acquire certain perceivable features that we apprehend as if they belonged to those objects: "True emotion [...] is accompanied by belief. The qualities conferred upon objects are taken as true qualities" (Sartre 1993, p. 73). Therefore, it is not the case that we *misjudge* expressive objects, but rather our emotions are responsible for the generation of an experience in which features determined by emotions are perceived as constituents of those objects.

---

[13] Sartre's inquiry certainly deserves a more precise introduction that is far beyond the possible scope of this work. A short remark concerning his method may nevertheless be useful to contextualise his proposal. In the aforementioned essay, Sartre accounts for emotions on the basis of phenomenological (namely Husserlian) premises, overtly arguing against the methods adopted by psychology. In particular, he declares himself sceptical about the capacity that psychological inquiries on emotions (and, allegedly, all human experience) would have to put forward for any meaningful general theory. Based on what it takes to be "mere facts" disconnected from one another, psychological inquiry is doomed to draw particular conclusions from particular analyses and is not in the position to provide a wider view on the world and the experience humans have of it. As an alternative, Sartre presents his method as *phenomenological psychology*, grounded in the description of emotions as *phenomena* provided with a *meaning* that the philosopher is in the position to decipher (Sartre 1993, p. 1–21).

Analogously to the pathetic fallacy approach, this account deals explicitly with occurring emotions that are deemed responsible for making the world appear in some way or another. It has already been mentioned that the capacity to account for the peculiar phenomenal character of expressive experience is among the desiderata for a good theory of expressiveness. Sartre's proposal points out that there is a specific way in which the world is perceived on those occasions. In so doing, he acknowledges that the experience of objects as affectively charged is characterised by a certain phenomenology. This phenomenology is not wrong or illusory, for it consists in the attribution of perceptual properties rather than in the misattribution of affective states to objects. A sad-looking landscape may look sad because of our being sad, but we ascribe sadness to it because of its specific way of appearing to us under certain conditions. Importantly, this specific character is such that properties that depend on our being affectively moved are perceived as belonging to the objects themselves. Therefore, Sartre's view can help to add a piece to the puzzle of expressiveness. Indeed, it accounts for the fact that we can describe expressive objects by taking their appearance seriously, instead of discarding the resulting experience as illusory.

This being said, the experience described by Sartre must not be considered the paradigmatic example of expressiveness, since it neglects those cases in which objects look expressive to subjects who are not feeling any emotion. And indeed, based on everyday experiences and introspection, we do not need to be in the grip of any emotion in order to perceive inanimate objects as expressive of affective states: we might be perfectly serene and hear a funeral march as mournful or a jingle as cheerful. The next step of this overview will deal with precisely this aspect of the experience of expressiveness, finally presenting the analytic debate about expressive experience.

The first account of expressive experience that is worth introducing is Richard Wollheim's theory of projection. It is one of the few works in analytic philosophy that explicitly and thoroughly addresses the problem of expressiveness not so much in the arts, but rather in the experience of nature. In his 1993 article "Correspondence, Projective Properties and Expression in the Arts", Wollheim adopts a perspective which seems to echo that of Sartre. Wollheim's view shows an awareness of the importance of distinguishing expressive experiences that take place when the subject is moved from expressive experiences in which the subject does not feel any occurring emotion. He is interested in those cases in which objects in the external world seem to *correspond* to certain emotional states, i.e. cases where psychological predicates are attributed to nature and to works of art.

Wollheim borrows the notion of *correspondence* from Charles Baudelaire's famous poem *Correspondances* (1857), and describes the content of the experience of correspondence as the experience of something that appears *of a piece with* an affective state. Accordingly, if something shows this sort of correspondence, then it is perceived as instantiating *projective* properties. Projection is a psychological mechanism that Wollheim explains by appealing to developmental psychology in a Freudian vein.

Significantly, Wollheim had previously faced the topic of projection in his 1986 lecture "From Voices to Values: The Growth of Moral Sense", while discussing ethical and psychological problems in the light of Freudian theories. According to the theory that Wollheim develops in both works, we perform projection processes from infancy. In the early stages of our development, we tend to find relief from oppressive and generally unpleasant affective states, such as anxiety, by projecting them onto what surrounds us, either on people or objects. Projection can then give rise to beliefs that follow from the achieved condition of relief, so that: "On the level of judgement, projection [...] can be represented by the speaker's applying to someone or something else a predicate that he himself satisfies" (Wollheim 1986, p. 214).

However, unlike Sartre, Wollheim considers these experiences of projection psychologically and philosophically uninteresting. He believes that episodes in which attributions of emotions to inanimate objects correspond to the subject's occurrent psychological state do not tell us enough about correspondence. As in those cases described by Sartre, we can feel sad and *project* our sadness on our surroundings, so as to perceive them as sad, but this is not the core case of what Wollheim calls "projective experience". We can see or hear expressive objects even when we are not in the grip of any emotion or when we are feeling completely different emotions from those that we ascribe to objects. Therefore, Wollheim focuses on what he terms "complex projection", the projection of emotions having as its output the ascription of an expressive character to objects, but which does not imply that the subject undergoes any emotional state.

Complex projection takes place only insofar as there is something inherent to the appearance of the world that makes it possible: "There has to be a real match of correspondence between [the outer world and the inner world]" (Wollheim 1986, p. 214), an *affinity* already present between the object which is taken to be, say, sad and the affective state of sadness, even though sadness is not the emotion felt by the subject at the time of the experience. So, when complex projection is in play, the subject recognises an object as apt for the projection of a certain affective state on the basis of some existing affinity. The question is, thus, what such an affinity amounts to. Once more, Wollheim appeals to developmental psychology to answer this question, arguing that affective projections, which are randomly applied during infancy, become more precise as we grow up. As time passes we tend to select the objects on which to project. This progressive selection both provides the basis for and depends on the affinity such objects seem to share with emotions.

Here is a first controversial aspect of Wollheim's account. On the one hand, he claims that the affinity that should make certain objects apt for the projection of emotions is a "brute fact", something about which it is impossible to say more; but on the other hand our projections are meant to become more stable as time passes, so that we tend to project and attribute expressive traits in a more stable and systematic fashion. This progressive stabilisation creates and enhances the conditions for certain things to be recognisable as expressive, say, to show a certain affinity with projectable emotions. When we recognise something as expressive we recognise it as the object on which we *have* or *may have projected* our emotions in the past. And there is a sense in which the object lends itself to this experience precisely in virtue of the fact that we have projected our emotion on it (or similar objects) in the past.

Wollheim appeals to the notion of affinity because he does not want to limit the experience of what he calls *projective properties* to those objects on which we have *actually* projected emotions in the past. Such a limitation would make it impossible to account for those cases in which we see as expressive an object that we encounter for the first time.

> That is evidently too restrictive, for we can and do perceive nature as of a piece with our feelings in cases where we can no longer recall having projected those feelings on to it and, indeed, in innumerable cases where we have not done so. (Wollheim 1993, p. 153)

Something in the experience must make it possible for a completely new object to allow for the projection. Therefore, Wollheim suggests that it is not only memories of past projections that the object triggers, but even the "intimation of the projective origin" that the experience could have that could be responsible for the experience of an expressive object.

> When such experiences do not – and most of them do not – intimate how they came about, they do intimate how experiences of the sort they exemplify come about in general. A [...] comparison may help to clarify this claim. [...] Most experiences of bodily pain intimate specifically how *they* originate: that is, in damage to part of the body where they are felt. But there are some individual pains that do not arise in this way: the part of the body where they are felt is undamaged or has been amputated. But such pains [...] intimate how pains in general arises. Experiences of the sort that they exemplify arise, they tell us, from damage in the body. (Wollheim 1993, p. 150)

However, the thesis regarding the intimation that an experience can make of its origin also proves to be problematic on two counts. Firstly, it is not clear how such an intimation should partake in our experience. Secondly, the fact that it is impossible to specify how an object should look in order to show some affinity with certain emotional states (and so to entertain a correspondence relation with the inner world), makes it difficult to release Wollheim's projectivism from a radically idiosyncratic view of expressive experience. Let us expand on these two points. The first point has been raised by Malcolm Budd who is concerned about the way in which the alleged projective origins of the experience manifest themselves: "Presumably, for an experience to intimate something about itself the intimation must be an aspect of its phenomenology. But what form does the intimation assume?" (Budd 2008, p. 245). If one follows Wollheim, it seems that the intimation about its own origin that the expressive experience is supposed to provide is part of its phenomenal character, say, of what the experience is like for a subject. It should then be specified *how* it enters the experience.

> What is needed is a conception of an emotion that someone does not actually feel on a certain occasion yet is present in the person in an occurrent sense that enables it to modify a perception from not being a perception of correspondence to being such a perception.
> (Budd 2008, p. 249)

Spanish philosopher Francisca Pérez-Carreño has provided an interpretation that aims at clarifying and supporting Wollheim's view. She suggests, in a Wollheimian vein, that emotions enter perceptual experiences of expressive objects in the form of a "thought content" (Pérez-Carreño 2017). She accordingly argues that something we *believe* or *know* about emotions, can enter the perceptual experience we have of certain objects, either because they trigger an associative mechanism linking current perceptual experiences to past projections of emotions, or because they are thoughts intimating the origin of the current expressive experience in possible projections. Yet – this is Budd's point – our experience does not attest that the capacity to recognise such an origin is required to undergo an expressive experience. In other words, it does not seem that, in order to recognise something as expressive, we should possess the *concept* of "intimation of a projective origin". Furthermore, it is far from obvious that even if we reflect on the experience after it took place, we end up with a thought concerning the intimation of its origin in projection.

> [...] if an experience intimates something about itself this intimation must announce itself to us when we reflect on the experience in order to determine if it tells us this about itself. For reflection on the experience of expressive perception – at least, reflection on my own

experience of the expressive perception of nature or the perception of the expressive properties of works of art – fails to reveal a thought concerning complex projection.
(Budd 2008, p. 246–247)

As stated above, the second problematic aspect of this projectivist account is its inability to specify how an object should appear to be akin to an emotional state. Wollheim puts forward an explanation that appeals to memories and background knowledge of projections. Yet he needs to acknowledge that the appearance of the involved objects plays some determinant role in the experience. In fact, either one must claim that any object can be experienced as expressive of any affective state or something in the appearance of the objects should be taken as binding.

Wollheim is aware that the first alternative is difficult to endorse. Firstly, there seems to be some strong intuition about objects and features that are liable to certain attributions instead of others: Richard Wagner's *The Valkyries* is hardly experienced as a cheerful piece, whereas, usually, *Jingle Bells* is not considered mournful. Secondly and more importantly, Wollheim is well aware that attributions of expressiveness refer to the perceivable look of an object, to its appearance. Despite being convinced that such appearance must trigger memories of past projections or associated thoughts that lie beyond the perceivable surface, the latter should be able to bear some strong connection to those states and contents, on pain of an intrinsic randomness that expressive experience does not prove to have. The following example can make the whole point more perspicuous. Suppose two persons are listening to Richard Wagner's *Ride of the Valkyries*; while the first person hears the piece as solemn and, occasionally, threatening, the second person finds it ridiculous and pompous. Both listeners have good reasons to attribute those affective features to the piece, and among those reasons are the memories and thoughts – allegedly different ones – that they associate with it. Nevertheless, they are referring to *the same* piece of music, this sameness consisting in the same structure and audible features. If the two persons were asked to convince each other of the correctness of their attributions, the common ground on which they would probably base their arguments would be the perceptual surface of the *Ride*, its tempo, rhythm, melody, and so on.

This example captures an important aspect of our experiences of expressive features, namely the fact that, in spite of possible disagreement, what we refer to in order to justify our ascriptions is the way objects look, rather than (or prior) to our personal associations. Although Wollheim is aware of this problem, he is reluctant when it comes to saying how an object has to be in order to be expressive. On his view, as well as merely perceptual properties, projective (i.e. expressive) properties that are responsible for expressiveness both *cause* our experience and are *what the experience is about*. But, he thinks, holding that the expressive aspect of a perceived object depends on its perceptual features would imply that expressive properties may be reduced to merely perceptual ones. If this were the case, there would not be any need to explain *correspondence* as a *sui generis* phenomenon.

> If what is wanted is information about how exactly nature has to look in particular cases if it is to be apt for the projection of this rather than that feeling, then this demand must surely go unsatisfied. For how could we convincingly describe what it is about some aspect of nature that makes it suitable for the projection of some particular feeling without upgrading the mere affinity into the projective properties of which it is – at any rate on my view – the mere substrate? (Wollheim 1993, p. 154)

Thus, Wollheim claims, it is just a brute fact that certain objects appear as apt for the projection of certain emotions. Projection is precisely the mechanism that allows non-expressive features to become expressive as it establishes a connection between the perceptual appearance of an object and the emotions that can be projected on it. But since the affinity is at least partly dependent on repeated projections made by the subject onto the same or similar objects according to personal vicissitudes, preferences, or simply casual associations, two subjects are likely to establish quite different projective connections with those same objects. And once they become able to recognise those objects as expressive in the absence of any occurrent projection, the two resultant experiences are likely to be incommensurable with each other.

Therefore, the projectivist theory put forward by Wollheim can account for those cases in which our personal affective states are currently projected onto or associated with inanimate objects, by means of our own memories. However, this view has problems in accounting for those cases in which we experience something as expressive for the first time, without being in the grip of any emotion. It is certainly true that, as claimed both by Wollheim and by Sartre, our occurrent affective states can influence the way in which we perceive certain objects, so that we recognise some of their features as being expressive. This allows the two philosophers to deal with the apparent contradiction of expressive objects by acknowledging that, although they do not literally possess emotions, inanimate objects can look compatible with or, in Wollheim's words, "of a piece" with felt emotions. But when it comes to the experience of expressive objects in the absence of a (previously or currently) felt emotion, projectivism so conceived does not hold. As we have seen, this proposal does not clarify how the hinted projective origin of expressive experience partakes in the phenomenal character of the experience and, moreover, it does not account for the fact that the way an object looks determines (at least in part) the expressive experience one can have of it.

1.6 Arousalism: Matravers, Ridley, and Robinson on Art and Emotions

The second approach to be listed among the theories of expressive experience is *arousalism*. It stems from the intuition that the emotions that we attribute to objects do depend on those objects, but only as long as they provoke some affective reaction in us. This family of accounts finds its ideal pioneer in Wassily Kandinsky. In his *Concerning the Spiritual in Art* (1912) he wrote:

> Colour directly influences the soul. Colour is the keyboard, the eyes are the hammers, the soul is the piano with many strings. The artist is the hand that plays, touching one key or another purposively, to cause vibrations in the soul. (Kandinsky 1912 [1997], p. 45)

On this view, perceptual aspects of objects – especially artworks – are capable of arousing emotions in the audience. As a result, one ascribes expressive values to artworks, be they visual or auditory.

In his book *Art and Emotion* (1998) Derek Matravers takes on this intuition and puts forward a more thoroughly articulated arousalistic theory. The explicit assumption of his proposal is that if expression is available only for those beings that can *feel* emotions as internal states, then human expression of emotions must serve as a paradigmatic "central case" for expressive experience. According to Matravers, the standard reaction of human (or, more generally, sentient) beings when confronted with an emotional expression is the feeling of a certain emotion in turn.

> We do not characteristically react to the expression of emotion with the bare formation of a belief. As a general rule, such a reaction would be inappropriate; the characteristic response to such situation is another emotion, whether of the same or of a different type.
> (Matravers 1998, p. 26)

Suppose we see someone manifesting her sadness: if we are not victims of any relevant affective disorder, Matravers says, we ought to react with an appropriate emotion such as sorrow, pity or compassion.

Matravers' theory derives the case for inanimate objects' expressiveness from this paradigm of human expression: some objects trigger in us feelings of the same kind as those elicited by human expression of emotions; these reactive feelings are in turn meant to cause our beliefs about the expressiveness of those objects. Therefore, we call the features of objects that actually arouse certain feelings in us *expressive properties*. In order to develop his theory, Matravers focuses on the case of music:

> A piece of music expresses an emotion e if it causes a listener to experience a feeling a, where a is the feeling component of the emotion it would be appropriate to feel (in the

central case) when faced with a person expressing *e*. Hence music expressive of sadness will cause the listener to feel sad (or maybe the feeling component of pity if that is a different state), and this feeling will cause him to believe that the work expresses sadness.

(Matravers 1998, p. 149)

It is undeniable that we happen to feel moved by inanimate objects: let us think about particularly moving pieces of music and also, for example, the deeply emotional reactions that many people say they have when contemplating Rothko's paintings; extremely desolate or extremely dramatic landscapes also provoke affective reactions in beholders, not to mention the emotions we might feel with respect to objects that are linked to some especially touching episode in our lives. Peter Kivy describes this as "the 'our song' phenomenon", referring to the arousal that a piece of music may trigger, due to associative mechanisms that tie that very piece to some affectively charged memories (Kivy 1989, p. 30). Moreover, in such cases we may tend to justify our attributions of expressiveness to inanimate objects by referring to the emotions those objects make (or made) us feel. Admittedly, arousalism captures the intuition that, in order to experience something as being affectively charged, and especially expressive, one has to be involved in a properly affective experience that, in principle, implies some form of arousal.

However, as already pointed out when discussing projectivism, it also happens that we attribute expressive properties to objects without feeling moved by them: we could acknowledge that a piece of music we listen to is very sad, but still feel happy or lack any affective state. Let us think about the *Ride of the Valkyries* once again. In assigning to the piece an expressive value, one can be deeply affected and moved to exaltation or anxiety, but it may also be the case that one goes through the piece without having any emotional reactions. In light of this consideration, and as already suggested, actually felt emotions should not be considered a necessary condition to experience something as expressive.

Nevertheless, Matravers insists that the feelings triggered by expressive objects are ultimately responsible for our ascriptions. He contends that those feelings are not something we need to be aware of. On the contrary, feelings can remain completely unknown to the subject, and we can infer their presence and nature on the basis of the beliefs that they are able to cause. However, this view lends itself to an objection, of which Matravers himself is aware: "Because the feeling aroused by [an expressive object] is only causally connected to it and is thus independent of it, it follows that the feeling could be aroused by other means" (Matravers 1998, p. 169).

In other words, arousalism does not account for the link between the phenomenal character of the experience and its causes. In fact, it does not say how an object should look in order for it to cause an affective reaction and therefore be experienced as expressive. Accordingly, the phenomenal character of the expressive experience could be identical with the phenomenal character of the perceptual experience of the same object, save the fact that such an object or (some of) its features elicit reactive feelings.

As with Wollheim's proposal, it is worth taking a moment to consider the aspect of the theory that seems less compelling. According to Aaron Ridley (1995), Matravers' account is intrinsically incapable of explaining how the way the expressive object looks is linked to the belief one forms about its being expressive. Ridley argues that Matravers' arousalism is committed to the "heresy of the separable experience", this phrase coming from Malcolm Budd (1985). We will deal directly with this heresy in Chapter 3, but it is useful to introduce it here, in order to discuss Matravers' view. According to Budd – and to Ridley who applies this same criticism to Matravers – one commits to such a heresy when one describes a work: "as being related in a certain way to an experience which can be fully characterised [and valued] without reference to the nature of the work itself" (Budd 1985, p. 123).

Arousalism accepts the idea that the causal chain resulting in the belief that an object is expressive starts with the perceptual features of that object. But if the connection between those features and the resulting experience is merely causal, one cannot determine what they should look like in order for the object to appear sad rather than cheerful to an observer. Thus, in principle, expressive experience may be obtained by other means that do not necessarily involve those objects that the experience seems to be about. If this sounds obscure, suppose one is under the effect of a drug capable of triggering affective reactions such that the subject undergoes an expressive experience. In this case, the link between the objects' appearance and the experience in which they feature is absolutely contingent, so that the latter cannot be justified by referring to the former. Reducing the connection to causality does not leave room for a normative link between the experience and the objects' perceivable features.

Matravers addresses this lack of normative constraint on the experience of expressiveness by appealing to two distinct factors. On the one hand, he maintains that there is a specific way in which perceptual expressive features trigger affective reactions, a way that distinguishes such experiences from the one that may be caused by a drug: "A piece of music, then, is a structure, the identity and the value of which will not reside in any particular part, but rather in the relations between its parts" (Matravers 1998, p. 178). So that: "The experience of expressive music is the experience of an organized structure of sounds and the corresponding feelings it arouses" (Matravers 1998, p. 177). It is the very complex structure of music that provokes affective reactions in the listener, in such a way that a drug or any other simple causal stimulus could not obtain the same result.

On the other hand, in order to establish a normative link between the perceived aspect of the object and the feeling aroused, doing justice to the phenomenal character of the experience, Matravers appeals to the constraint of "appropriateness" (Matravers 1998, p. 146). The feeling aroused by the expressive object – however complex it is – is the non-intentional component of the emotions that it would be appropriate to feel when confronted with an expressive *person*. This is to say that, analogously to how we react to certain behaviours and, subsequently, judge them as melancholy or as nervous, there are objects that lend themselves to certain attributions rather than others. Matravers' arousalism accounts for both kinds of experiences (the experience of sad music and the experience of sad behaviour) in the same way, namely, by appealing to causal reactions: as there are affective reactions to human expressions whose appropriateness can be explained in physiological terms and evolutionary standards, so there are affective reactions to the perception of certain features of objects that, in principle, can be explained in the same or in an analogous way.

Both these arguments, which are basically meant to explain the experience of expressiveness in more complex causal terms than one would use to explain a bump on a toe, deserve some discussion. The complexity condition introduced by Matravers against the drug counterargument seems to avoid the problem rather than to deal with it. It is true, as will be discussed later in further detail, that emotions are multi-componential items that include non-intentional feelings, i.e. physiological reactions that may be devoid of intentional objects and therefore lack any content. Therefore, to consider mere non-intentional feelings as responsible for the merely causal connection between expressive objects and our attributions of expressiveness is consistent with such a widespread assumption. Moreover, unlike the projectivist perspective, this view locates the origin of the experience in certain perceivable features of objects, rather than in the subjective projection of emotions upon them.

Nevertheless, the drug counterargument remains. In principle, such an objection points at the link between the appearance of an expressive item and our beliefs about the appearance. Even if one is disposed to accept that the responsible causal relation is more complex than the one linking the sharp edge of my chest of drawers and the pain in my toe caused by bumping into it, the problem persists: there may always be other means to arouse the same feeling reaction and subsequent judgements in the absence of the intentional object of the experience. Thus: why should our attributions of expressiveness be about those same objects that our experience seems to be about?

1.6 Arousalism: Matravers, Ridley, and Robinson on Art and Emotions — 35

There are further complications with this view. As we have just seen, the second way in which Matravers tries to account for the specificity of expressive experience resorts to the idea of *appropriateness*. Indeed, our experience of expressive objects attests a certain degree of normativity. So, the appeal to appropriateness should account for the fact that certain pieces of music are appropriately deemed sad, while others are appropriately deemed happy. But on which basis should one accept that the appropriate way to react to the *Ride of the Valkyries* is by having (consciously or not) the feeling component of fear, which will in turn cause the judgement that the piece is threatening? If the criterion to affirm that such a reaction is more appropriate than another is the mere fact that most of us tend to respond in this way, then this explanation falls short of establishing a normative criterion.

Despite being himself an upholder of arousalim, Aaron Ridley calls "strong" arousalism the approach according to which the disposition of music to provoke feelings "exhausts the meaning of all descriptions of music in affective terms" (Ridley 1995, p. 51). He argues that strong arousalism condemns our beliefs and judgements about expressive objects to be nothing more than an unjustifiable "linguistic muddle" (Ridley 1995, p. 52). Such a theory focuses on the *causes* of arousal rather than on its *reasons* and, in so doing, it does not fit the requirements of a theory of expressiveness.

> To ascribe dispositional predicates to a thing is not to attribute to it any expressive qualities. We need not, for example, think expressive of irritation a dentist who, irritatingly, hurts us – though it might be true that the dentist is irritating. (Ridley 1995, p. 52)

Ridley argues that a theory of expressive experience should be able to distinguish between the causal power that objects can have on our emotional states, and the way in which we perceive expressive objects to be. In other words, we may agree that the causal elicitation is necessary to make us think that a piece of music is expressive of sorrow, yet this would not be enough to say what such an object must look like in order to elicit such a reaction. A sharp distinction between these two aspects of expressive experience has been famously drawn by Peter Kivy, who stated:

> [...] we must separate entirely the claim that music can arouse emotion in us from the claim that music is sometimes sad or angry or fearful: in other words, we must keep apart the claim that music is expressive (of anger, fear, and the like) and the claim that music is arousing in the sense of moving. (Kivy 1990, p. 153)

Kivy is saying that affective arousal and the experience that consists in recognising affective features in objects are conceptually distinct. No one can deny that music arouses feelings (perhaps one may argue that the feelings that it arouses are of some distinct quality from those aroused in other situations), but this is not a good reason to believe that aroused emotions are what make us experience music as expressive of emotions.

Ridley proposes a weaker version of musical arousalism, according to which we hear a piece of music as being expressive primarily owing to its perceivable structure. On his view, expressiveness is experienced in virtue of those perceptual qualities of musical pieces that he calls *melismatic gestures*. "Melisma" or the "melismatic gesture" is the unit of musical pieces that resembles emotional expressions on the basis of the quality of timbre and on that of musical motion (Ridley 1995, p. 49). Accordingly, expressive experience takes place as long as one perceives melismatic gestures in music as resembling human expressions. He writes:

> Sometimes the resemblance is to *vocal* expressive behavior, as with the sharply rising horn arpeggio at the climax of the slow movement of Brahms's Horn Trio, which sounds like a cry of anguish. At other times, and probably more commonly, the resemblance is to *physical* expressive behavior, as when the musical movements of the *marcia funebre* resemble the movements of someone resolute but heavy of heart. (Ridley 1995, p. 49)

Unlike Matravers, Ridley accounts for expressiveness by characterising the appearance of expressive objects as being similar to human emotional expressions. Resemblances are, therefore, what makes expressive appearance *sui generis* compared to standard perceptual features, and the recognition of melisma is deemed ultimately responsible for the experience of expressive music.

Why call him an arousalist, then? Because, although his proposal strives to do justice to the specific appearance of expressive objects (music in particular), Ridley is convinced that such an experience requires an additional component in order to take place, namely the arousal of emotions. According to Ridley's analysis, arousal is a sympathetic mirroring of the detected melisma. When one listens to a piece of music that – given the quality of the timbre and motion constituting its melismatic gesture – resembles the human expression of sadness, one experiences that piece of music as expressive of sadness as long as one mirrors the emotion of sadness in oneself. For example, Ridley argues that when listening to the Funeral March from Beethoven's *Eroica* symphony: "[...] in attending to the musical gestures I come to be aware of their heavyhearted, resolute quality through the very process of coming myself to feel heavyhearted but resolute" (Ridley 1995, p. 52).

This sympathetic arousal is, in Ridley's view, the same sort of mechanism that allows for the recognition of other people's expressions as being expressive of internal states, rather than as mere perceptual patterns. His concern is patent: while in principle perceptual patterns such as melismatic gestures might be recognised and correctly associated with affective attributions, e.g. by computers, expressive properties mobilised in expressive experience must bear some robust relation to our *inner life*. So, on Ridley's account, the arousalistic perspective acquires a more refined shape. The reason why felt emotions and expressive experience cannot be kept separate is that only sentient beings that are aware of what it means to undergo a certain emotion can also fully and adequately understand what it is for someone – and therefore for something – to be expressive of that affective state.

Before moving on to the next family of theories, it is worth mentioning one last but particularly influential supporter of arousalism, that is American philosopher Jenefer Robinson. Robinson embraces a theory very close to Ridley's, with a key difference, namely that she rejects the sympathy requirement. On her view, Ridley is right in considering emotional arousal as a necessary component of expressive experience, especially the idea that such an arousal is what enables us to detect very specific shades of emotions that music can express. Incidentally, she is not convinced that the sort of arousal in play is a sympathetic one. Indeed, she observes that the emotions felt by the listener are not always those expressed by the piece of music: a piece may express nostalgia while evoking melancholy in the listener, or express joy and provoke amusement in the listener (Robinson 2005, p. 358). However, this can be taken as a minor disagreement between the two arousalistic perspectives, that are quite of a piece regarding the role of felt emotions: they both claim that musical expressiveness is something we hear thanks to the capacity that music has to evoke emotions in us.

Let us recall the paradox by means of which the topic of objects' expressiveness was introduced. The contradiction is meant to show that, if one takes expression of emotions to be the outward manifestation of internal conditions, it is inconsistent to believe that inanimate objects can be expressive. The solution proposed by Matravers is simple: it is not the case that inanimate objects *really* express emotions; it happens instead that they provoke emotions (or at least elicit their non-intentional components) in sentient beings who will automatically be led to attribute affective characters to those objects. Thus, expressiveness is a matter of ascription of affective states that *we* feel, to objects that cannot feel them. Ridley and Robinson rephrase the same solution in a subtler way. Indeed, they also claim that the central case of expressive experience is the attribution of affective states to other human beings on the basis of our capacity to feel (through some mirroring mechanism) those states. The case of expressive objects is therefore a derived experience that involves the same capacities and mechanisms that are in play in the central experience.

Thus, recognising perceptual patterns as expressive is a matter of being able to lead a merely perceptual experience back to our emotional, inner life. Once again, objects would not express emotions, but they would at best resemble human expressions that we can recognise only provided that we feel the corresponding or related emotions.

1.7 Resemblances and the Contour Theory: Kivy and Davies

Among the theories that aim at accounting for the expressiveness of music is the *contour theory*, according to which music can be heard as expressive in virtue of those features that make it similar to human emotional expressions. Contour theory accounts for expressiveness in terms of those resemblances that hold between its perceivable profile or contour – analogously to what Ridley calls melisma, constituted by the auditory properties of a piece of music – and the typical profile of human emotional expressions. The key idea, originally expressed by Peter Kivy, is that we perceive music as expressive insofar as it resembles typical vocal expressions and behaviours that human beings perform when experiencing and expressing emotions.

In this sense, two dimensions of the musical contour are particularly relevant. Firstly, it seems that some musical features sound like human voices (Kivy 1989): an acute, stable sound, brilliant and well articulated may appear similar to a joyful voice, whilst a sound full of dissonances is typically experienced as a vocal manifestation of anguish or despair. Secondly, some features of the contour, such as melody, rhythmic cadence, agogics, and so on, resemble visible aspects of human behaviour, like gestures and bodily movements (Kivy 1989; Davies 1994, 2010). According to Kivy in particular: "We hear [musical sounds] as human utterances, and perceive the features of these utterances as structurally similar to our own voices when we express our own sadness in speech" (Kivy 1980, p. 51). While according to Davies: "In general, music resembles gaits, carriages, or comportments that are typically expressive of human occurrent emotions" (Davies 2005, p. 181). And, more extensively:

> [...] music is naturally expressive because the dynamic character of music is experienced as significantly similar to human behavior expressive of emotions. Movement is heard in music. The relative highness and lowness of notes provides a dimension in aural space within which music moves through time. Thus, if the characteristic behavioral expression of an emotion, *X*, has the dynamic form *Y*, and if a musical work is heard as having the same dynamic form, then *X* is heard in the music. (Davies 2005, p. 132)

1.7 Resemblances and the Contour Theory: Kivy and Davies

Both Kivy and Davies consider musical expressiveness a matter of *perceivable features*. Expressive qualities reside, in their view, in the configurational aspect of music, in the way it, its notes, pitches, rhythm, and chords perceptually present themselves to listeners.

As it is made clear by the term *contour*, the resemblance in question holds between the perceptual structure of music on the one hand, and the perceptual profile of emotion manifestations on the other. This latter point is worth noticing because it is overtly in contrast with another theory of musical expressiveness that relies on resemblances, yet in a quite different way. Malcolm Budd (1995) has argued that the resemblance that is responsible for making music expressive is the resemblance that holds between music and emotions *as internal psychological states*. He wrote that, when we hear a piece of music expressive of an emotion [E], we:

> hear the music as sounding like the way E feels; [...] So the sense in which you hear the emotion *in* the music – the sense in which it is an audible property of the music – is that you perceive a likeness between the music and the experience of the emotion.
> (Budd 1995, p. 136)

According to Budd, expressive music resembles our feelings, namely the phenomenology of feelings felt from a first-person perspective.[14] Music is taken to mirror the affective component of emotions: it resolves its tensions in a way that corresponds, for example, to the satisfaction of desires; it trembles and so resembles the way in which we waver and feel uncomfortable when overtaken by agitation; a syncopated musical rhythm may mirror feelings of anxiety, and so on. Even if he declares himself open to a variety of ways in which musical expressiveness can be experienced (including arousal, imagination, and the intersection of the two), Budd's fundamental claim is that we perceive this sort of cross-categorical resemblances between the way music sounds and the way emotions feel, and that this peculiar kind of perception is ultimately responsible for expressive experience.

Questioning those theories that ground the experience of expressive music in resemblances, Saam Trivedi has argued that Budd's view loses the connection to our ordinary concept of *expressiveness* understood as an external manifestation:

---

14 Admittedly, Budd's view is indebted to Carroll C. Pratt's seminal *The Meaning of Music* (1931). Pratt explains musical expressiveness in terms of musical movement. Given that emotions involve bodily modifications perceived first-personally, Pratt argues that music displays those very same movements that characterise felt emotions. In sum, music can be agitated, restless, triumphant or calm since it shares characteristic movements with felt agitation, restlessness, triumph, calmness.

> Our ordinary concept of expressiveness involves the outward manifestation of inner mental states. As a species of expressiveness in general, musical expressiveness must relate somehow to this ordinary concept. (Trivedi 2001, p. 412)

Accordingly, the appeal to resemblances must not overshadow the idea of an outward manifestation on pain of disconnecting the expressiveness of music (and, more generally, of objects) from what we usually consider expressive, namely, expressive behaviours. Resembling inner felt states (whatever this resemblance amounts to) does not imply resembling what in an emotion is visible or audible (that is its manifest expression).

One could try to defend Budd's theory by insisting that, on his view, expressive music is not taken to resemble those feelings felt and injected in music by its creator nor by its listener. What is relevant is rather that expressiveness belongs to the perceptual aspect of music. The fact that it does so in virtue of a resemblance to felt emotions in general (and not experienced in the occurrence of expressive experience) preserves the idea that expressiveness is something other than actual expression of felt emotions.

But this move is not sufficient for saving this resemblance-based account from criticisms. Trivedi offers a perspicuous analogy:

> For example, an extremely hot and spicy food may taste the way extreme anger, or anguish, feels in that there may be a "fiery, burning" affect common to both; similarly, a soothing beverage may taste the way calmness, or contentedness, feels in that there may be a "pacifying, cool" feeling in common. [...] if indeed there are such likenesses between some foods and some emotions, and if indeed we perceive them, that alone does not suffice to show these foods are expressive of these emotions, nor that they are, or should be, judged to be so. (Trivedi 2001, p. 412–413)

Having something in common with an emotion, sharing some component or resembling some features of an emotion is not enough to be considered *expressive of* that emotion. The same criticism about Budd's account is raised by Paul Noordhof, who states:

> A resemblance, however strong, is not sufficient to explain how something is heard as expressing that which it resembles. At best, resemblance makes something appear expressive if it resembles something which is expressive. (Noordhof 2008, p. 332)

It is not the case that *any resemblance* accounts for expressiveness. Thus, if one intends to account for musical expressiveness in terms of perceivable similarity, one should better focus on what is expressive in the first place, namely, expressions. If Trivedi's and Noordhof's criticism is right, then the term of the resemblance is to be sought in those components of emotions that are manifest and perceivable. Accordingly, contour theorists insist that the relevant resemblance holds between the perceptual structure of music, say, its profile, and the perceptual profile of emotion manifestations. Stephen Davies has termed such a profile "emotion characteristics in appearance" (Davies 2005).

Contour theory explicitly assumes the distinction between expression and expressiveness introduced above as a requirement for a theory of expressiveness. Robinson's distinction and the rich range of examples that she offers do not provide an exhaustive definition of expressiveness, nevertheless she seems to indicate a direction of inquiry. Two aspects of this phenomenon are important to her: firstly, that expressiveness, contrary to expression, "depends on how effectively the artwork reveals to a (suitable) audience what that emotion is like" (Robinson 2007, p. 36); secondly, that it is "a *cognitive* notion. Expressions reveal something about the nature of the emotion expressed" (Robinson 2007, p. 30). Thus, despite being understood as conceptually distinct items, expression and expressiveness cannot be considered as completely disconnected from one another. Consistently, Stephen Davies points out that musical expressiveness would be completely uninteresting if it did not bear any relation to human emotions:

> If the expression of emotion in music is seen as one of music's most important features, then it can be only because we *recognize* a connection between the emotions expressed in music and in life, because musical expressiveness reflects and reflects on the world of emotions. (Davies 2005, p. 135)

Contour theory is precisely concerned with the relation that holds between the *manifest components* of emotions and musical expressiveness. In accordance with Tormey and Robinson, Davies observes that we also tend to isolate expressiveness from expressions in the case of human beings. For instance, we say that someone's face is *sad* without implying that the person is feeling and expressing her sadness; we attribute joy to the behaviour of an actor, without attributing the feeling of joy to the actor on the stage; we may describe folk dances as cheerful and enthusiastic, but we are ready to believe that the dancers are rather serious and concentrated on their performance. Since felt emotions need not be expressed, and they can be experienced privately:

> The emotion characteristics in a person's appearance are given solely in his behavior, bearing, facial expression, and so forth. [...] there is a legitimate and common use of the word 'sad' in such sentences as 'He is a sad-looking person' that does not imply that the person feels sad or is prone to feel sad and, therefore, that does not refer to the person's felt sadness or proneness to feel sad. This no-reference-to-feeling use refers solely to the person's look. That is, emotion words can be used, are regularly used, and can be understood by others as being used without even implicit reference to the occurrence of feelings.
> (Davies 2005, p. 136)

Relying on linguistic practices, Davies claims that when making such attributions we refer to emotion characteristics in appearance, say, typical gestures and behaviours that have an original intimate connection to emotions. However, this does not imply that we ascribe felt emotions every time we recognise an expressive behaviour. Emotion characteristics in appearance are therefore one term of the resemblance and the other term relates to the structural perceptual properties of music.

The experience of musical expressiveness consists therefore in the perceptual recognition of *this* kind of resemblance – which is not crystal clear. In fact, the questions arise of what these perceptual features exactly amount to and of what this perception of resemblances precisely consists in. Consistent with the identification of musical perceivable "profile" as being responsible for expressive experience, Kivy and Davies maintain that expressive features are perceptual (more specifically, auditory) gestalt properties, that is, complex patterns emerging from and exceeding the sum of simpler perceivable properties of a piece of music. So far so good: as we will see, most scholars agree on this basic level of the analysis. But even assuming such a general description of a musical expressive profile, one has to explain where and how resemblances come into play.

Given the appeal that its upholders make to resemblances, one can easily retort against contour theory that we do not necessarily *perceive a resemblance* when we hear (or see) something as expressive. It can be true that, sometimes, we notice resemblances between certain musical tones and typically expressive tones of voice, but this does not amount to saying that when we experience a piece of music as melancholy we necessarily experience it as resembling a melancholy behaviour. Rather, intuitively, things might work the other way round, that is, in virtue of the expressiveness of music, we might be led to compare it to an expressive behaviour and determine the similarities. Noticing resemblances seems not be a necessary condition to experience an expressive piece of music. As Paul Noordhof (2008) has pointed out, contour theory reflects in the phenomenal character of expressive experience a resemblance that is not (always) manifestly there.

Even though a more detailed discussion of this problem will be developed in the next chapter, I shall give contour theorists the opportunity to briefly respond. A possible strategy to address this criticism appeals to an evolutionary explanation. According to Kivy (1989 and, in a more sceptical fashion, Kivy 2002), we are forced to hear the contour of a piece of music as an expressive behaviour in virtue of an existing resemblance, even when we do not recognise any actual relation of similarity. In other words, the invoked resemblance that is maintained to explain our expressive experience need not be consciously detected. Rather, it is supposed to lie at an unconscious level as the remains of an evolutionarily favourable mechanism. Such a mechanism is compatible with the idea that in our minds we tend to animate objects as much as possible. Kivy makes the case of a twisted branch partially hidden in the grass and suggests that we have a natural tendency to perceive it as a living snake, which could potentially be dangerous (Kivy 1980, 57–58). This supposition is compatible with an evolutionary explanation: for our ancestors it was probably convenient, for the sake of survival, to behave as if perceptual inputs were mostly produced by intentional beings. That is, transposed into the auditory domain, to run away when hearing a noise that sounded *as threatening as* the one produced by a truly threatening animal. Traces of these same mechanisms may have survived humankind's development.

Evolutionary stories about musical expressiveness are usually more refined than the one proposed by Kivy (see for examples Cross and Morley 2009).[15] In particular, most of them relate the tendency to perceive music as expressive to the role played by music in promoting group cohesion and wellbeing (e.g. Roederer 1984; H. Papoušek 1996). Still, evolutionary arguments plausibly support Kivy's claim that a useful tendency to perceive patterns as animated might have resulted in some unconscious mechanism generating expressive experiences.

Even accepting that resemblances can, in one way or another, justify expressive experiences of music and other inanimate objects, another objection can be raised against contour theory's appeal to resemblance. This second criticism concerns the explanatory level of expressive experience and has been put forward in similar ways by Saam Trivedi (2001) and Paul Noordhof (2008). In short, they contend that it is not clear why the resemblances between musical perceptual contour and expressive behaviour should be more salient than other possibly existing similarities. One can indeed argue that a piece of music, or a passage, resembles a dialogue, a fight, a journey, a series of events, the fury of the elements, rather than emotional expressions; that a piece of music is better described by appealing to the resemblances it bears to other objects, events, structures, rather than to behavioural manifestations of emotions. So, the philosopher who intends to justify expressive experiences by appealing to resemblances needs to explain why resemblances to expressions come prior to or prevail on other possible resemblances. Moreover, contour theorists should answer the question of how it is possible that the numerous differences that can

---

[15] For an insightful challenge to Kivi's appeal to evolutionary arguments, see Ravasio (2018). An attempt to provide some psychological support to contour theory can instead be found in Benenti and Meini (2017).

be observed between the audible contour of a piece of music and typical emotion manifestations do not undermine the emergence of expressiveness.

Even in this case, it seems that an evolutionary stance may provide some consistent explanation for the priority of the recognition of objects' features that resemble human expressions, over others. The interest in the recognition of emotion as an evolutionarily relevant phenomenon can be traced back to Charles Darwin's seminal study (1871). Famously, according to Darwin, the expression of basic emotions is rooted in biology, cross-cultural and mostly conveyed by facial expressions. Basic emotions are taken to have typical expressions, which conspecifics are able to detect rapidly and automatically. This ability is not surprising from an evolutionary point of view: a highly social species like ours gains extensive selective advantages from being able to recognise others' emotions as quickly and as automatically as possible. A plausible outcome of this mechanism could be our tendency to prioritize the detection of features of the environment that resemble emotional expressions.[16]

However, as will become clearer later on, contour theory does not manage to settle these problems. The explanatory and the phenomenal role of resemblances are definitely not self-evident and, more generally, the exact relation between the phenomenal character of the experience and the mechanisms that make it possible deserves further clarification.

1.8 Imaginative Theories: Levinson and Noordhof

Pure music has been and continues to be especially interesting for those who intend to explain the expressive features of inanimate things and their relation to our emotions. One of the most influential views in the philosophy of music that seeks to account for the experience of expressive music is the so-called *persona theory* and Jerrold Levinson is the most prominent supporter of this theory. His account of musical expressiveness is well summarised by the two following quotes:

> [...] a passage of music P is expressive of an emotion E if and only if P, in context, is readily heard, by a listener experienced in the genre in question, as an expression of E.
> (Levinson 2006, p. 93)

---

[16] The perceptual recognition of emotional expressions will be discussed in more detail in Chapter 5.

That is:

> [...] music expresses an emotion only to the extent that we are disposed to hear it as the expression of an emotion, although in a non-standard manner, by a person or person-like entity. (Levinson 2006, p. 93)

Levinson explicitly shares the concern that "expression" is, by definition, the manifestation of inner states through outer signs, performed by sentient (especially human) beings. Given such a premise, the link between human expression and musical expressiveness requires the appeal to some psychological mechanism that accounts for the fact that musical expressiveness cannot be the expression of any occurring internal state, for music is an inanimate object.

In order to fill in the gap between human emotional expression and musical expressiveness, Levinson introduces the notion of a fictional character that we are meant to imagine whenever we experience a piece of music as being expressive. The term "persona" is not chosen by chance: this Latin word refers to the mask that used to hide the actor's face when performing a play. The "persona" is therefore the fictional character of a play who mimics behaviours, especially affective manifestation, on the stage. Consistently, we experience expressive music *as if it were* the expression of emotions and feelings on behalf of such a fictional character. Levinson's explanation appeals to our capacity to *perceive* (hear, in the case at stake) something *as* something else. What an experienced listener does when she hears a sad piece of music, is hear it *as* a behavioural expression of the emotion of sadness on behalf of a fictional agent.

Levinson treats the experience of *hearing-as* as an imaginative experience that is anchored in perception. According to his perspective, expressive properties are dispositional properties that listeners (at least experienced ones) recognise by virtue of the capacity these properties have to trigger the appropriate imaginings that, in turn, can make listeners hear merely perceptual properties *as* the expression of someone's emotions. When understood in this way, expressive experience is taken to involve (i) the perceivable features of the piece of music, such as its notes, chords, melody, rhythm, and (ii) what Levinson calls the "modifier" of the perceptual content of the experience, that is, what makes the perceivable features of music sound in a *sui generis* way, i.e. expressive of emotions. This modifier, according to Levinson, "plausibly belongs to the content of a subsidiary thought on the expressing we hear in expressive music, not part of the content of the core experience" (Levinson 2006, p. 95). And in order for such a modifier to actually modify the perceptual content of the "hearing as expressive" experience, the intervention of *imagination* is required. In particular, Levinson writes that, although defining the experiences of perceiving-as or perceiving-in is a difficult task:

> [...] it suffices to locate hearing-as and hearing-in among perceptual acts that partake freely of, or that substantially enlist, the *imagination* [...] To hear music as such and such is, perhaps, to imagine *that* the music is such and such, and more specifically, to imagine *of* the music, *as* you are hearing it, that it is such and such. (Levinson 2006, p. 95)

This statement needs to be unpacked. According to this view, it seems to follow that imagination is responsible for the fact that the content of our experience involves expressive features. This intervention consists in the propositional imagining that a person or person-like entity expresses her affective states through the piece of music. As a result, what could be the experience of a mere arrangement of perceptual features is turned into the experience of expressive features.

If this interpretation is correct, then we should think about the experience of expressive music as the experience of certain perceptual properties that are capable of triggering propositional imaginings having an expresser (the *persona*) in their content. However, such a content is not necessarily part of what we experience, but it has the power to modify it and make it a *sui generis* perceptual content.[17] Levinson insists that "immediacy is a proper desideratum for an account of musical expressiveness" (Levinson 2006, p. 101), meaning that expressive experience is, so to speak, perception-like for what concerns its phenomenal immediacy. In other words – for reasons that will become clearer in the discussion below – the expressive features of a piece of music will appear to a listener with the same immediacy of its perceptual structure. Expressiveness is therefore maintained to be the conjunction of two factors. On the one hand, perceptual features of music are meant to trigger the propositional imagining *that someone is expressing her own felt emotions through music*; on the other hand, the resulting experience is a *sui generis* perceptual experience whose perceptual features are "readily" recognised as being expressive.

One of the problematic aspects of the persona theory is that it appeals to an imaginative experience with quite distinctive content and phenomenology, such that it predicts that we should be able to consciously experience an expressive persona. Stephen Davies (1997), Kendall Walton (1999), Jenefer Robinson (2007), and Paul Noordhof (2008) have put forward four various versions of this same

---

[17] Levinson does not explicitly distinguish between content and character, but I take his view to imply that we experience only some features of the experience's content – namely those that result in the phenomenal character. In the next chapters I will try to make this distinction clearer.

criticism, that is effectively captured by Tom Cochrane (who nevertheless endorses the persona theory):

> The main criticism of the persona view is that it places too great a demand on what a listener is experiencing when he or she hears music as emotionally expressive. We may agree that a listener can imagine that the emotion in the music belongs to a person. We might also grant that his or her imagination can be passively stimulated to do as such, rather than deliberately engaged on most occasions. But this is far from agreeing that listeners necessarily imagine a persona. (Cochrane 2010, p. 264)

Although we can undergo experiences where we imagine fictional characters within music, most of our experiences of expressive music do not bear witness to such a content and to the related phenomenology: most of the time we do not imagine any persona expressing herself through music.

Levinson replies to this objection by appealing to an extremely thin notion of persona. He suggests that we think of the fictional character "hidden" behind the music as one who is devoid of specific features that must be imagined. Rather, it should be imagined as the mere capacity of animated beings to express themselves through movements and behaviours.

> [...] this agent or persona, it must be stressed, is almost entirely indefinite, a minimal sort of person, characterised only by the emotion we hear it to be expressing and the music gesture through which it does so. (Levinson 2006, p. 93)

And in the same vein, Cochrane insists that:

> In general, this minimal sense of self intrinsic to emotional experience is all that we should consider necessary to the musical persona. We appeal to the persona only insofar as it is required in order to explain the bare connection between music and emotions. (Cochrane 2010, p. 264)

The required persona is therefore a "minimal self" provided with the capacity to express affective states. Such a persona would be neither a fictive composer, nor a fictive musician then.

Describing this view as "hypothetical personalism", Lopes remarks that it is so trivial that nothing can prevent one from accepting it. The only requirement for something to be a "persona", on this view, is that it possesses those emotions that we see expressed in the work. If the work in question is expressive of anguish, then the only feature characterising the persona that we are meant to imagine in order to perceive such an anguish, will be the capacity to express anguish. But if this is the case, then the only reason why it is worth appealing to a persona to explain expressiveness is conformity with the rule that expressed emotions must be attributed to persons (Lopes 2005, p. 65).

As Noordhof points out and as Lopes seems to suggest, one is tempted to ask whether, once it has been reduced to such a residual notion, the fictional character that we are expected to imagine is still a useful explanatory tool (Noordhof 2008, p. 334; Lopes 2005, p. 65). Still, however minimal and vague the persona is taken to be, Levinson's theory requires the listener to engage in an imaginative experience in order to hear music as expressive of emotions. Although the object of this experience could be no more than an x without specific features, it remains a required integral part of the imaginative engagement, a part that not all experiences of expressive music seem to witness.

Notice that this objection does not amount to denying that certain pieces or kinds of music can or should better be attended as if they were someone's emotional expression. For instance, Jenefer Robinson observes that:

> [...] it is appropriate to look for musical personae only in Romantic and post-Romantic music that can plausibly be interpreted this way either because the composer explicitly encourages such an interpretation, as in the *Symphonie Fantastique*, or because the composer is working in light of this kind of precedent. (Robinson 2007, p. 27)

There exist experiences of expressive music that may allow for the imaginative engagement predicted by the theory of persona. Moreover, as Robinson (2005) has argued extensively, certain works advise listeners to attend to the music by means of this kind of engagement. But this is not enough to claim that such an engagement is required to hear a piece of music as expressive.

An analogous consideration can be put forward for other sorts of expressive items. One may take Jackson Pollock's dripping canvas to be expressive of anxiety, while Mark Rothko's grey and black paintings to be expressive of despair. But do we need to imagine them as being the expression of some real-life (the painters') or fictional character's anxiety or despair in order to see them as expressive? Once again, the phenomenology of our experiences hints a negative answer.

As with contour theory, this difficulty in reconciling the perception-like phenomenal character of expressive experience and the mechanism that is meant to explain it, has been pointed out by Paul Noordhof in his insightful article (2008). He proposes to distinguish two different tasks that a theory of expressiveness has to fulfil: to account for the content of the experience at stake (roughly, what the experience of expressiveness is about) and to elaborate on the explanatory mental mechanisms that make the experience possible. Therefore, according to his analysis, Levinson fails in distinguishing between these two levels of the explanation. Because whereas he acknowledges that the experience of expressive music is perception-like, as it consists in an immediate and spontaneous recognition (Levinson 2006, p. 95), he accounts for the specificity of the experience (its being perceptual but is a special way) by "reflecting, in the phenomenal content of expressive perception, features which, at best, are part of the explanation of expressive perception or analytic commitments of our notion of expression" (Noordhof 2008, p. 332).

Although he criticises Levinson, Noordhof is still persuaded that imagination is what one should appeal to in order to explain expressive experience. His entire argument stems from the idea that:

> [...] it makes little sense to suppose that something may be experienced as expressive quite independently of how we respond to it; that our experience of expressiveness can be simply an experience of features of the world. (Noordhof 2008, p. 342)

The intuition here is that the sadness that a piece of music seems to express does not belong to the piece in the same way in which its rhythm, notes, and pitches do. *Sadness* is something that cannot be literally heard as a "feature of the world", that is, as a perceptual property of the piece of music, while auditory properties are. In other words, notes and chords are perceptual components of music independently of the subjects' responses, whereas sadness seems to be more dependent on the way subjects respond or are disposed to respond to the piece. The task is therefore to appropriately describe the content of the experience of expressiveness so as to characterise as precisely as possible the explanandum of the theory. After casting light on the specificity of the content, it is possible to provide a consistent explanation that should be compatible with both phenomenological observations and experimental data.

With regard to the content of the experience, Noordhof claims that it should be described differently from Levinson's account: it is not *as if* the music were expressing emotions (through some fictive persona), but rather certain perceptual properties of music are experienced *as potentially expressive*, and:

> [...] it is in virtue of this potential, that the properties in question are part of the realisation of expressive properties. [...] we simply experience the fact that they could be used to express something in much the same way that the potential uses of many things in our environment signal themselves to us. (Noordhof 2008, p. 332)

Accordingly, the peculiarity of this experience consists in the perceivable expressive potential of certain "merely perceptual" features instantiated by objects. Let us consider again Pollock's famous paintings realised by means of the so-called "dripping" technique. Noordhof's suggestion is that we experience the perceptual pattern constituted by its stains of colours and manifold shapes as being *potentially* expressive. Once he has characterised the content of expressive experience, he focuses on the related explanatory level. Consistent with his scepticism about the possibility to explain expressive experience in terms of mere perception, he argues that expressive properties are better characterised as response-dependent properties. In order to avoid the difficulties encountered by the persona theory, Noordhof's account relies on *sensuous imagination*. This kind of imagination presents several advantages compared to the propositional imagining employed by Levinson. Before explaining them in detail, an elucidation is required about the notion used by Noordhof.

In the recent debate, sensuous (or, as it is more often called, "sensory") imagination is maintained to be a subclass of mental imagery, namely the kind of imagination that implies the formation of mental images. The specificity of sensuous imagination is such that it *recreates* in imagination a perceptual experience, that is to say, it *re-presents* features that can be perceptually experienced but that need not be directly presented to the subject at the time of the sensory imagining. "Visualisation" is an instance of sensuous imagination. When I visualise a landscape, I form the image of such a landscape in its absence, and the image that I form is meant to instantiate those features that I may perceive if the landscape in question were actually in front of me. Thus, we should think about the content of sensuous imagination as being significantly related to perception. Compared to perception, sensuous imagination is less immediate, that is, unlike when we perceive an object, when we imagine it we do not have the impression to be directly, *immediately*, in contact with its features.[18] Moreover, by definition, imagination requires some kind of engagement: we can to some extent decide what and how to sensuously imagine. Therefore, sensuous imagination, unlike perception, is "relatively under our control" (Noordhof 2008, p. 337). These three characteristics of sensuous imagination – its closeness to perception, its lack of immediacy and its dependency on will – are, according to Noordhof, apt to account for the phenomenal features of expressive experience.

Firstly, the fact that sensuous imagination recreates perceptual features in imagination matches the content of expressive experience, namely the fact that it seems to represent those shapes, colours, and sounds that are mobilised by the perceptual experience of the same objects. Secondly, in the words of Noordhof: "[...] our perceptual experience of expressive properties, while attributing them to objects, does not have the immediacy of our perceptual experience of colours say" (Noordhof 2008, p. 337). And he takes sensuous imagination to be responsible for this alleged difference in immediacy

---

18 As we will see in Chapter 2, immediacy, along with vivacity (or vividness) and determinacy, are often considered those phenomenal qualities that help us to distinguish between perceptual and imaginative experiences (on this characterisation see Dorsch 2012, Ch. 3).

that distinguishes standard perceptual experiences from expressive experiences.[19] Thirdly, expressive experience is not as stable and as independent of our will as standard perceptual experiences (such as those of mere sounds, chords, shades, or shapes) seem to be. To some extent we can decide whether to experience an artwork as expressive or as affectively neutral. Noordhof writes:

> It is possible to hear music as inexpressive noise, [...] especially if you are not attending to it. It is tempting to think that the difference arises from whether or not our imaginations are engaged. The fact that our imaginations are relatively under our control explains how it is also relatively under our control whether we experience expressive properties.
> (Noordhof 2008, p. 337)

Thus, sensuous imagination meets three fundamental requirements that the phenomenal level of expressive experience sets up, namely: (i) the fact that it instantiates perceptual features, (ii) the fact that its character lacks the immediacy and vividness of perceptual character and (iii) the fact that it is relatively under our control. This is meant to make sensuous imagination the best candidate to account for expressive experience.

On this basis, Noordhof can elaborate on the most intriguing and intricate part of his theory. He suggests that, when we experience a work of art as expressive of some affective state, we *sensuously imagine the emotion-guided creative process* that is or might have been responsible for making expressive certain merely perceptual features of the work (Noordhof 2008, p. 330). These imaginings do not imply that we imagine *someone*, like a fictive persona, who creates the work in such a way that makes it expressive; nor do we need to imagine that we ourselves are engaged in a creative process. Instead, we can imagine how certain features that constitute the work we are attending to might be the result of a process of selection and arrangement that is guided by emotions – even if such a process never took place. According to Noordhof, when we perceive the expressive features of a painting, we are actually sensuously imagining those features as being the result of an intentional creative process that was put in place under the guidance of the emotional state we see expressed. Last but not least, the very fact that we experience expressive properties is taken by Noordhof as evidence that there is a sensuous imaginative project going on. This process involves what he calls the *phenomenal skeleton*

---

19 Notice that this intuition about the lack of immediacy is in contrast with what most authors think, namely that expressive experience is perception-like in character. This disagreement about the phenomenal character of expressive experience will be the object of an in-depth analysis in the next chapter.

of emotions, i.e. the causal power they have to generate expressive gestures that can, in turn, result in a creative process.

The problem with the persona theory that Noordhof had pointed out was that the imagined persona is not part of the phenomenal character of the experience. In other words, most of us on most occasions would not acknowledge that we are engaged in the imaginative project of considering a fictive, expressive character when attending to expressive music or paintings. *Prima facie* one might address the same criticism to Noordhof's theory, arguing that it is definitely not the case that, when perceiving an expressive work, we are aware of imagining a creative process. Noordhof replies by appealing to the distinction between judging *whether* we are or are not imagining, and judging *what* we are imagining (if actually we are): "My claims about the plausibility of attributing one content or another are thus independent of the question of whether or not we are aware that we are imagining" (Noordhof 2008, p. 342). We may accordingly be wrong about the fact that we are imagining rather than perceiving something, but not about what such a mental state is about.

This view, applied to the case at hand, means that we might be perfectly right about the music sounding sad, but not about the fact that the mental state we are in is an imaginative one. The content of our expressive experience is in fact constituted by perceptual properties that we recognise as apt for being the result of a creative process, so that we grasp their expressive potential. The fact that such a content is the result of an imaginative process is something we do not need to be aware of. Accordingly, what we are aware of – the phenomenal character – is only the expressive potential that imagination made available. So, unlike the theory that implies that one imagines a persona, Noordhof's account is apparently safe from criticisms that address the way it is like for a subject to undergo the experience.

In order for an imagined creative process to make perceptual features expressive, the imaginings that are triggered by such non-expressive features should partially "involve states with phenomenally similar (but not identical) content to our experience of our own emotions" (Noordhof 2008, p. 344). This means that certain features of emotions, namely their power to cause expressive behaviours (the *phenomenal skeleton*), will be part of the content of the imaginings, which are in turn responsible for perceptual features resulting expressive: "In brief, we will sensuously imagine the phenomenal skeleton of an emotion that guides the creative process" (Noordhof 2008, p. 344). Noordhof carefully specifies that we do not need to imagine we ourselves undergoing an emotion guiding an expressive behaviour resulting in a creative process. On his view, expressive experience does not require an imaginative engagement from a first-person perspective, so that we can well imagine the phenomenal skeleton of the emotion without imagining that emotion to be *our own* emotion. All is needed is that we recognise the phenomenal skeleton of an emotion leading the process, meaning its causal power to give rise to certain expressive behaviours. According to this hypothesis, we need to recognise something as ultimately generated by such a causal skeleton; put simply, we need to be able to imagine something as resulting from an emotion.

Both Levinson and Noordhof put forward theories of expressive experience that use imagination as a powerful explanatory tool. With this in mind, we should focus on the way they relate to IOE, i.e. the intuitive paradox of expressive objects. It can be maintained that the persona theory introduces the imagined character (i.e. the minimal persona) precisely in order to solve the contradiction: emotions and therefore their expressions do not belong to music and other inanimate things, hence imagination is required to explain how such things can be expressive. Namely, imagination introduces in the experience what cannot be "out there" in reality and consequently what simple perception cannot give us: emotions and their expressions as belonging to inanimate objects. Similarly, Noordhof presents expressive experience as requiring the imagination of an *action* performed under the guidance of an *emotion* that, by definition, can belong only to a sentient being. In both cases, the intervention of imagination is required to solve what is still felt as a paradox, analogously to what illusion, projection, memory, and arousal did in the cases of pathetic fallacy, projectivism, complex projectivism and arousalism, respectively. Despite distancing itself from Wollheim's standard projectivism and from Matravers' standard arousalism, the imaginative projectivism supported by Noordhof shares an important supposition with these views: expressive features of objects cannot be features of the world because objects cannot literally possess emotions. Therefore, when we perceive expressive properties of objects we are not experiencing something that actually belongs to those objects. As a consequence, emotions (namely their causal power resulting in gestures) are projected on objects so as to fill the gap between the animated and the inanimate.

To conclude this overview, it seems relevant to point out that contour theory takes the distinction between expression and expressiveness more seriously than the rest of the presented accounts. In fact, its supporters do not appeal to the subjective capacity to evoke fictive characters or memories of past experiences in order to fill the gap between actual human expression and objectual expressiveness. Rather, they acknowledge that expressiveness must be analysed as distinct from actual expression and as pertaining to the look of things (and of people). Still, the appeal to resemblance between expressiveness and expressive behaviours as what does justice to the affective relevance of expressiveness is problematic. As argued by critics of resemblance accounts, despite being able to explain some experiences, similarities are not always available, not even upon reflection. The appeal to similarity limits the explanatory power of contour theory to features that are complex enough to be compared (or comparable) with behavioural manifestations. This limitation is further attested by the difficulties it has to account for elementary but nevertheless expressive features such as pitches, chords, notes, colours, and simple shapes.

Chapter 2
The Phenomenology of Expressive Experience

When we examine the most relevant theories of expressiveness that are central to the analytic debate, a constellation of perspectives emerges that share some intuitions but diverge on several points. These accounts can now be compared and tested against the *desiderata* to see whether and to what extent they satisfy those requirements. In § 2.1 we will see that there is a general agreement about the phenomenology of expressive experience, namely its perceptual phenomenal character. However, some ambiguity arises when it comes to the role played by imagination in relation to phenomenal character (§ 2.2), and disagreement becomes evident in the discussion about the role of felt emotions (§ 2.3). This is discussed in more detail in § 2.3.1. In § 2.4 the phenomenal character of expressive experience is assessed in terms of its relation to time (§ 2.4.1), movement (§ 2.4.2), and the degree of complexity of the phenomenology (§ 2.4.3).

2.1 Some Agreement: The Perceptual Character of Expressive Experience

The first requirement that a theory of expressiveness should meet, is an accurate account of its specific phenomenal character, meaning *the way it is like* to undergo an expressive experience. Most philosophers of expressiveness agree to some extent on the phenomenal character of expressive experience. In particular, they share the view that expressive experience is a perceptual experience, albeit on that is *sui generis*.

Contour theory is the only theory to consider expressive experience as a perceptual experience *tout court*. Consistently, contour theorists have devoted much attention to the phenomenology of expressive experience. As already pointed out, both Peter Kivy and Stephen Davies claim that expressive experience of music is analogous to the perceptual experience of structural features of the pieces. Davies writes:

> [...] the claim is that the expressiveness is a property of the music itself. This property resides in the way the music sounds to the attuned listener, just as happy-lookingness can be a property displayed in a creature's face or movements. (Davies 2005, p. 181)

On this perspective, expressive qualities are perceivable components of musical structure and are experienced as such. They are neither the result of affective arousal, nor of imaginative engagement. Rather, they are heard *in* music.

Accordingly, the perceptual phenomenology of expressive experience consists in the recognition of profiles or contours.

Remarkably, this is held to be true of music as well as of other objects, regardless of their being natural objects or artefacts. Indeed, even though most philosophers who deal with expressiveness focus on auditory experiences, they often take their theories to apply also to other sensory modalities. Levinson, for example, declares that his view on expressive properties "is apt not only for music, but for non-representational art generally" (Levinson 2006, p. 102), and Davies relies on episodes of visual experience to make the case of expressive music more perspicuous, arguing that: "[...] when we attribute emotions to music we are describing the emotional character it presents, just as we do when we call the willow sad or the car happy" (Davies 2005, p. 181). Finally, Dominic Lopes explicitly applies contour theory to paintings (Lopes 2005).[20] Arguably, the phenomenal character of expressive experience consists therefore in the auditory or visual perception of features that is as immediate and as unreflective as the perceptual experience of sounds, colours and shapes.

Arousalism inevitably struggles with this view. As suggested, strong versions of arousalism are difficult to defend, particularly if they imply that one has to be aroused in order to undergo expressive experiences. Phenomenology speaks against this claim, as we do not always *feel* aroused when we hear a relentless piece of music or contemplate a lively scene. However, this version of arousalism is neither the sole arousalistic account that exists in the literature, nor the most refined. As already seen, Ridley (1995) has shown that one can hold an arousalistic position about music's expressiveness without neglecting the link between the structure of music, its contour, its auditory features and the sort of emotions that it is capable of arousing in listeners. He adopts Kivy's idea that we experience music as being expressive if it bears some resemblance to typical expressions of emotions performed by humans. Interestingly, despite his rejection of the idea that musical expressiveness can be reduced to a merely perceptual experience, Ridley acknowledges that contour theory establishes the necessary conditions for expressive experience to take place, namely that a musical contour resembles, in some relevant aspect, the human expression of emotions. Jenefer Robinson, shares the same intuition: "Of course, in listening to music we may also be *noticing* expressive contours and *figuring out* how the expressive character of the music unfolds" (Robinson 2005, p. 374). Thus, even

---

[20] This is Lopes' own formulation: "[def.] minimal contour theory of pictorial expression: a pictorial design, a depicted figure, or a depicted scene expresses E if and only if it is an expression-look of E." (Lopes 2005, p. 71).

if she doubts Kivy's account and believes that felt emotions must aid expressive experience, she acknowledges that 'the cognitive mode of understanding' expressive contours of music plays a necessary role in the experience of expressiveness. Overall, the idea is that at least a relevant part of the phenomenal character of expressive experience is a matter of perceptual experience of certain features, be they a contour, a profile, or a melisma.

Further support for this idea is provided by imaginative accounts. According to Levinson, we experience music as being expressive so long as its perceivable features trigger the propositional imaginings that someone is expressing oneself through music. This requires a preliminary step consisting in the perceptual recognition of certain features of the piece, namely the "appearance of human emotion" that the structure of music resembles:

> In addition to presenting an array of sonic features, simultaneously and successively, much music offers the appearance of human emotion, or of persons outwardly manifesting emotional states; arguably, that is what the expressiveness of music largely consists in [...] The degree of resemblance between the shape of music and the behaviors through which emotions are commonly expressed in life will have something, though not everything, to do with our being disposed to hear music in such ways. (Levinson 2006, p. 50)

Even though he does not content himself with this endorsement of the contour theory's proposal and invokes the imaginative solutions already mentioned, Levinson is quite explicit: the "shape of music", which means its perceivable structure, is an important part of expressive experience as it bears resemblances to expressive behaviours. More specifically, Levinson claims that when we experience music as being expressive, we perceptually experience its gestures:

> Gesture in music serves as the crucial middle term between musical movement and musical expression. It is because music often presents the appearance of *gestures* of various sorts that it can be heard, by analogy with the role of physical gesture in behavioural expression of emotion, as if it were *itself* an expression of emotion. (Levinson 2009, p. 420)

The experience of gestures as what makes music expressive cannot be accounted for appealing to *inferences*, Levinson says, rather it is a special sort of perceptual experience as reliably attested by its *immediacy*:

> basic musical expressiveness – though perhaps not all sorts of expressiveness, such as that more typical of literature, involving articulate states of mind, nor that perhaps attaching to works of music as wholes – is something directly heard, not inferred, [...] immediacy is a proper desideratum for an account of musical expressiveness.
> (Levinson 2006, p. 101)

As I shall recall, *directedness* and *immediacy* are commonly maintained to be peculiar features of what it is like to perceive something. In his characterization of the phenomenology of expressive experience, also Noordhof relies on these features, the phenomenological ascertainment of which grounds the claim that expressive experience is a kind of perceptual experience.

2.2 Some Ambiguity: The Imaginative Character of Expressive Experience

Paul Noordhof uses the term *expressive perception* to describe expressive experience that requires the interplay between perceptual and imaginative contents and attitudes. Phenomenally, expressive experience consists in the perception of potentially expressive features of artworks. Yet, as said, phenomenological considerations about the specific character of expressive experiences are precisely meant to support the imaginative intervention. To recap: expressive perception is taken by Noordhof to be: (i) less immediate than normal perception, (ii) relatively under our control, unlike normal perception, but (iii) such that it presents the same phenomenal features of perception (colours, shapes, shadows, sounds, and so on). Features (i) and (ii) are worth questioning. In particular, it is worth trying to show that such a phenomenology does not automatically imply the intervention of imagination. On the contrary, these features can be considered features of the phenomenal character of a perceptual experience. If this is true, then the appeal to imagination should find its foothold somewhere else than in the phenomenal character.

Let us first focus on the difference between perceptual and sensuous imagery experience. It is very common to introduce this distinction starting from the lack of immediacy and of vividness of the latter compared to the former. Fabian Dorsch writes:

> That sensory imaginings (as well as sensory memories) lack the immediacy of perceptual experiences means, first of all, that they do not present their objects as being there before us in our actual environment. When we see a tree, it seems to be right there before our eyes. But when we visualise a tree, we do not have a similar impression of its presence in our actual environment. (Dorsch 2012, p. 83)

On this interpretation, immediacy is understood as some sort of feeling of presence that accompanies every perception, whereas it is lacking, or at least is diminished, when we undergo imaginative experiences. Noordhof buys into this distinction when he appeals to sensuous imagination considered as a "paler version" of perception. According to such an admittedly Humean view:

> [...] seeing an apple seems to have a certain phenomenal oomph that is missing in the case of imagining the apple. This phenomenal oomph is often described as feeling of

presence. When we see an apple, we have this feeling of presence. When we have mental imagery of it, we don't have this feeling of presence. (Nanay 2016a, p. 128)

However, Bence Nanay insists, this paradigmatic distinction admits for intermediate cases where the "oomph" criterion is not applicable:

> I don't see any reason to take the difference in the feeling of presence to be a mark of the difference between the phenomenology of perception and mental imagery. It sounds right that perception is, at least when conscious, accompanied by a feeling of presence. But I see no reason to think that mental imagery in general is not accompanied by a feeling of presence. (Nanay 2016a, p. 129)

Thus, one may argue that the difference in terms of immediacy (oomph, feeling of presence) between sensuous imagination and perception is not granted, thereby undermining one of the reasons for appealing to imagination in order to account for expressive perception. In addition, even if one accepts this criterion to distinguish between the two, it does not indisputably apply to expressive experience.

It has been noticed that we do not hear the sadness of a musical gesture less immediately than how we hear the gesture itself, nor the liveliness of a landscape less immediately than how we see its colours and slopes. Sadness or liveliness are no less immediately presented in experience than colours or shapes, nor experienced in a later moment compared to the auditory structure of music. Instead, it seems that: "It takes as long to hear the music's expressive properties as it takes to hear the passages in which those properties are articulated" (Davies 2005, p. 181). It does not take more to hear the "noble and restrained passion" expressed by the principal theme of the First Movement in Gabriel Fauré's Piano Quartet in C Minor, Op. 15, than it takes to hear the underlying "strings with syncopated interjections from the piano" (Levinson 2009, p. 422). Expressive qualities are apprehended as immediately as the merely perceptual features of musical pieces. Therefore, even if one endorsed a view according to which the object of mental imagery is not phenomenally present to the subject as the object of perceptual experience, it is not clear that the objects of expressive experience should fall within the former instead of within the latter category.

One may interpret Noordhof's view more charitably, as claiming that expressive experiences are not as *vivid* and as *stable* for a subject as perceptual experiences are. Accordingly, the sadness expressed by a sonata would be perceived as being phenomenally fainter than the sounds and rhythm that constitute it. Vividness is indeed a phenomenal characterisation of experiences that may be taken to belong either to their representational content or to their phenomenal character. In the former case, vividness concerns the degree of vagueness of the *information* provided by the representational content, whereas in the latter case, vividness affects the *experience* we have of the objects and of their features.²¹ In either case, it can be argued that, as a qualitative aspect, vividness remains a matter of degrees: "[...] it is not clear whether there could not be, on the one hand, perceptions [...] which are faint and, on the other hand, sensory imaginings which are vivid" (Dorsch 2012, p. 82). Thus, nothing guarantees that vivacity or vividness is enough to distinguish perceptual episodes from imaginative episodes. It is at best a typical qualification of the phenomenology rather than a criterion for the classification of different mental states (Dorsch 2012, p. 82). Hence, even if we interpret the appeal to immediacy as an appeal to vividness, it does not offer any good reason to affirm that expressive experience has an imaginative rather than a perceptual phenomenology.

Let us now take what can be called the *manipulability* of expressive experience, that is, its being relatively under our control. As said, this phenomenal quality prompts the idea that mental imagery is best suited to account for expressive experience. According to a general and widely accepted characterisation, the main distinction between perceptual states and imaginings is that, whereas the latter are subject to the will, the former are independent of the subject's will or agency.²² Along this line, Paul Noordhof points out that there are occasions in which we can deliberately decide whether to experience the same piece of music as being expressive or affectively neutral.

It must be noticed that the claim is not that we are totally free to imagine the same piece of music as expressive of whatever affective state we please – which would imply a denial of any constraint of the perceptual, non-expressive structure of the piece on its expressive features. Rather, the idea is that we can control our experience and obliterate, so to speak, its expressive component in favour of a neutral and merely perceptual experience. This remark captures an important phenomenal quality of expressive experience, namely that it is more dependent on the subject than other perceptual experiences. It is indeed true that, while we cannot decide whether to experience Malevič's *Black Square* (1915) as being "black" or not, we have some control over our experience when it comes to seeing it as being or not being "disquieting". And even if we ourselves can't help experiencing it as disquieting, it is not difficult to imagine that the art historian

---

21 For discussion about blurriness and fuzziness of perceptual experiences, see Boghossian and Velleman 1989; Tye 2003; and Calabi 2014.
22 See, for example, Dorsch 2012 for an exhaustive account of imagination characterized as motivated action. He ascribes what he calls the "Agency Account" to Richard Wollheim, Jerrold Levinson, Amy Kind, and Colin McGinn.

who studies the painting, focusing on its shape and on the contrast between the black of the square and the white of the frame, will be able to neglect its expressive character in favour of an affectively neutral experience.

Accepting that the expressive character of things is phenomenally not as independent of our will as colours are, however, is not *ipso facto* to rule out perception in favour of imagination. A fruitful strategy in support of this objection consists in considering perceptual experiences in which we exercise some control but that are not usually explained in terms of imagination. The example that I wish to analyse is perceptual attention and shifts of attention from certain perceptual saliences to others. Suppose we are looking at a depicted landscape such as *Der Nachmittag* (1821–1822) by Caspar Friedrich, and suppose that, at a first glance, we do not see the horse pulling the wagon at the centre of the canvas. Then, all of a sudden, we notice it. We shift the focus of our attention, perhaps in virtue of a chromatic discontinuity on the canvas, and we perceive features of which we were previously unaware. Once we are aware that there is a horse pulling a wagon in the picture, it might also be the case that we shift our attention again and we focus on other elements of the work, such as the compositional structure, or chromatic range displayed on the canvas, so that we once again neglect the depicted wagon and the horse. This experience does not require that one engages in an imaginative project such as to determine features of the painting that are not actually part of the painting. It is just a matter of looking more attentively at the surface and picking up certain saliences.

An immediate objection to this example is that it concerns a change of the visual focus that leaves a certain particular feature of the painting out of sight. If so, this would not be a counterexample to the idea that controlling one's experience makes this experience an episode of imagination. Rather, it would merely suggest that we can direct our gaze to different items in our environment and that, owing to spatial considerations, it is not possible to have all of them in sight at once. What is needed instead is a perceptual experience that allows us to neglect certain features in favour of others, while nonetheless keeping our gaze fixed on the same portion of the canvas.

A more fruitful way to show that there are perceptual experiences in which we exercise some control without necessarily mobilising imagination appeals to bi-stable (or multi-stable) figures perception. As is well known, we can experience figures such as the Jastrow's duck-rabbit either *as representing x* or *as representing y*, depending on the perceptual saliences on which we focus our attention. They are perceptual patterns that lend themselves to being perceived in different ways. Seeing-as experiences are explained in terms of "seeing" or "noticing an aspect": "I contemplate a face, and then suddenly notice its likeness to another. I *see* that it has not changed; and yet I see it differently. I call this experience 'noticing an aspect'" (Wittgenstein 1986, p. 193). Such a noticing, as well as the recognition of the duck in the duck-rabbit figure, or of Voltaire's portrait in Dalí's *Slave Market with the Disappearing Bust of Voltaire* (1940), is often maintained to be perceptual in character and sometimes involving the voluntary focus of attention (see for instance Gombrich 1960; Wollheim 2003; Nanay 2010; Jagnow 2011; Voltolini 2015). Yet it is also relatively under our control:

> True, we may be able to stop seeing a picture as a picture (e.g. by attending to it in a certain way); and we may have some control over whether we see the duck-rabbit drawing as a depiction of a duck or as a depiction of a rabbit. (Dorsch 2016, p. 234)

This characterisation of aspect perception suffices to point out that a phenomenology that entails voluntary control is not peculiar of imagination, it does not indicate *per se* that imagination is involved. Undeniably, the fact that (i) vividness and (ii) manipulability feature in the phenomenal character of expressive experience must be taken into account. Expressive qualities may appear less vivid and more subject to will than colours, say. But these features are not specific enough to distinguish the phenomenal character of expressive experience from that of standard perceptual experience.

So far, I believe I have shown that most accounts more or less explicitly converge on the idea that our expressive experiences are perceptual in character, despite providing different explanations for this view. They exclude in one way or another that the ascription of expressiveness to objects is the ascription of fully-fledged emotions to them (in what would be a sort of illusory, systematically erroneous or hallucinatory experience), and they try to deal with the fact that the expressiveness of objects is primarily a matter of perceptual recognition, whatever this implies. However, this experience is taken to be distinct from standard perceptual experiences, such as the perceptual experience of patterns of sounds, pitches, chords, or rhythms (or, in the case of visual features, as the perceptual experience of colours and shapes). In order to account for the specificity of expressive experience, two further phenomenal features are usually discussed. The first is what we may call the *affective load* of expressive experience, while the second is the *degree of complexity* of expressive features.

2.3 Some Disagreement: The Affective Load of Expressive Experience

Curiously enough, there is no agreement among philosophers about the affective load that is meant to qualify expressive experience. Whereas many tend to agree that expressive experience is perceptual in character, some believe that such a phenomenal character is distinct from the perceptual recognition of a shape or of a shade of colour because it occurs *along with*, or *in virtue of* some felt affective state. But the relationship between the perceptual and the emotional character is far from clear.

Many authors conceive of the affective component of expressive experience as being an emotional arousal. Derek Matravers insists that the arousal of the feeling component of an emotion is required to undergo expressive experience. However, according to his perspective, such an arousal is neither part of the content nor of the character of that experience. Rather, the aroused feelings responsible for our attributions of expressiveness can be understood as mere causal triggers that do not enter into the phenomenology of expressive experience. Analogously, Noordhof's appeal to arousalistic insights is limited to the mechanism that he believes is in play when we experience expressive objects. It does not affect us emotionally, that is, it does not make us *feel* emotions, not even through the mediation of imagination. All we do, according to Noordhof, is recognise expressions by means of a simulation mechanism of which, as we will see below, one can well remain unaware.

In the same spirit, in his 1999 essay "Projectivism, Empathy, and Musical Tension", Kendall Walton accounts for musical tension and relaxation and for the way they are experienced by listeners. In a nutshell, Walton distinguishes between two sorts of musical (and, more broadly, aesthetic) properties that explain the expressive experience of music. At the basic level he places properties such as tension and relaxation (which one may also want to call, depending on musical genres, description, culture, context: *force, intensity, stress, restlessness, stability, calmness, repose*. See Walton 1999, p. 409). These properties are experienced by means of simulation processes that make one feel the changing tension of music as if it were one's own tension. They are dispositional properties that music possesses, which trigger analogous reactions in listeners, and thus such properties are experienced. On top of tension and relaxation, Walton locates expressive properties – at least some of them – that can result in the experience when the simulation process of tension and relaxation takes place and we, so to speak, *empathise* with music.

Empathy as Walton conceives of it is not a new idea in the history of philosophy. The concept of empathy originally emerged in German philosophy precisely for the purpose of explaining our relation to inanimate objects (see for instance Geiger 1911), rather than in connection with mindreading. It is worth noticing that Walton's account closely resembles Theodor Lipps' theory of empathy (*Einfühlung* in German). In his *Ästhetik* (1903), Lipps argues that empathy is our primary and most direct way of approaching objects in our environment, and that it consists in the subject "filling in" the objects with her own feelings. Literally, *einfühlen* means "to feel in", evoking the idea that one may feel oneself *in* something – or someone – else. Lipps is not clear, at least from an empirically demanding perspective, about how the *Einfühlung* takes place. He rejects the view that it might involve bodily movement and simulation and tends to consider it a matter of psychological resonance (1903, p. 105). However, this is not the point here. What is instead especially interesting is that in Lipps' theory as well as on the Waltonian view, the process of projection taking the shape of an empathic relation is not random, i.e. we do not project whatever feeling we like on any sort of objects. Instead, empathy for objects is always led by perceptual features that trigger and lend themselves to projection. So, the being *tense, relaxed, straight, curved, expanded, agitated, rising*, and *falling* of inanimate objects is what allows for projections of feelings and for the empathetic experience of such objects. These features are taken to have the dispositional power to elicit mechanisms of resonance and consonance in subjects while not necessarily reaching the level of consciousness.

Thus, although both views require *empathy* as the special reaction that allows us to experience expressive properties of objects, neither view seems to require that the subject of the experience *feels* any more definite affect than tension, relaxation and the like. And, in principle, the mechanisms of simulation of tension and relaxation need not be something we consciously experience as being an emotional reaction. Rather, they might remain fully off-line processes.[23] Both in Lipps' and in Walton's view, we may not experience any affective state in expressive experience, which may still consist in recognising perceptual features as being apt for the ascription of some affective character.

Talking about empathy for objects, Gregory Currie points out: "Simulation may do its causal work without reaching the threshold of consciousness, or may produce a very dim conscious experience that easily goes unnoticed" (Currie 2011, p. 91–92). Thus, the claim that we must be aroused to some extent – that is, that some mechanism of behavioural simulation or empathy must be triggered and is responsible for the ascription of affective features to objects – does not coincide with the claim that expressive experience entails that *we feel* emotions in turn. For the purpose of understanding the extent – if any – to which emotions enrich the phenomenal character of expressive experience, making it *sui generis*, this is a relevant point. Indeed, one may accept that some causal connection to

---

[23] Noordhof, who appeals in turn to simulation mechanisms akin to arousal, adopts an even more radical stance on this point: he excludes not only that we must be emotionally aroused in order to experience expressive features, but also that our simulation mechanisms must be held from a first-person perspective (Noordhof 2008, p. 345).

emotional states can play a role, but this does not entail that such mechanisms affect the phenomenal character of expressive experience.

The claim that felt emotions are components of the phenomenal character of expressive experience is instead overtly vindicated by Jenefer Robinson and Aaron Ridley. They argue that expressive experience of music is not limited to the perceptual recognition of features – such as melismatic gestures or contours – but that it is an inherently affective experience, provoking an emotional arousal in the listener. True, we perceive those features of music that make it similar to human expression, but a recognitional, perceptual process is not enough. For this reason, that is, because it denies that any form of arousal is required for an experience to be considered expressive, Robinson and Ridley deem contour theory reductive.

According to Ridley, either we are aroused – namely, the appropriate feelings are elicited in us – or we do not recognise what is expressed. This is held to apply to humans in the first place and to music derivatively. Ridley is especially concerned about the distinction between merely perceptual recognition, which may equally be performed by an adequately instructed computer, and expressive experience, which – he seems to think – can only be performed by someone who can feel emotions. He supports his view via two sets of arguments. On the one hand, he appeals to the origins of meanings of emotion words observing that, unless some or even most of us had responded affectively to musical melisma, the application of expressive predicates would have never been extended to music. This implies that we might have learnt to associate those predicates to certain perceptually distinct patterns in such a way that does not require any arousal. But the semantic shift of emotion words from felt emotions to patterns to which we ascribe expressive features must have originally occurred on such a basis, that is, it must sooner or later have involved some arousal (Ridley 1995, p. 54).

Intuitive as it is, this argument does not play in favour of an arousalistic account of expressive experience. For even if it were true that linguistic habits originated in affectively loaded experience, this would imply that every expressive experience producing expressive ascriptions originates in the same way.

On the other hand, Ridley appeals to the conditions under which we can recognise perceptual signs as expressive. He writes:

> [...] the recognition of expressiveness (and not merely of one kind of sign among others) is conceptually related to our capacity to feel. If I judge someone's behavior to be expressive of, say, melancholy, then I am saying at the same time that I know something of what [one's] melancholy is like, what it would be like to be in the state which [one's] gestures reflect; my judgment is partly felt [...] My response is a part of my recognition of those qualities. (Ridley 1995, p. 53)

Ridley is claiming that the full understanding of emotion concepts requires that one feels, is capable of feeling, or knows what it is like to feel the emotion in question. Accordingly, we cannot attribute expressive values, unless we affectively respond (or know what it is like to respond) to the perceptual stimulus to which we attribute this value. That means, although we may learn to recognise certain traits as typically associable to affective values and we can perform the association as computers do, expressive attributions require that we feel or know what it feels like to undergo the related emotions. Expressiveness is, according to Ridley, not just a perceivable sign that bears some connection to felt affective states. It is instead intrinsically (conceptually) related to felt emotions. There is more to expressiveness than mere perceptual recognition of a pattern and the required extra bit consists in actual or potential arousal. Commenting on Ridley's view, Robinson affirms: "[...] we never merely recognize dispassionately what music expresses; we identify what a piece of music expresses partly by the way it makes us feel" (Robinson 2005, p. 354). Emotions aroused by music, says Robinson, help us *understand* its expressive character, guiding us and setting our expectations about expressive musical development. The following example may clarify the point:

> In the Brahms Intermezzo Opus 117 No. 2, the A theme makes me feel anxious and uneasy, which helps me to recognize the yearning quality in the theme. When the B theme arrives I am relieved and pleased, and this helps me realize that the B theme is more stolid and reassuring than the A theme it replaces. (Robinson 2005, p. 366)

According to these two accounts, emotions are not mere reactions to stimuli that may occur sub-personally. They are taken to be affective states with a phenomenology that contributes to the phenomenal character of expressive experience and makes it a *sui generis* experience.

So, weak arousalistic theories provide convincing reasons in favour of their view. Nonetheless, the disagreement between these accounts and contour theory, as well as theories such as Noordhof's, Walton's and Levinson's is striking. It seems indeed that they do not share the same view about the phenomenology of the experience they want to account for. We may grant that expressive experience involves subjective variables that deserve to be explained: there may be differences between experts and non-experts in experiencing expressive music, as well as differences owing to personal and subjective associations. However, the aim of theories of expressiveness must be to explain expressive experiences as having some common ground by determining their necessary conditions.

On this perspective, the disagreement about the required phenomenal ingredients of expressive experience cannot but raise doubts: because this disagreement occurs at the phenomenal level, it is reasonable to think that philosophers have in mind different kinds of experiences. Indeed, a number of different experiences can fall under the label of "expressive experience". Expressive experiences may indeed differ in duration, intensity, richness, capacity to generate behaviours and to justify assertions and beliefs, degree of clarity and vagueness, consistency with the subject's set of beliefs, her taste, and her background knowledge. It must therefore be acknowledged that what Robinson describes in the passage quoted above may take place, namely that those affective states that music arouses lead us and orient our experience of the piece. Analogously, it may well be the case that we get a better insight in the expressive value of van Gogh's *Wheatfield with Crows* (1890) if we let our emotions influence and guide our judgements. Regarding Ridley's argument that felt emotions are required to fully understand the meaning of emotion words and therefore to use them appropriately, there may well be a sense in which knowing what it is like to feel an emotion helps to ascribe it (its manifest expression) more accurately to an object. But before committing to the idea that these conditions are necessary for expressive experience, some remarks about the phenomenology of emotions can be of help.

2.3.1 The Phenomenal Character of Felt Emotions

What is it like to feel an emotion? By responding to this question, we may indeed find out whether, on a phenomenological perspective, expressive experience presents the phenomenal character of felt emotions and how this merges with its eminently and widely acknowledged perceptual character.

Traditionally, the phenomenology of emotions is held to involve at least two aspects: bodily feelings and the intentional representation of some objects. Moreover, *modes* or *attitudes* are often considered part of the specific phenomenology of emotions. Bodily feelings are usually considered fundamental components of emotion episodes. The etymology of the term "emotion" alludes precisely to movements, agitations or disturbances that take place and that we feel when we undergo emotions. Some of the most relevant elements that cause those feelings are heart rate, breathing, blood pressure, and adrenaline. Also, emotions as feelings of bodily changes are described in terms of kinaesthetic sensations and muscular feedback (Deonna and Teroni 2012, p. 3). William James is considered the pioneer of theories of emotions conceived as feelings of somatic changes. He famously claimed that emotions consist precisely in our feelings of bodily changes that occur when facing certain situations or objects (James 1884 and 1890). Relying on his view, Jesse Prinz takes affective states to consist primarily in the representations that bodily changes provide of the relations between the organism and the environment (Prinz 2004). Less radical views that nevertheless assign bodily feelings a central role, have been put forward confirming the importance of this aspect of phenomenology (e.g. Barlassina and Newen 2014). More generally, even those philosophers who consider emotions eminently judgemental mental states integrate this aspect of the phenomenology in their theories (see for instance Solomon 2004).

However, bodily feelings do not necessarily nor inherently characterise every emotional state. For example, it is hard to distinguish an episode of *pride* from an episode of *satisfaction* on the basis of the bodily feelings that accompany them. Moreover, bodily changes may occur without the subject noticing it, that is, they might be unconscious. This is true both if one believes that changes in the brain or at the neural level are among the bodily changes required by a somatic theory of emotions, and if one thinks about those cases in which we are simply *not aware* of our feelings and related emotions as they occur, but we may get to acknowledge them afterwards.[24] Therefore, one should also contemplate cases in which emotion phenomenology does not amount to bodily feelings, or at least is not limited to them.

The second aspect of emotion phenomenology is related to the intentional nature of affective states. In this respect, emotions are usually taken to be evaluative attitudes. They represent objects as having evaluative properties: intentional objects of fear episodes are represented as fearful, intentional objects of shame episodes are represented as shameful, intentional objects of episodes of enthusiasm are represented as thrilling or exciting, and so on. According to an intentionalistic perspective, we experience the forest as fearful, a gesture as shameful and the plane's take-off as thrilling, and the phenomenology of these experiences – their typical what-it-is-like – is determined by evaluative properties such as fearfulness, shamefulness and thrill that are represented in their content.[25] This latter point can be better understood by analogy with intentional theories of perception, according to which the phenomenal character of perceptual intentional states is determined by the sort of properties that are represented in the content of the experience. In both cases, the idea is that those properties that the experience is about, are responsible for the experience appearing to the subjects in such and such a way. Evaluative properties, such as the property of "being shameful"

---

[24] See Deonna and Teroni (2012, p. 16 ff.) for a clear overview of what "unconscious" emotions amount to.
[25] For a discussion about the objects of emotions see De Sousa (1987).

of a situation would therefore be responsible for producing a certain effect on the subject, namely the specific "what-it-is-like" of experiencing that situation as shameful.

Whatever stance one takes on this – be it a version of dispositionalism for evaluative properties (Kriegel 2002), an Edenic theory of affective properties (Mendelovici 2014) or a pure intentionalist view – it has been noticed that it is unlikely that the intentional content of emotions *exhausts* their specific phenomenal character (Lutz 2015). In point of fact, it seems reasonable to think that feeling ashamed or, on the contrary, proud, amounts to experiencing a certain feature as capable of triggering some kind of "affective attunement" in the subjects, rather than producing a merely "cognitive" reaction – as would be the case in perceptual experiences of, say, colours. Thus, if on the one hand, bodily feelings are not enough to phenomenally characterise emotional experiences, on the other hand it seems that the mere recognition of evaluative properties requires some connection to feelings if it is to characterise emotional episodes.

It is presumably for this reason that a third candidate has been introduced that could characterise emotions as intentional mental states: their intentional *mode*. The most enthusiastic proponents of a theory of emotion phenomenology as depending on modes have been so far Swiss philosophers Julien Deonna and Fabrice Teroni. They believe that emotions are characterised by a specific intentional mode, namely, an evaluative intentional mode. They claim that emotions are evaluative in virtue of their phenomenology, which peculiarly involves bodily feelings. Therefore, they conceive of emotions as particular attitudes towards objects instantiating evaluative properties. Their theory seems to accommodate the idea that the phenomenal character of emotions is eminently "felt" with the fact that it must also involve the phenomenal characterisation of intentional objects. Accordingly, they provide descriptions of the phenomenal character of several emotions in terms of bodily feelings oriented towards objects that exemplify evaluative properties:

> In anger, we feel the way our body is prepared for active hostility to whatever causes the anger. In shame, we feel the way our body is poised to hide from the gaze of others that typically causes the shame. In an episode of loving affection, we feel the way our body is prepared to move towards cuddling the object of one's affection. In disgust, we feel the way our body is poised to prevent the object from entering into contact with it. And in sadness, our body is given to us as though prevented from entering into interaction with a certain object. (Deonna and Teroni 2012, p. 80)

We can finally figure out what it is like to undergo an emotion. In particular, we have seen that emotions are mostly taken to entail bodily feelings. Also, they are mostly taken to have intentional objects instantiating evaluative properties in such a way that may imply specific attitudes. We can thus return to the question that originally motivated this brief detour about the phenomenal character of emotions, that is: are felt emotions required in order to experience objects as expressive? In light of this sketched overview, claiming – as arousalism does – that felt emotions are required, amounts to claiming that at least some of the elements listed above (bodily feelings, evaluative properties of the intentional objects, evaluative attitudes connecting the two) are present in our experience.

Let us start from the view that the intentional object of an emotion might be responsible for its phenomenology, in conjunction with the specific attitude one takes towards it. We may consider the case in which a piece of music is experienced as fearful. The arousalist can insist that, in order for such an experience to occur, one must entertain a specific attitude that involves both bodily feelings and the representation of some evaluative features, namely the fearfulness of the piece. However, it is immediately clear that the case of fearful music must be distinguished from the case of a full-blown episode of fear, such as being afraid of a barking dog. Indeed, in expressive experience, objects are not the intentional objects of an affective experience, for it is not the case that we are *afraid of the piece of music*, that we feel tenderness *towards it*, that we are happy *about it*. In short, if arousalists want to argue that the capacity that music has to express emotions is connected to its capacity to provoke emotions, then they have to provide an account that preserves the distinction between full-blown episodes of emotions directed towards something and expressive experience.

Once it is clear that the way in which the phenomenal character of felt emotions contributes to the phenomenal character of expressive experience cannot depend on the intentional object of the experience, arousal theorists can insist that the phenomenal component of affective states that must be present in the phenomenal character of expressive experience is the "feeling component". Given the two versions of arousalism that we have considered, we may further unpack this requirement, dividing it into two alternative possibilities: the requirement that felt emotions are in place in the form of bodily feelings when we experience expressive objects may be understood in a strong or in a weak version.

The strong version of the requirement would entail that the constitutive feelings of the emotion are actually *felt*: hearing a piece of music as sad would accordingly require that we feel our body as being deprived of something, assuming a bowed-down posture and a weary attitude, lacking energy and disposition to action. And even if one follows Robinson by accepting that the kind of felt emotion required does not necessarily coincide with the one perceived in the object, the requirement would still be that some *consistent* feeling (pity, sorrow, melancholy, grimness) is actually felt by the subject. Moreover, if one follows the suggestion of Deonna and Teroni about unconscious emotions, one may allow for the case in which the subject is not *currently* aware of the feelings she is undergoing, but may become aware of them afterwards, by means of reflection and introspection. This strong version of the feeling requirement is therefore consistent with the weak versions of arousalism described so far, namely Robinson's and Ridley's.

The weak version of the requirement would instead entail that those feelings needed for an emotion to be in place might occur sub-personally, without reaching the level of consciousness or of bodily awareness. This hypothesis seems quite counterintuitive. Indeed, it goes against the "common-sense intuition that there always is something it is like to undergo an emotion" (Deonna and Teroni 2012, p. 17). Although this is a very controversial matter, the claim that feelings can be unconscious and still have a causal impact on our overall emotional state has been defended (Gardner 1993; Damasio 2000). Moreover, one may hold that neural activations correlating to feelings are enough to claim that the feeling component of an emotion is in place. Recall that, according to Matravers, we do not need to be aware of the emotions' feeling components when we experience expressive qualities. Rather, they can remain unknown to the subject, who becomes aware of them on the basis of the judgement that they cause (Matravers 1998, p. 150). According to this version, the claim that emotions are required by expressive experience would amount to the claim we must be aroused *sub-personally* in order to undergo such an experience. The weak view is therefore compatible with Matravers' strong version of arousalism.

Now, whereas the weak reading can only be corroborated or disconfirmed by empirical results – which nevertheless would lead us quite far away from the phenomenal level that is currently under scrutiny – the strong reading can be rejected on the basis of the following two phenomenological considerations. Firstly, as in the case of the persona theory, against which phenomenal reports could be fruitfully employed, we can consider introspective reflection about one's experience. Desolate landscapes, lugubrious colours, cheerful motifs can be experienced as being desolate, lugubrious and cheerful without necessarily resounding or echoing in us in the form of feelings of which we are aware. Nor these feelings are such that they can always be recognised afterwards, when reflecting on the experience. This is neither to deny that, as Robinson suggests, such feelings can "help" us listening to musical passages in the correct way (which I take to mean: in the richest way, possibly the one intended by the composer or the musician playing the piece), nor to claim that we are *never* aroused when we undergo expressive experience. On the contrary, it may well be the case that we are very often affectively involved when we hear emotionally characterised pieces of music, see expressive landscapes, decide whether to paint our walls white, yellow or grey. But it seems that our conscious experiences of expressive things do not attest that bodily feelings are necessary components of their phenomenal character.

Secondly, we can focus on the specific way in which bodily feelings are taken to be a fundamental part of emotions. In particular, we have seen that one of the problems with somatic theories of emotions is characterising the role of feelings as distinct from the role they play in other non-emotional experiences. Take *fatigue* for example: somatic theories must be able to explain why, despite being a bodily feeling, fatigue is not to be counted among emotions. It is precisely this worry that leads most supporters of somatic theories to account for the specificity of bodily feelings in emotions in terms of their relation to intentionality (Prinz 2004; Deonna and Teroni 2012; Barlassina and Newen 2014). They all argue that feelings are components of the phenomenal character of emotions as long as they put us in contact with the intentional (or formal) objects of emotions. Prinz, for instance, thinks that emotions: "use bodily states to represent organism-environment relations" or what he (following Lazarus 1991) calls "core relational themes", whereas feelings such as fatigue are mere bodily perceptions that represent nothing but some bodily condition (Prinz 2004, p. 190). In turn, Barlassina and Newen have provided a clear definition of what this *distinctiveness thesis* consists in:

> Emotions are interoceptive states, and what distinguishes emotions from non-emotional interoceptive states is that emotions are those interoceptive states that represent core relational themes (i.e., organism-environment relations that pertain to the organism's well-being). (Barlassina and Newen 2014, p. 18)

Moreover, Deonna and Teroni provide several descriptions of emotions as consisting of bodily feelings (namely readiness to action) intentionally connected to intentional objects with evaluative properties. Here are a couple of them:

> Fear of the dog is an experience of the dog as dangerous, precisely because it consists in feeling the body's readiness to act so as to diminish the dog's likely impact on it (flight, preemptive attack, etc.), and this felt attitude is correct if and only if the dog is dangerous. [...] Admiration is an experience of a given object as admirable, because it consists in feeling the way one's body opens up to sustained and expanding exploration of the object, and it is correct if and only if the object is admirable. (Deonna and Teroni 2012, p. 81)

Finally, Barlassina and Newen also argue that the way in which feelings contribute to the specific phenomenal character of emotions is via an integration (which may be cognitive or perceptual) with intentional attitudes. (Barlassina and Newen 2014, p. 24–27).

It is interesting to note that an analogous position is endorsed by Davies in discussing Robinson. He also distinguishes between *feelings* such as tension, relief, nervousness that might well "initiate" an emotional state, and (propositional) *attitudes* towards formal objects that "surround" those feelings.

> An overdose of caffeine might put me on edge, but if my state is one of nervousness, this is because my sensations become located within a wider cognitive context, one where I contemplate some future state or action with apprehension. Now, if music triggers reactions of nervousness, relief, disturbance, and reassurance – and thereby is unnerving, relieving, disturbing, and reassuring – it is far from evident that these qualities *connect* with a cognitive content delivered or directed by the music, as opposed to one created by and imported from the listener.
>
> (Davies 2005, p. 165)

According both to Davies' remark – explicitly meant to undermine Robinson's arousalism – and to numerous theories about the phenomenal character of emotions, if one considers feelings to be what attests the phenomenal presence of an emotion, then one must take into account that feelings can only play this role as long as they are significantly connected to some intentional object (namely an object that instantiates evaluative properties that make it the appropriate formal object of an affective experience) through appropriate attitudes. We have already seen that this cannot be the role of feelings within expressive experience, for expressive experience does not provide any intentional object that is adequately conceived as the formal object of a full-blown emotional experience. Once again, in spite of the possibility that we are causally aroused in expressive experience, felt arousal is not necessary. Moreover, it does not bear any necessary connection to the (broadly understood) intentional component that, so to speak, makes an emotion out of a mere feeling. It is therefore reasonable to believe that what Robinson and Ridley consider to be the paradigmatic case of expressive experience is only one example out of the many that can be put forward, namely the one that involves felt emotions. One can admit that this arousalistic experience is an example of expressive experience. It is perhaps what happens most frequently, but this is not enough to consider felt emotions a necessary ingredient of expressive experience.

If this is how things stand, then we can reconsider the question of how emotions might otherwise enter expressive experience. As most authors' main concern is to reconcile the perceptual aspect of expressive experience with its affective aspect, and felt emotions are not a good candidate, we shall examine further options. For this purpose, it is useful to focus again on the perceptual side of expressive experience.

2.4 The Phenomenal Character of Expressive Experience

So far, we have seen that the most convincing way to qualify the phenomenal character of expressive experience implies a perceptual mode of experience. Even in those cases in which such a perception is taken to involve imagination (as it is in Levinson's and Noordhof's accounts), we do not experience expressive features as if they were the result of some imaginative engagement. Therefore, imagination is not believed to affect the phenomenal character of the experience in paradigmatic cases. In order to focus on the qualitative phenomenal features that could be taken to distinguish expressive experience from other experiences at stake here, the assessment of those properties and mechanisms that allegedly result in such a phenomenal character can be delayed. Three phenomenal qualities seem worth analysing: (i) temporality, (ii) development through movement and (iii) degree of complexity.

2.4.1 Time

Philosophers of music legitimately aim at accounting for musical expressiveness. They standardly take the entire piece of music, such as a *sonata*, or a portion of a piece, such as a movement or *melismatic gesture* as the units to which expressiveness applies. As already seen, contour theorists focus on contours, profiles, gestaltic configurations, Ridley refers to *melisma*, Levinson to musical gestures. Unlike simpler features such as single notes or chords, these units unfold in time. *Temporality* seems *prima facie* what makes them particularly suitable targets of expressive experiences and ascriptions. Davies picks out this aspect when he affirms:

> Because music is a temporal art, its expressive character is revealed only gradually and can be heard only through sustained attention to its unfolding. It takes as long to hear the music's expressive properties as it takes to hear the passages in which those properties are articulated [...] In the case of music, this [expressive] 'appearance' depends on its dynamic topography, as this unfolds through time. (Davies 2005, p. 181)

On this view, temporality is the musical feature that grounds musical expressiveness. If so, that is, if expressiveness were dependent on time, then visual expressiveness would require an *ad hoc* account – for visual objects clearly entertain a different relation with time. Still, conceiving of musical expressiveness as a radically distinct phenomenon compared to visual expressiveness is unconvincing. Generally speaking, it is reasonable to think that visual and auditory features behave somehow differently: it is one thing to see a visual pattern and another thing to hear an auditory pattern, for instance in that they relate differently to spatial and temporal variables. Speaking about emotional expressions, it is reasonable to believe that different psychological mechanisms govern our ascriptions of emotions to people based on visual or auditory detection of patterns. However, when it comes to expressiveness, offering two different accounts that are nevertheless rooted in perception and in some conception of emotional expression would be a baroque and expensive move. True, music is by far the privileged object of inquiries about expressiveness and its allegedly special relation with emotions has been repeatedly stated, but an effort is nonetheless worth making to provide a unified account of visual and auditory expressive experiences. To this aim, music's relation with temporality can be questioned.

As Davies rightly points out, the development through time is an essential feature of music and music's appreciation. This feature appears to distinguish music from other artistic forms such as painting or sculpture, traditionally considered "atemporal" arts. Music is specifically constituted through time in such a way that makes it a *sui generis* – and therefore especially fascinating – item. The way in which music reveals itself perceptually consists in that its "being in time appears experientially as passing" (Forlè 2016, p. 178).

In his *Filosofia della musica* (1991), Italian philosopher Giovanni Piana provides an extremely precise and insightful description of the special relation of music with time. In short, such a relation consists in that music *exhibits temporality*, as opposed to what, more trivially, *takes time to be experienced*. Unlike visual patterns, he writes, auditory (musical) patterns are inherently temporal. In the case of painting, for instance, time is a phenomenological determination of our experience rather than of its object: visual features present themselves in time as our experience requires time to take place. But such features are objectively independent of the passing of time, that is, of the duration of our experience – they are rather intrinsically spatial. Music is instead temporal for it makes us experience *duration, beginning* and *end* as being intrinsic to music and independent of our experience: "Duration manifests itself concretely in perception" (Piana 1991, p. 154, my translation). It is not the experience of music that *requires* time, it is music itself that takes place as *passing*. With music it makes sense to talk about *simultaneous* and *successive* sounds, as simultaneity and succession are objective constituents of music, whereas they are at best qualities of our *experience of* paintings. As Forlè efficaciously sums up:

> [...] this passing appears as the sequence of the phases of one single phenomenon. The melody, in fact, is not just the static juxtaposition of sounds but emerges from the perceived relationships between the notes. In this way, perceiving a melody means in a certain sense perceiving the sequence of notes as the transition from one sound to another.
> (Forlè 2016, p. 178)

Since such musical passages are not randomly juxtaposed, but are rather characterised by an *internal coherence*, Piana suggests that, as movements in space attract our gaze, so the sounds that follow one another in musical passages attract our auditory attention by virtue of their directionality. On his view, the temporality of music manifests itself precisely because of its capacity to make our perceptual attention follow the transitions from notes to notes, the alternation of *openings* and *closures*, a *gestaltic tension* that, as such, displays a *teleological directedness*. This teleological orientation of the structure of music, rather than its temporal development, is actually responsible for musical expressiveness. Contrary to what Piana takes to be a common but superficial view, the temporality that is constitutive of music is not responsible for its expressive potential in the first place; rather, it is its *intrinsic dynamism* that makes it expressive and, *as a consequence* of its capacity to catch our attention, allows us to experience temporality.

Piana's phenomenological remark that the expressive value of music is to be searched in its dynamic structure prior to its temporal development finds support in empirical approaches to the same issues. Just to mention one example, discussing the evolutionary and social value of music, Ian Cross and Iain Morley conclude that the interaction between humans that is conveyed by music is grounded in the perceptual recognition of rhythmic structures that attract our attentional resources and make them "focus on specific moments and sequential patterns in the temporal unfolding of the music" (Cross and Morley 2009, p. 68).[26]

Granted, temporal development is fundamental to the inherent (metaphysical) structure and to the overall phenomenology of the experience of music – but it can contribute to the experience of its expressiveness only as a result of musical oriented tension. Once one focuses on expressiveness, it is what we can call the *dynamic* dimension of music that is at stake. If this analysis is correct, then the expressive potentials of auditory and visual patterns are closer than expected.

2.4.2 Movement

It is therefore true that music is essentially connected to time, but it is also true that temporality is not where we have to look if we want to find the source of expressiveness. This is not to deny that musical expressiveness is the special and philosophically interesting experience it is precisely because of its essential relation to time. On the contrary, the aim of a phenomenological examination is to find the layer of expressive experience that is common to auditory and visual objects. Only on such basis any kind-specific analysis can be taken forward.

---

[26] An analogous conclusion is drawn in Drake *et al.* (2000).

Let us reconsider the aforementioned quotation from Stephen Davies. Aside from temporality, he refers to the "dynamic topography" of music. *Dynamism* is in point of fact a characteristic that is commonly ascribed to music and that clearly refers to *movement*. Widespread spatial descriptions of music support this characterisation. I borrow from Forlè (2016) the following evocative excerpt:

> We say that a sequence of sounds rises or falls, or that one note jumps to another. We say that the leading tone displays the tendency to move towards the tonic, while the tonic shows no tension and acts as a resting point. In the same sense, we say that a cadence is suspended when it does not move to the tonic. We also talk of fast or slow tempos and we can define a musical piece as a dance or a gallop on the basis of its rhythm and metrical structure. (Forlè 2016, p. 175)

Dynamic features of music are, on this view, those elements that connect the temporal development of music with its allegedly spatial properties. It is thus easy to see how contour theory can appeal to resemblances between bodily movements (behaviours) and musical contours as presenting dynamic qualities.

Admittedly, despite insisting on music's intimate relation to time, Davies is aware that dynamism and movement are ultimately responsible for musical expressiveness. In particular, he takes this argument to support his resemblance-based account: "Music, like behavior, is dynamic. It is a straightforward fact about hearing that two notes an octave apart are heard as 'the same' and that notes are heard as relatively high or low" (Davies 2005, p. 140). Accordingly, music resembles expressive behaviours thanks precisely to this intrinsic dynamism:

> We experience movement and pattern in music [...] If music resembles an emotion, it does so by sharing the dynamic character displayed either in the emotion's phenomenological profile, [...] or in the public behaviors through which the emotion is standardly exhibited. (Davies 2005, p. 176)

However, the notion of dynamism as being part of the phenomenal character of expressive experience is not established. Although many authors share the idea that movement and dynamism are experienced in music, it is not clear what such an experience amounts to.

The most intuitive way to conceive of this analogy between dynamic music and movement is offered by *dance*. Piana, for instance, speaks about dance as the perceived "possibility of an internal relation with gesture and movement" that characterises listening to music as irreducible to "an act of pure contemplation" and as showing the "direct and immediate link with subjectivity [...] as vitality gushing out in bodily movement" (Piana 1991, p. 167, my translation). From a quite different, namely *enactivist*, perspective, Joel Krueger considers dance as the most adequate way to engage with music, precisely in virtue of the way in which bodily movements fit musical ones, providing a privileged experience of it: "Via dancing, the temporal regularities of melodic and rhythmical patterns within the music are physicalized within an array of bodily movements" (Krueger 2011, p. 75). Accordingly, the expressive potential of music finds its source in music's relation to *movement* rather than in its being a temporal art. If so, then *dynamism* could illuminate the path to follow in order to provide an account of expressive experience as a wider phenomenon that is not limited to music.

Enactivist philosophers stress the role played by interactive bodily engagement with musical features in the experience of music and of its expressive power. The following excerpt nicely summarises their views:[27]

> Bodily gestures in response to musical events can act as a kind of attentional focusing: the animate body, by interactively engaging with the piece, becomes a vehicle for voluntarily drawing out certain features of the piece, such as rhythmic beats or the progression of a melodic contour, by foregrounding them in our attentional field. This 'drawing out' is an enactive and exploratory gesture in response to felt affordances within the music. The listener perceives the inner space of the piece as a space that can be entered into, experientially, and by doing just this shapes how the experiential content of the piece-as-given becomes phenomenally manifest. (Krueger 2011, p. 73–74)

The parallel with contour theory and with Robinson's (weak) arousalist approach is here well suited. With regard to the former, contour theory shares with this enactivist account the idea that bodily movements are somehow responsible for musical expressiveness. Both theories take bodily movement to provide the paradigm of dynamism. According to contour theory the dynamism is perceived in music as long as it resembles bodily movement, whereas according to Krueger dynamism triggers the interactive engagement that makes music animated. Regarding the latter, instead, both enactivism and weak arousalism exploit the idea of an active psychological engagement that guides the experience of expressive music. But while, for Robinson, our felt emotions guide us through perceptual saliences of music, Krueger ascribes this guiding role to the body.

All these accounts focus on those features that make music resemble, as closely as possible, psychological and bodily emotional dynamics. Forlè agrees with the enactivist perspective to the extent that it accounts for what she calls *dynamic qualities*, which are "enacted" by perceivers who become bodily engaged with musical patterns. However, she argues, although enactivists are in

---

27 Francesca Forlè (2016) offers a critical introduction of this approach to musical expressiveness, whose main proponents are Noë (2004); Cochrane (2008); Krueger (2009, 2011), Schiavio *et al.* (2017). I will not deal with these accounts of musical perception and expressiveness here, but they are definitely worth mentioning, especially given the importance they ascribe to movement.

a good position to explain a specifically immersive and bodily involving experience of the dynamic qualities of music, there are certain features that they cannot adequately account for.

> If we can say that dynamic musical qualities are enacted by our virtual or actual motor engagement, what is exactly that we track with our movement in music? Which are those music features that afford our movement? It seems that we already need to perceptually recognize a musical structure that allows our bodily entrainment in order for the enactive constitution of dynamic qualities to take place. (Forlè 2016, p. 177)

In particular, she argues that in order to undergo this experience of music we need to apprehend certain dynamic perceptual structures that are conditions of possibility for the bodily-centred experiences mentioned above. Such a precondition, she claims, cannot be accounted for by Krueger's theory. On the contrary, as it clearly emerges from Piana's view, *openings*, *closures*, *downbeat* and *upbeat*, *impulse* and *quiet* that characterise musical gestures are what makes music describable in terms of movement. This movement, however, is neither an enacted movement, nor a simulated one. In other words, it does not require any specific bodily engagement. Rather, it can be perceptually recognised by subjects as being the intimate structure of music.

The main virtue of Forlè's criticism is that it provides a distinction between the possibility that musical expressiveness is enacted and the necessary role played in this experience by the perceptual recognition of certain structural regularities. The phenomenal character of expressive experience may accordingly be enriched by the contribution of bodily involvement, analogously to what can happen when emotions drive our psychological engagement with music. Nevertheless, expressive experience consists primarily in a perceptual experience of some kind of dynamic qualities. If this account is correct, it may be the case that there is a minimal level of the experience of musical expressiveness that does not entail a bodily-characterised phenomenology.

An interesting parallel with visual experience can also be traced at this point. For this purpose, let us take the example of *action painting*, also known as "gestural painting" as it is quite a well-known style that is usually taken to convey very expressive works. The term identifies the work of a group of American abstract expressionists who, starting around 1950, employed a particularly direct, instinctual, and dynamic technique in painting, involving the spontaneous – and otherwise automatic – application of vigorous brushstrokes along with dripping and spilling paint onto the canvas. Jackson Pollock, Willem de Kooning, and Franz Kline are among the best-known action painters.

Setting aside historical and critical considerations, it seems reasonable to think that we engage with these works by bodily simulating the actions that might have realised them. In other words, it may well be the case that the best appreciation one can have of this kind of painting requires some form of bodily engagement, possibly with their alleged creative process.

In his essay about style, Kendall Walton generalises this intuition to most aesthetic experiences. Arguing against what he calls the "cobbler model" (namely the idea that aesthetic fruition implies a relationship between a producer, a product, and a consumer who values the product on the basis how it fits her needs), he claims that aesthetic appreciation mostly consists in the appreciation of the creative process that one believes has realised the artwork; and that if this is obvious for music and dance, it is also true for painting. In short: "we 'see' in a work the action of producing it" and "The action of interest is in many cases that of behaving as though one is creating and/or displaying a valuable aesthetic object" (Walton 2008, p. 225).

So, it is possible that we experience even the expressive character of paintings by means of some bodily engagement, which may well take place by means of simulation processes. This kind of engagement is likely to enrich the aesthetic appreciation of action paintings, and perhaps many other artworks. Still, the same criticism addressed to the enactivist approach applies to this case. In order to engage with the expressive properties of paintings that trigger our bodily reactions, we must be able to perceptually recognise some features of the works as "affording" such reactions. In other words, our experience of expressive properties must be taken to be, also in this case, the perceptual experience of the object's features which may (or may not) trigger our bodily reactions.[28]

Let us take stock. On the one hand, we have seen that the development through time is inherent to the structure of music, but that when it comes to the experience of expressiveness, temporality is not necessarily a qualitative aspect of expressive experience. This is even more evident when we experience static visual objects such as (expressive) paintings. Our experience of paintings might require time, the experience of it as expressive might take place as quickly as the experience of its colours. Temporality is not a constitutive aspect of the experiences' phenomenology, any more than it is a constitutive aspect of the recognitional experience of its perceivable traits. On the other hand, motoric interaction with music is an enhancing factor of such a phenomenology. It makes certain dynamic or kinetic qualities of music more salient owing to our capacity to mirror musical gestures. Nevertheless, bodily engagement implies

---

[28] Freedberg and Gallese (2007) famously addressed this kind of appreciation from a neuroscientific standpoint. Further support for a simulationist perspective can be found in Umiltà et al. (2012), whereas criticisms have been put forward by Casati and Pignocchi (2007). An amended proposal, focused on *analytic painting*, that accepts simulation based on a preliminary detection of gestaltic structures can be found in Benenti and Fazzuoli (2018).

the perceptual recognition of such gestures, or at least of some components of those gestures. If this is the case, then the phenomenal character of expressive experience is perceptual in the first place, i.e. undergoing an expressive experience is like undergoing a perceptual experience, although a number of integrations and enrichments are possible and often do take place.

Now, before asking – and trying to answer – the question of what kind of properties are those that make the experience of expressiveness possible, there is still one point that needs to be discussed. Namely, there seems to be a difference between experiencing something like a painting, a landscape, or a melody as expressive, and something like a colour or a sound as expressive. Intuitively, one may say that the phenomenology of the former kind of experience is much more complex and demanding than the latter kind.

2.4.3 Expressive Experience of Simple and Complex Features

Musical expressiveness is often considered as an issue concerning pieces of music having either a significant duration, or at least offering the possibility to be compared with expressive gestures. Along this line of thought, Peter Kivy believes that a distinction should be made between the experience of complex and simpler expressive features. His point is not that simple features cannot be experienced as expressive, but rather that their expressiveness cannot be accounted for in terms of resemblances to behaviours. He therefore suggests that the experience of chords or keys sounding sad or happy requires a different explanation. Specifically, he claims that the "anguished" or "restless" sound of the diminished triad, is a matter of *convention*:

> [...] in its context, during a long period in the history of our musical tradition, it is an "active" chord; it has to go somewhere, lead to something [...]. We can now see why the diminished triad can, in a proper musical context, present an anguished quality that can be accounted for on the contour model. (Kivy 1980, p. 80)

Simple features are too indefinite and ambiguous to be expressive *per se*, and they require the appropriate context within a cultural tradition to acquire their expressive value. Analogously, Kivy treats colours as simple features whose expressive value is to be accounted for in a different way from music (and, presumably, visual complex patterns). He thus appeals to allegedly associative mechanisms that are corroborated by repeated uses within the same culture and which provide the ground for further analogous associations between certain perceptual features and emotional states (Kivy 2002). So, while colours are *conventionally* happy, sad, mournful, music is happy, sad, mournful in a more complex way, such that we can justify our ascriptions by pointing at the resemblances that a piece of music bears to expressive behaviours.

As previously seen, contour theory cannot claim that resemblances are part of the specific phenomenal character of expressive experience. Indeed, it is not the case that we auditorily or visually perceive a resemblance each time we hear or see something as expressive. This is precisely the reason why, after introducing and endorsing contour theory, Kivy casts doubt on it and ends up supporting an impoverished version of this position (Kivy 2002). He appeals to sub-personal mechanisms capable of processing similarities and allowing for a phenomenal character that does not require the manifest recognition of resemblances. Moreover, he maintains that, in order to experience a piece of music as expressive, we need not be aware of what components of the piece make it expressive – be they its rhythm or its key. This implies that, on his view, there is nothing specific on the phenomenal level that makes the expressive experience of a piece of music different from the expressive experience of a chord. Therefore, although the expressiveness ascribed to chords – and analogously to colours – and the expressiveness ascribed to pieces of music require different explanations, Kivy's theory implies that they have a similar phenomenal character. Colours and simple sounds might be experienced as expressive owing to conventions (whose intervention remains under the level of awareness) and pieces of music might be experienced as expressive because of certain resemblances.

On the one hand, Kivy claims that the expressiveness ascribed to complex items depends on simpler features (notes, chords, rhythm, keys in the case of music) that may well be non-expressive *per se*. According to this perspective, musical expressiveness would *emerge* or *supervene* on standard, non-expressive features. On the other hand, he admits that simple features (both auditory and visual) can also look expressive, but that this is due to conventional mechanisms of association. But even if one believes that simpler and more complex things are expressive owing to different reasons and must be treated differently – as Kivy does – this does not seem to entail any significant difference for the phenomenology in question.

Firstly, one might be tempted to say that temporality is what distinguishes the expressive experience of complex items from the expressive experience of simple items. But, as we have seen, temporality does not affect the phenomenal character of expressive experiences in any essential way. At most, when one perceives objects (such as music) that only exist throughout time, one's expressive experience of those objects will *last* as long as the objects themselves. But this does not speak for the complexity of the experience' phenomenal character.

Secondly, one may think that complex expressive items such as music are more likely to resemble gestures and behaviours. But, as we have seen, the recognition of resemblances to bodily movements is not always required in order to undergo expressive experience. It is perfectly possible that certain musical gestures or certain lines on a canvas resemble human behavioural expressions and that we tend to associate expressive values with such gestures owing to our capacity to recognise resemblances. Still, expressive experience is phenomenally distinct from the experience of the resemblance holding between contours.

Thirdly, one can think that the experience of a piece of music may trigger significant bodily involvement, whereas the perception of a chord or of a sound does not. Although bodily involvement can be a particularly useful way to provide a phenomenally rich expressive experience, it is not required by all expressive experiences. So, even if articulated expressive objects (like many artworks are) are more likely to trigger these sorts of bodily reactions, we can undergo expressive experience even in those cases in which we are not bodily engaged.

Therefore, all the phenomenal differences between hearing a simple sound as sombre and hearing a musical gesture or a complex piece of music as sombre do not seem to affect the experience in such a way that it allows for a distinction between an expressive and a non-expressive experience. It might be a longer lasting, more intense, more involving or intriguing experience, but the degree of complexity does not account for its being expressive.

Thus, what is the phenomenal character's ultimate specificity in the experience of expressiveness? It seems that most criteria that can be found in the literature do not fulfil the task of explaining what is so special about expressive experience. What is left to address is therefore its specific content, i.e. the kind of properties that the experience mobilises, along with the mental and the affective properties that it involves.

Chapter 3
The Content of Expressive Experience

The previous chapter was meant to show that expressive experience has the phenomenal character of a perceptual experience. At the phenomenal level (what-it-is-like to experience expressive things), expressive experience involves neither an imaginative engagement – although such an engagement can enhance and enrich the character of the experience – nor a phenomenally relevant affective arousal – even if we are often aroused by expressive objects, and despite the contention that felt emotions may in turn make expressive experience more detailed. Moreover, temporality and bodily movements do not seem to necessarily characterise expressive experience either. However, the previous discussion was comparatively neutral regarding the *content* of the experience at stake, that is, about the kind of properties mobilised by such an experience and their relation to the phenomenal character.

In the present chapter the problem of expressive experience's content will be framed within representationalism broadly conceived. I will address the relation between the phenomenal character and the representational content of expressive experience in terms of a relation between standard perceptual properties and expressive properties (§ 3.1), dealing with the widespread assumption that expressive properties are inherently "response-dependent" (§ 3.2). § 3.2.1 focuses on the hypothesis that imagination is the kind of response involved and that perceptual properties play a causal role. Two mechanisms that may account for expressive experience are discussed, namely a cognitive intervention and a simulationist strategy, both effectively employed by Noordhof (§ 3.2.2). Then the problem of causal triggers is addressed and dealt with following Budd's "heresy of the separable experience" (§ 3.3 and § 3.4). In § 3.5 I suggest that a perceptual strategy helps to avoid the heresy and I introduce a distinction between three sorts of expressive experience, namely the case of the *weeping willow* (§ 3.5.1); the case of the *musical gesture* (§ 3.5.2) and the case of the *minor chord* (§ 3.5.3). Finally, I suggest that dynamic perceptual properties are mobilised by the content of expressive experience (§ 3.6).

3.1 The Problem of Content

In order to assess the problem of what exactly expressive experience is about, the discussion must be framed within the contemporary literature. This issue is rarely addressed explicitly by authors as being a problem of "content". However, most authors seem to adopt what has been called the "content view"[29] about expressive experience. In other words, they account for expressive experience in terms of those properties that are related to a certain phenomenology and that constitute the content of that experience. Accordingly, their theoretical framework implies some form of representationalism.

The representationalist approach to the experience of expressive properties can be understood in two distinct although related ways. Firstly, there is the idea that speaking of content implies speaking of adequacy conditions. In this case, some properties of the world should be taken to satisfy the experience of something as being expressive. Such properties would be responsible for our experience being veridical and for certain experiences being more or less correct than others. Secondly, there is the idea that phenomenal properties of experiences can be *reduced to* properties of their content, in which case one should either claim that expressive properties are properties of the world, or that they are phenomenal properties that can be reduced to perceptual properties of the world. Importantly, one may hold the first view without committing to the second. One may indeed claim that there are adequacy conditions in the world that verify our expressive experiences, but that the content of expressive experience is not exhausted by those properties that ground such conditions. In what follows, this latter approach is deliberately adopted. The first consequence of this adoption is that, even if one is disposed to accept that experiencing something as expressive is phenomenally like *perceiving* it as expressive, one can still ask whether the kind of properties that one is perceiving are standard perceptual properties – such as colours or shapes or sounds – that one represents in a particular way, or if they belong to a different kind of properties that, nevertheless, convey a perception-like experience.

The present chapter will explore the tension between two poles of expressive experience: on the one hand, accounts of the content of expressive experience must do justice to those constraints that reality puts on it. Expressive experience is not a sort of daydreaming or phantasy where one is free to ascribe whatever expression to whatever object; rather, it appears to be related to objective features of objects. This suggests that some adequacy conditions are

---

[29] The content view is usually defended against so-called naïve realism or direct realism, although it has been argued that some inclusive versions of the content view may also accommodate these latter theories, at least to the extent that they allow for a description of experiences in terms of phenomenal properties (Siegel 2010). I will not deal directly neither with non-representationalist nor with anti-representationalist theories of perception.

required. On the other hand, such accounts must do justice to the relational and therefore "subjective" nature of the experience, that is, to the fact that important differences might subsist between two expressive experiences of the same object on behalf of different subjects. The same painting can look sad to someone and simply dull to someone else. Although the margin of agreement about expressive properties of things is wider than most authors believe, this relativity of expressive experience is not easy to discard. On the contrary, it seems peculiar of expressive experience that the disagreement about expressive properties of objects cannot always be solved by pointing at their standard perceptual features.

3.2 Response-Dependence

A widely endorsed way to deal with this tension is to consider expressive properties as depending on the specific reaction they trigger in the observer for their instantiation, whether such a reaction is an affective or an imaginative one. The relevant kind of response is the intervention of a mental state that interacts with perception in one way or another. Whereas standard perceptual properties are normally agreed to be mostly independent of who is experiencing them, when they are experienced, the background knowledge and emotional condition of the subject, expressive properties are mostly understood to be intrinsically dependent on these sorts of factors. This is why philosophers try to account for their nature in terms of the kind of reaction these properties trigger in us. They are usually considered response-dependent and the relationship that they are taken to entertain with their subject varies from account to account.

As argued, imaginative accounts appeal to imagination in such a way that the phenomenology of our experiences does not always bear witness to. Yet, claiming that imagination does not necessarily affect the *phenomenology* of expressive experience is not denying that imagination contributes to expressive experience. Thus, even if one agrees that the phenomenal character of expressive experience is perceptual, one can insist that, for a phenomenally perceptual experience to be the experience *of* perceptual features, an independent argument must be provided. This is the case of those imaginative accounts that explain the nature of expressive properties in terms of their capacity to trigger some imaginative reaction in the subject. Both Jerrold Levinson and Paul Noordhof deal with this problem along these lines.

Let us focus on Noordhof's account first. The imaginative mechanism that he believes is in play when one undergoes an expressive experience can be further analysed and fruitfully discussed by focusing on what he considers the experience's content.[30]

3.2.1 Imaginative Responses

Noordhof addresses the problem of content after drawing the distinction between the *explanandum* and the *explanans* of expressive perception. Philosophers, he says, should acknowledge this distinction and preliminarily describe the experience, then they should consistently account for it. After describing expressive experience in the way thoroughly discussed in the previous chapter, he puts forward his account of expressive perception in terms of "sensuously imagining an emotion-guided creative process". On his view, when we hear an expressive piece of music, we perceive its expression in virtue of our imagining the process guided by the emotion that might have led to the creation of such a piece of music. Our seemingly perceptual experience is therefore actually an imaginative process whose content is a creative behaviour, the act of *making*, under the guidance of some emotion.

On this perspective, there are three ways to account for the content of expressive perception, namely (i) a non-representational approach, (ii) an "experiencing-as" approach, and (iii) the sensuous-imagination approach. Noordhof believes that the first two paths can be discarded, whereas the third should be endorsed. His rejection of the idea that expressive experience could be a matter of non-representational content, stems from his endorsement and defence of representational theories of experience (Noordhof 2008).[31] With regards to the second option, Noordhof writes:

> […] we might take imagining an emotion-guided creative process to characterise a different way of perceiving what are, in fact, non-expressive properties. According to this view, expressive properties would not literally be part of the representational content of perceptual experience. (Noordhof 2008, p. 343)

If one assumes – as Noordhof does – that expressive perception cannot *merely* consist in the perception of features of the world, one can conceive of sensuously imagining an emotion-guided creative process as a specific way of experiencing

---

[30] I shall underline a terminological issue regarding Noordhof's paper: he uses the locution "phenomenal content" when talking about experiences. In discussing his view, I will adopt the term "content" or "representational content".
[31] I do not have any strong argument against anti-representationalist theories of perception, but I will not address them here, nor will I question Noordhof's rejection.

merely perceptual features. Accordingly, the content of expressive experience would involve standard perceptual properties *experienced-as* expressive, possibly owing to the intervention of imagination. Therefore, expressive properties would be perceptual properties that are experienced in a specific way – as through a distorting lens. Although this may seem an intriguing hypothesis, for it preserves the perceptual constraint to the look of objects by placing the burden of expressiveness on the experience modality, Noordhof jettisons it. He claims that this view does not do justice to the fact that expressive properties figure in our experience *as if they were properties of the object*, rather than features of the experience. Contrary to Noordhof, this second path will remain open and be developed it in the next section.

As for the third path, that is, the solution based on sensuous imagination, it stems from the worry that, although expressive properties cannot be features of the world, they appear as if they were so:

> It seems literally true that expressive properties are part of the content of our perceptual experience. Moreover, our experience of expressive properties presents them to be features of the world. (Noordhof 2008, p. 344)

The appeal to sensuous imagination is meant to vindicate the apparent mind-independence of expressive properties. Indeed, by definition it represents features as belonging to objects. In the specific case of expressive experiences, features that are represented as belonging to objects *are* expressive properties. Yet, what kind of properties should we take them to be? What is actually represented in the content of expressive experience?

> We might take the type of representational property responsible for the representation of expressiveness to *be* imagining an emotion-guided creative process. Here expressive properties would be part of the representational content of our perceptual experience.
> (Noordhof 2008, p. 343)

This is probably the most delicate passage of the theory and requires some effort to be correctly interpreted. Once it is triggered by perceptual properties of artworks, sensuous imagination provides the overall experience with a content that amounts to the imagined creative process. Moreover, such a creative process is not whatever process that might have given origin to the perceptual features of the work; rather, it is the creative process that would have originated under the "guidance" of an emotion, so providing the work with that very appearance. The guidance in question is the automatic, causal guidance that the expression of a felt emotion may generate. Emotions generate behavioural expressions that may turn into creative activities, actions, and gestures. Thus, experiencing a piece of music as expressive of sadness means to imagine the perceptual properties of the musical matter as if they were the result of a creative process that might have taken place under the impulse of an emotion. Noordhof calls this guidance the "phenomenal skeleton" of an emotion, say, what an emotion is typically able to cause. Imaginings of these phenomenal skeletons are therefore an integral part of the content of expressive experiences as long as they consist in the recreation of the productive capacity of emotions.

At this stage, some further discussion regarding the notion of phenomenal skeleton is required. It might be thought that the phenomenal skeleton, which is imaginatively experienced as guiding the creative process, consists in the behavioural profile of an emotion. This would place Noordhof's imaginative account closer to the contour theory and to the persona theory. Because if what is needed is a way to bind the perceptual aspect of things to some perceivable aspect of emotions, it seems that behavioural expressive profiles could do the job. Moreover, it must be recalled that Noordhof himself criticises Malcolm Budd's account based on resemblance, insofar as it appeals to a first-person phenomenological perspective on emotions, the what-it-feels-like to undergo that emotion (Budd 1995, p. 136), rather than the expressive component of emotional episodes (Noordhof 2008, p. 332).

However, Noordhof's proposal is different and lies somewhere in between these two views. Indeed, the phenomenal skeleton constitutes the causal component of an emotion, what in the emotion is responsible for its outward expression. We can simulate this component in such a way that it remains an off-line or facsimile emotion, that is, in such a way that the simulation does not cause us to perform any behaviour (Noordhof 2008, p. 332). Yet this simulation must not be understood as the introspective experience of the phenomenal skeleton – which is a (simulationist) way to interpret Budd's view. Instead, based on the fact that Noordhof takes sensuous imagination as not necessarily involving a first-person perspective (Noordhof 2002, following Williams 1973), he can insist that sensuous imaginative engagement does not imply any sort of introspection.

So, to take stock, experiencing an artwork as expressive of melancholy consists in simulating in imagination the causal skeleton of an emotion that might have guided a creative process so as to shape the perceivable structure of the artwork in that precise way. Sensuous imagination is therefore responsible for representing such a creative process when triggered by certain perceptual properties. This is what expressive properties would consist in and how they can be taken to be literally instantiated in the content of expressive experience.

Noordhof's account accommodates the perceptual phenomenology of expressive experience and provides an explanation for its relation to affective states, without requiring any arousal, but is also capable of accounting for those cases in which arousal occurs. Indeed, the appeal to the truncated causal power of simulated emotions allows for those cases where simulation results in an effective arousal (Noordhof 2008, p. 346).

If this is how things stand, however, no adequacy conditions can be found for expressive experience. The following example emphasises this point: the same landscape could look desolate to somebody and cheerful to somebody else, and these two ascriptions could never be verified by actual properties of the landscape, because the experience would entirely consist in the responses the two subjects would give to the same causal stimulus. At best, causal conditions may explain the rise of certain expressive experiences whose content would not find in the world any criterion to establish its correctness. This view does justice to the subjective character of expressive experience. However, it is not in a position to capture its more objective side, that is, our tendency to ascribe the same or similar expressive features to objects, or, at least, our tendency to appeal to the way objects *perceptually look*, in order to justify our ascriptions.

If one accepts this view, the first problem that arises is explaining how standard perceptual features can cause an observer to engage in the imagining of a creative process. That is, if one considers standard perceptual properties such as the chromatic shades of a painting, its slopes, the spatial relations on the surface, as responsible for the initiation of the off-line simulation of an expressive behaviour resulting in the activity of creation, then the role of standard perceptual properties must be further explained. Otherwise, the account risks allowing for a radically relativistic outcome, according to which any perceptual configuration may give rise to any expressive experience. I try to delineate two possible ways out of this problem, patterning them after Noordhof's argument. The first path consists in putting weight on the cognitive impact of background knowledge on the experience – in the spirit of Wollheim's projectivism. The second path consists in putting weight on the affective component of the experience, rooted in automatic mechanisms. Both paths present some difficulties.

3.2.2 Cognitive and Affective Requirements

In order to account for the relationship between standard perceptual properties and the specificity of expressive experience that they give rise to, one may be tempted to adopt a perspective that is analogous to Richard Wollheim's projectivist view based on the notion of "correspondence". As previously mentioned, Wollheim believes that associations taking place somewhere in memory are ultimately responsible for things looking expressive. According for instance to Francisca Perez-Carreño (2017), that account appeals to "thought-contents" associated with perceptual inputs, namely those cognitive contents of background knowledge and memories about emotions and projections undergone and performed in the past. Such contents associated with perceptual stimuli would result in expressive experiences.

Along the same lines of the debate about the recognition of musical properties, and in particular following Budd (2008, p. 138), it is legitimate to interpret the notion of thought content as amounting to that of "recognitional concept". According to Brian Loar (1990) a recognitional concept is the disposition to make minimal judgements about objects being *of a certain kind*, i.e. to *classify* objects (Loar 1990, p. 87). Applied to the case at stake, claiming that a recognitional concept associated with the perceptual input is required to undergo an expressive experience, implies that one must be able to classify the experience one is undergoing as being *of the same kind* of past analogous experiences. We have already seen, following Budd's criticism, why this mechanism is problematic. In particular, it implies that one has at least a minimal concept of what it is to project one's feeling onto an inanimate object, to experience it as a case of "correspondence", and that one also has the ability to use the concept to classify new occurrences of correspondence.

Given the developmental (namely Freudian) approach adopted by Wollheim, his notion of projection could even be understood as allowing for an automatic mechanism of association which would not require that one is aware of performing an association. Rather, the association would take place automatically and possibly at an unconscious level. Still, it would require a classificatory ability. In which case, the two projectivist accounts at stake would look even closer to each other. According to Wollheim, standard perceptual properties can cause an expressive experience in virtue of their capacity to trigger recognitional concepts about past, analogous experiences. Similarly, according to this first interpretation of Noordhof's account, standard perceptual features could cause an expressive experience in virtue of a recognitional mechanism based on background knowledge about creative processes and, possibly, emotional causal skeletons. For example, when confronted with William Turner's *Snow Storm: Steam-Boat off a Harbour's Mouth* (1842), one's experience of the painting as agitated would amount to one's knowledge about the way in which agitation can result on a canvas through an allegedly artistic creative process. If this were actually the case, simulation would take place only provided that one is sufficiently equipped with knowledge about how sounds, colours, plastic materials can be juxtaposed to obtain possibly expressive results. At least a minimal degree of knowledge (if not that of experts or experienced subjects) about how material things can be creatively manipulated under the guidance of an affective state (real or pretended) would be needed.

It must be recalled that Malcolm Budd argued against Wollheim by claiming that recognising the intimation of the projective origin of that experience in the content of expressive perception (even in the reflective aftermath of the experience) is too demanding a requirement and does not find sufficient confirmation in our introspective reports of expressive experiences (Budd 2008, p. 246 ff.). Analogously, one may argue against Noordhof that recognising an emotion-guided creative process in our expressive experience is highly demanding in that it requires additional knowledge about artistic creation. Moreover, our introspective experiences hardly attest this sort of recognition. By endorsing this view, we restrict the range of people capable of undergoing expressive experience to those who are well acquainted with processes governing artistic creation. On the contrary, even artistically lay people seem to be able to perceive music and paintings as expressive of emotions.

One additional criticism can be raised, that is, if one accepts that only subjects with a sufficient degree of expertise about creative processes can undergo expressive experiences, then what about expressive experiences of natural objects? In other words, what about expressive experiences of objects that are not the result of a creative process guided by emotions? Interestingly, rather than considering this a counterexample to his view, Noordhof takes it to be the confirmation of our natural tendency to engage in this sort of imaginative processes. Indeed, he argues that natural objects are experienced as expressive as long as one is able to imagine them as being the result of some intentional creation. The problem with this supposition, I suspect, is that such an engagement would be even more cognitively demanding than the one allegedly triggered by expressive artworks. Indeed, besides the capacity to recognise something as the product of a creative process, it would require the ability to apply this category also to non-artefacts. So conceived, this conceptual shift is as demanding as the capacity to recognise the "intimation of the origin in analogous experience" postulated by Wollheim.

As the reader might have already guessed, endorsing simulation as the process underlying sensuous imagination serves the purpose of avoiding such a limitation. Consistently, the second interpretation of Noordhof's account that I would like to consider places the burden of explanation on the phenomenal skeleton of emotions. It exploits the idea that emotions are automatic, unreflective processes and that their behavioural expressions are immediately recognised – with different degrees of accuracy – since an early age by means of simulation.

As it is well known, simulation theory of mindreading consists in the view that our ability to understand the minds of others can be explained in terms of our capacity to simulate their manifest behaviours. Simulating gestures, movements and expressions can accordingly give us access to others' intentions and mental states in a quick and automatic way (e.g. Heal 1986; Meltzoff and Gopnik 1993; Goldman 2006). Importantly, simulation processes need not be conscious.

They can and mostly do take place sub-personally, that is, in the form of "systems that operate within the person, are not directly under personal control, and the workings of which may be inaccessible to consciousness, though they may give rise to conscious experiences" (Currie 2011, p. 85).

In the case of sensuous imagination that is involved in Noordhof's proposal, in particular, off-line simulation is taken to generate mental states whose contents are very similar to perceptual ones. And the automatic and non-reflective character of this recognition, which may occur by means of simulation, is stressed by Noordhof as being one of the main virtues of his account.[32] This view is particularly consistent with evidence regarding the ability of young children to grasp the emotions of others by means of non-cognitive simulations of their behaviours and expressions. Furthermore, very young children – who allegedly lack complex background conceptual knowledge about emotions and creative processes – can perform attributions of affective states to others (Meltzoff and Moore 1977, 1983, 1989; Bavelas et al. 1987).

With regard to the application of this mindreading framework to Noordhof's imaginative theory, let us recall that, firstly, what is simulated in expressive experience is the phenomenal skeleton of an emotion, capable of causing creative processes and that, secondly, simulation accounts for our capacity to attribute mental and affective states to others. On this basis, off-line simulation of emotions can be taken to explain the fact that, even without a specific cognitive background concerning creative processes, one may simulate the phenomenal skeleton of an emotion as guiding gestures. The kind of mechanism in play in expressive experience would be the same or analogous to the one in play when we understand others' mental states. We automatically come to understand what is on someone else's mind thanks to the fact that we are triggered to simulate certain manifest qualities of their behaviour. The same would hold for expressive experience: certain manifest qualities of artworks would trigger the simulation of emotions (facsimile emotions running off-line) resulting in the representation of expressive properties as perceivable properties of artworks.

So, according to this latter solution, standard perceptual features cause the observer to simulate a creative process neither because they are associated with past experiences, nor because they are integrated by background knowledge about creative activities. Insisting on mechanisms of simulation that may be in play helps avoiding the appeal to background knowledge or, more generally, to

---

[32] I must specify that Noordhof is not trenchant in his endorsement of simulation theory as the best available theory of mind. He just notes that it is particularly compatible with his own account of expressive projection.

cognitive integrations. Perceptual properties would instead function as causal triggers of an automatic and mostly sub-personal simulation.

3.3 Causal Triggers

If perceptual properties are merely causal triggers of an expressive response, then their capacity to evoke an expressive experience is a matter of empirical study. And in point of fact, both Noordhof's account and Wollheim's account remain silent about what perceptual properties must look like in order to cause an expressive reaction. Whereas Wollheim's worry is to avoid the reduction of expressive properties to standard perceptual properties (Wollheim 1993, p. 154), Noordhof explains this point appealing to brute factuality:

> My response is that emotion-guided creative processes find certain features natural for expression and others not. This is a brute fact. [...] There may be no explanation in nature apart from this for why pieces of music and human behaviour share expressive properties.
> (Noordhof 2008, p. 345)

The search for the reasons why certain perceptual features cause the experience of expressive properties is doomed to lead nowhere but to causal relations, that is, to "brute" facts. Thus, if the simulation processes can be explained as the result of causal stimulations, then the account is not committed to the appeal to knowledge about emotions or creative processes. In order to perceive an artwork as expressive we just need to be naturally equipped with working mechanisms of simulation, apt to respond to particular stimuli in a particular way. The content of those sensuous imaginings that we entertain is a process whose (causally generated) expressive profile is capable of making expressive properties out of merely perceptual ones. Such perceptual properties are assigned a trigger-role, that is, they *cause* the imaginative mechanism, but it is not the case that the subject *represents* perceptual properties *as* expressive. Importantly, if the latter were the case, we would be able to justify our expressive experiences in terms of the involved merely perceptual properties. Instead, all we can say is that certain perceptual properties can *cause* imaginative responses of the kind just described.

When framing the problem of the relation between standard perceptual properties and expressive properties, Noordhof acknowledges that a relationship between the two might exist that goes beyond mere causality. He does not intend to:

> deny that we cite certain features of the music as bound up with our perception of the music's expressive properties. Indeed, we might cite these features to explain and partially justify our responses [...].
> (Noordhof 2008, p. 348)

Such a "bond" would therefore serve the purpose of "justifying" our expressive responses. But, he continues, he doubts that:

> the features we identify are both specific enough to explain why our imaginings are triggered by a piece of music but not the pattern of rainfall on the roof, and yet general enough to be common to all those works which have a certain expressive property.
> (Noordhof 2008, p. 348)

This is probably the most relevant problem that must be faced when trying to assess the content of expressive experience. All accounts should deal with this issue and many of the available theories try to find their own way out. Contour theory's appeal to resemblances between musical profile and people's expressions can be understood as an attempt to solve this problem. It is meant to provide a rationale between the merely perceptual structure of music and our experience of it as being expressive. According to this view, we would in principle be able to detect similarities between music and forms of behaviour (even if this does not necessarily happen whenever we undergo an expressive experience) and our expressive experience would be grounded in these similarities. But as we have already seen, it is easy to contradict this grounding, for there are many cases of expressive experience in which resemblances cannot be found. Consistently, Noordhof argues against the role ascribed to resemblances and is, at best, disposed to allow for some sub-personal detection of resemblances that could trigger the simulation process.

Interestingly, this idea is already present in Kivy's seminal book, where he writes that resemblance: "must lie at some deeper, nonconscious and pervasive level, although we can, of course, bring it to consciousness by analysis and scrutiny" (Kivy 1989, p. 173). This idea of a mechanism working sub-personally is radicalised in Kivy (2002), by the appeal to evolutionary mechanisms that do not necessarily make the resemblance available for conscious scrutiny. Yet, he can only support his claim with suppositions about how these mechanisms could work, according to the evolutionary assumption that it is more advantageous to perceive as many stimuli as possible as being animated (especially threatening), rather than inert. Even in this case, the causal explanation is adopted, although supported by reasons of evolution.

There seems to be a stage of the explanation where the appeal to a "black box" is unavoidable: justifications are no longer possible, because in principle one may never be able to consciously recognise the resemblance that makes expressive experience possible; all that can be said is that there are stimuli capable of causing certain reactions. Once the explanatory chain gets to this point, two options are available. Firstly, it is possible to reject the idea of a rationale for the relation between perceptual properties and expressive properties. Derek Matravers agrees on this view:

> I cannot see that we have any reason to think that the cause of our experience of expression should also be its object. The object of the experience of expression would, presumably, have to fall within a reasonably narrow range fixed *a priori*. By contrast, there is no reason to suppose that there are a priori limits on what properties of music can cause the experience of expression, nor that some of those properties will not turn out to be quite unexpected, even bizarre. (Matravers 2007, p. 98–99)

On Matravers' view, the debate about expressiveness is doomed to be irreducibly split: causal stimulus on the one hand, intentional objects on the other. The problem when one tries to find a relation between the two is that we are not able to establish *a priori* what a stimulus must be like in order to evoke an expressive experience. Expressive experience of sadness is plausibly caused by a number of different stimuli, variously composed, not to mention the contextual variables that can intervene. Stimuli fall therefore within the causal space, they are brute facts, whose relation to experience can at best be dealt with empirically. The task for philosophers is instead to offer phenomenological descriptions of experiences and of their contents that should be as consistent as possible among themselves and as compatible as possible with empirically testable causal reactions (Matravers 2007, p. 96).

Does this approach to expressiveness settle the issue? Is there any work left to do for the philosopher who aims at accounting for the not merely causal role of perceptual properties? The alternative option we have consists in peeping inside the black box, that is, providing more detailed descriptions of what kind of stimuli and contextual variables evoke expressive experience in people. Taking this path means acknowledging that the appeal to the black box or to the inevitable split of the explanation of expressive experience does not justify the cessation of philosophical inquiry about expressive experience.

3.4 The Heresy of the Separable Experience

As anticipated, when it comes to accounting for the relationship between perceptual and expressive properties, one strategy consists in focusing more closely on perceptual properties. The working hypothesis is that such a focus may provide a better explanation of the content of expressive experience. The original question from which the problem of the relationship between perceptual and expressive qualities stems is nicely phrased by Paul Boghossian:

> Sounds are heard as having the expressive properties they have *because* they are heard as having certain musical properties: it is something about the shape of the melody

which opens the fourth movement of Tchaikovsky's Sixth Symphony that makes us hear it as sombre. So what we are asking is: how could possessing certain musical properties amount to expressing a state of mind? (Boghossian 2007, p. 121)

The way in which Boghossian develops his answer is antithetical to the one embraced by Matravers. Indeed, he argues against those views according to which a rationale between these two kinds of properties cannot be provided. Boghossian insists:

> The point is that the expressive properties of music are clearly grounded in its purely musical properties. It is *because* a passage has certain musical properties that it is heard as having certain expressive properties. (Boghossian 2007, p. 124)

Even if he does not develop his positive account further, Boghossian is sympathetic to resemblance theories. In particular, he argues that judgements of musical expressiveness are justifiable by listeners in terms of resemblances and that the fact that one might not always be able to indicate the extent to which music must resemble a behaviour in order to be expressive is not problematic. The simple fact that we tend to point at resemblances in order to justify such judgements is enough, on his view, to ground an account of expressiveness on resemblances. Boghossian draws the emphasis back to the problem of justifying expressiveness in terms of underlying perceptual properties. But since he does not provide any knock-down argument in favour of resemblances, I take his as descriptions of a widespread tendency to justify expressive ascriptions by pointing at the perceptual structures of objects. Such perceptual structures are accordingly the place to look for more robust and detailed justifications.

The tension between the idea that the relationship between perceptual and expressive properties can be clarified and the idea that it is doomed to remain mysterious is adequately stressed by Budd's argument against what he calls the "heresy of the separable experience". This argument has been introduced in Chapter 1, for it is exploited by Ridley to criticise standard arousalism. According to Budd, a theory of expressiveness is flawed by the heresy if it represents a work: "as being related in a certain way to an experience which can be fully characterised without reference to the nature of the work itself" (Budd 1985, p. 123). Budd argues against those theories that explain values such as musical expressiveness in terms of the experience music can generate, but without providing an explanatory link between the experience and the nature – that is, the perceivable structure – of music.[33] As a result, these

---

[33] In the text, Budd targets the so-called "communication theory of emotions" that he ascribes to Leo Tolstoy and to Deryck Cooke.

accounts cannot provide an explanation of the experience as being the experience of that very work and of its features. In principle, characterising the experience in causal terms implies that such an experience can be undergone even without experiencing those features. In the case of expressive music, for instance, we would end up with two distinct experiences, one in which we are confronted with the "nature of the work", that is, its intrinsic, allegedly perceptual qualities, the other which is the reaction to such qualities, and that may entail imaginings, feelings, memories, projections and so on:

> [...] music can be valued as music in virtue of its expressive aspect only if the experience of music as expressive of a state of mind is not thought of as a mere combination of experiences – an experience of the music which does not relate it to the state of mind and an experience of the state of mind – each of which would be possible without the other."
>
> (Budd 1985, p. 124)

Instead, Budd claims that: "the obligation to provide an independent description of the experience can never properly be discharged" (Budd 1985, p. 123). Such an independent description must therefore account for expressive experience in terms of the specific character and content of the experience, that is, in terms of those properties (of music or of whatever object) that the experience is about. This implies that the causal strategy, although it can provide some insight into those mechanisms that are activated and that arguably implement the experience, cannot fulfil this task.

As the drug counterargument undermines arousal theories (as shown in Chapter 1), an analogous objection inspired by the heresy of the separable experience might be raised against Noordhof's account and also against Kivy's hypothesis of the "black box". According to both of these views, the content of expressive experiences consists of perceptual properties whose expressive potential is determined by psychological mechanisms functioning at an unconscious level and is responsible for those features appearing in a *sui generis* way. These sub-personal mechanisms need not be represented in the phenomenal character of the experience, but can be invoked as an explanation as long as they are compatible with the phenomenal description of expressive experience. As well as Noordhof's explanation relies on the capacities of certain perceptual features to cause imagination, contour theory also delegates the task of detecting similarities to unconscious mechanisms. As the heresy suggests, however, the appeal to causal mechanisms does not allow one to account for the specificity (e.g. the expressive character) of what is perceived, but can only present us with a combination of two separate experiences.

3.5 Dealing with the Heresy

In order to deal with this heresy, one of the approaches discarded by Noordhof can offer a way out, namely the idea that expressive properties can be explained in terms of perceptual properties represented in a specific manner. Noordhof believes that this strategy does not do justice to the fact that expressive properties figure in our experiences as if they belonged to the object of the ascription. In other words, expressive properties do not seem to characterise *the experience*, but rather *its objects*. It is not the case that we experience a sunset *sadly*, or a piece of music *cheerfully*, rather, we experience sad sunsets and cheerful pieces of music. The idea to be developed further is that this might consist in the experience of certain perceptual properties as being expressive, without necessarily implying that so conceived expressive properties appear as belonging to the experience and not to the objects. Importantly, this approach promises to account for the link between perceptual and expressive properties without falling prey to the heresy of the separable experiences.

If expressive experience amounted to the perceptual experience of certain perceptual properties that we represent *as being expressive*, those perceptual properties would provide minimal adequacy conditions, doing justice to our tendency to justify ascriptions of expressiveness by reference to perceptual properties.

As we have seen, most philosophers agree that perceptual properties play a role in expressive experience. However, most approaches consider them to be the causal trigger of expressive experience, rather than part of its content. Among these positions, the resemblance approach is the one that explicitly acknowledges the relevance of perception not only for the phenomenal character of expressive experience, but also when it comes to its content. It indeed contends that we not only have a perceptual experience of expressive properties, but also that these properties bear a resemblance relation to standard perceptual properties. The difficulty consists in "locating" this perceived resemblance.

Contour theory holds that we perceive expressive qualities as long as we detect resemblances between objects and expressions. Yet resemblances are not always available. In order to see whether the perceptual approach designed by contour theory can overcome the theoretical difficulty concerning the experience's content, it is useful to distinguish three paradigmatic cases, each of which stands with resemblances in a specific relation. Firstly, there is the case in which resemblances actually and manifestly enable us to ascribe expressiveness, let us call it the case of the *weeping willow*. Secondly, there is the case in which the resemblance relation between the perceived object and the emotional expression is not consciously experienced by the subject. Still, in principle, the subject might be able to justify her experience afterwards, by reflecting on it, finding out that *there are* resemblances to which she can appeal. Let us call this the case of the *musical gesture*. Thirdly, there is the most mysterious case in which resemblances are not even available upon reflection, what I would call the case of the *minor chord*. By addressing these examples one by one, the role of resemblances and of perceptual properties will become clearer.

3.5.1 The Weeping Willow

Why do weeping willows look sad? One plausible answer appeals to manifest resemblances. We probably ascribe sadness to the weeping willow *because* we see it as resembling the posture of a sad person. In this case, expressive experience would consist in the perception of manifest resemblances between the structure of the weeping willow and a sad posture. The content of such an experience accordingly mobilises a sufficient number of perceptual properties that the object (the weeping willow) has in common with a typically expressive posture (the bodily expression of sadness). As long as we consider such a posture to be inherently expressive of sadness, we might end up representing the weeping willow as sad in virtue of such a manifest resemblance. Take by analogy the case of children resembling their parents, or of elder people resembling their younger selves: when we undergo a recognitional experience of this kind, that is, when we recognise someone as resembling her or his father, or as resembling her or himself in an old picture, the recognitional process can amount to some form of comparison resulting in an experienced resemblance. Analogously, at times, we see something resembling an expression and *therefore* we deem it expressive; in these cases, manifest resemblance is what expressive experience is about.

A strategy to deal with resemblances in expressive experience that has been exploited consists in considering them through the lens of so-called *seeing-as* experience or *seeing-an-aspect*. Stephen Davies, for example, presents his version of contour theory in terms of aspect perception, based on the idea that, as in the case of the recognition of expressive behaviours of human beings, when we experience expressive objects we do not need to connect the expressive appearance to any mental state (Davies 1994, 2005). Instead, we just recognise certain perceptual patterns as being similar to typical perceptual patterns displayed in human expressions. He preliminarily draws a relevant distinction relating to expression recognition in humans that is worth recalling. When we see someone "hopeful-looking", Davies argues, two possible explanations are available: either, we might be seeing the person's look while entertaining the belief that she is feeling and expressing hope; or we might be seeing her look without entertaining the belief that she feels hopeful. This latter case is, according to Davies, an example of aspect perception for, although we are not inferring the presence of a mental state, we are seeing the behavioural pattern as being the expression of such a mental state that can nevertheless be absent. Consider, for example, the rehearsals of the actor who produces with her body, face and voice a wide range of expressions without feeling them. We would probably see those movements and hear those sounds as being expressions, yet we would suspend any belief about the actor actually *feeling* the corresponding emotions.

Given these two cases, Davies claims that both if we attend the actor's rehearsal and if we encounter a "hopeful-looking" friend, we see their behaviours and gestures *as if* they were the expression of some emotion, that is, as potentially connected with some felt emotion. Instead – and this is a third possibility – when one experiences someone's "hopeful-look" without willingly suspending the belief about the mental (affective) state that the person is undergoing, one is perceiving what Davies calls the "emotion characteristics in appearance". Such a seeing-as experience does not involve any ongoing nor suspended belief about the expressed mental state. Rather, we perceive certain traits of the person's look as expressive of hope. To prove that this is what happens, Davies invites us to think that the same look may be experienced in different ways, that is, as "hopeful" or, for example, as "dreamy". This does not (always) depend on the belief one has about the person's actual or potential feeling.

> The perception of an emotion characteristic involves the recognition of an aspect of the appearance that bears the emotion characteristic. As with other instances of aspect perception, it is sometimes possible to see an appearance as presenting first one emotion characteristic and then another. Because of the possibility that the same material object of perception may be seen under more than one aspect, aspect perception differs from 'ordinary' seeing despite remaining a perceptually based experience.
>
> (Davies 2005, p. 139)

Let us therefore focus on the weeping willow case again. When we ascribe a sad look to the tree, we do not actually entertain any thought about it feeling and expressing its sadness, but we perceive some of its structural properties. One might disagree or be unable to see the weeping willow as sad. The very fact that this is possible speaks in favour of the explanation of the perceptual resemblance theory in terms of seeing-as.

The weeping willow case paradigmatically shows that expressive experience might take place in virtue of manifest resemblances, once a comparison is carried out. However, the argument also casts light on this being at most one of the possible kinds of expressive experience, the one whose content instantiates the perceptual structure of the object (the weeping willow) triggering a mapping process which results in the recognition of a similarity.

On the one hand, it can be objected that it is one thing to experience the weeping willow as resembling someone expressing sadness and another thing to experience it as sad (Noordhof 2008, p. 332). Alternatively, one can adopt a more liberal stance and accept this sort of experience within the range of expressive ones. In any case, however, it is easy to see that most experiences of expressiveness do not consist in the conscious mapping of the features of inanimate objects upon the expressive profile of persons. Instead, when we hear a sad song, look at a serene sky, choose a colour in virtue of its liveliness, resemblances are not what we actually recognise – at most, they can be found out afterwards, upon reflection, in the search for a justification.[34]

3.5.2 The Musical Gesture

Seeing-as experiences do not necessarily entail the manifest grasping of similarities and most expressive things are not experienced as such on the basis of the conscious detection of a manifest resemblance. Unless the amount of shared features between, say, a lament and a musical gesture strikes us as being a manifest resemblance, resemblance is unlikely to be phenomenally manifest to the subject who is undergoing the expressive experience of that musical gesture as lamenting. Therefore, we must assess the expressive experience of things that do not present themselves as resembling actual expressions.

This second case is what Christopher Peacocke has in mind when he discusses his theory of metaphorical experience (Peacocke 2009; 2010). It is worthwhile to linger over his view, because it sheds light on a relevant aspect of our problem. Rejecting the idea of metaphor as a merely linguistic device, Peacocke

---

34 This treatment of resemblance is inspired by Christopher Peacocke's account of depiction in terms of "experienced resemblance" (1987). On his view, experienced resemblance between an object and its depiction amounts to the similarity of the portion of the visual space occupied by a silhouette on a bi-dimensional surface to the real (or supposedly real) visual space. As Peacocke himself admits, however: "To see [an inkblot and its reduced copy] as having the same shape is to have a certain kind of visual experience: it is not a matter of consciously working out the similarity or of noticing matching features. *Certainly, one does have sometimes to work out consciously that two perceived things have the same shape: this may involve conscious mental rotation and comparison of parts. But not all cases are like this*" (Peacocke 1987, p. 386. Emphasis mine).

puts forward the notion of "metaphorical content" of experience as being a *sui generis* content that can be represented in perception as well as in imagination or in thought. Importantly, such a content "cannot be reduced to a combination of visual experience of some other kind with an element of imagining that something is the case" (Peacocke 2009, p. 259).

The metaphorical content characterises those experiences in which we identify certain objects as other objects, belonging to different domains. We happen to see a solitary tree as a lonely person, to imagine dark, stormy clouds as an army, to think of an artichoke as a warrior. Metaphorical content is embedded in all these experiences and especially in expressive experiences as long as we hear a musical gesture – that belongs to the domain of perceivable sounds – as the expression of an emotion – belonging to the domain of affects.

These sorts of experiences may well be considered instances of *experiencing-as* where what is seen or heard is not a manifest resemblance. Therefore, according to Peacocke, they require a specific account that explains how we can see, hear, imagine, think of things as being other things. This premise seems to rule out automatically Levinson's endorsement of a seeing-as perspective combined with imagination. He speaks of "ready-hearability-as-personal-expression" (Levinson 1996, p. 91, later confirmed and explained in 2006) arguing that we can hear expressive music only as long as we are disposed to hear it readily as if it were the expression of someone's emotion. Accordingly, the perceptual structure of music can be heard-as an expression, provided that one engages in an imaginative project about some fictive character who expresses her or himself through the music. Although this imaginative approach has the virtue of considering perceptual properties to be what is actually mobilised by the experience's content, it does not account for such a content being "integrated" as it should – according to Peacocke.

Peacocke's idea is that a process of "mapping" takes place establishing the link between distinct domains. More specifically, he claims that metaphorical content entails the detection of some *isomorphism* between these domains, i.e. the recognition of a structural resemblance that can take place at some sub-personal level and involves establishing a correspondence between the mental representations of such things (Peacocke 2009, p. 267). Subsequently, the metaphorical experience of X as Y does not entail the conscious representation of X as *resembling* Y.

> Metaphorical thought, imagination, or experience exploits a correspondence, rather than representing it. When you think of life as a journey, various features of your representation of a journey are mapped onto your representation of a life. The mapping is exploited, rather than being thought about or represented. (Peacocke 2009, p. 260)

One can examine the case of music: according to Peacocke's account, hearing a piece of music expressive of the transition from a negative to a positive emotion is a process that relies on and exploits an isomorphism between the domain of music and that of psychological states without representing it (Peacocke 2010, p. 189). Here is the elaborate description of the mapping process:

> Under the correspondence of mental representations between the two domains, some representations of the metaphorically represented domain are copied to some special kind of storage binding them with their corresponding mental representations (of the representing domain) in the sub-personal state underlying an experience, imagining, or thought which has the metaphorical content. Thereby their content enters the metaphorical content of that mental state or event [...] Detection of the isomorphism is causally active in producing that state with metaphorical content, but no representation of the isomorphism itself enters the content of the state to whose underlying realization various mental representations are copied. This is why one who enjoys the mental state with metaphorical content may have to work out consciously what the isomorphism is.
> (Peacocke 2009, p. 267 ff.)

This way of dealing with resemblance can explain the case of the expressive musical gesture: the perceptual structure of the gesture is metaphorically represented as expressive of an affective state as long as it triggers the sub-personal mapping from the domain of expressive behaviours to the one of organised sounds. Unlike in the case of the weeping willow, this mapping process takes place sub-personally, so that it is not necessary that one is aware of the resemblances that make it possible in the very moment in which the experience occurs. As a consequence, the resemblance will not feature in the phenomenal character of the experience.

The sub-personal mapping process hypothesised by Peacocke draws on a "special kind of storage", that is, on allegedly cognitive resources whose nature must be empirically specified. As Peacocke writes, the reference to the special kind of storage is an "empty box" (Peacocke 2009, p. 267) with the sole functional role of distinguishing the metaphorical recognition (of X as being Y) from the standard recognition (of X as being X). The activation of a mapping process from one domain to another is responsible for this distinction. Such an activation is causally determined by the perceptual structure of the musical gesture, so that the mapping process and the storage on which it draws can be understood in different ways. As to this, Peacocke seems disposed to endorse a solution to fill in the "empty box" that appeals to imagination: "We can say that in some very broad sense, the ability to experience one thing metaphorically-as another involves imaginative powers" (Peacocke 2009, p. 267).

However, he also insists that a sharp distinction should be drawn between imagining something in the music and perceiving it as belonging to the music.

So, the "very broad sense" to which he refers implies that the resulting experience must present expressive features as belonging to the objects, without requiring that the subject engages in an imaginative project. Therefore, the metaphorical view appears to be compatible with Noordhof's appeal to simulation and sensuous imagination generating an integrated experience. Accordingly, isomorphism would trigger the simulation of salient phenomenal features of, say, cheerfulness, and sensuous imagination would perform the mapping of such features onto the perceptual structure of the stimulus. The result would be the metaphorical representation of the musical gesture as cheerful. This hypothesis is worth exploring via two alternative paths. Firstly, the idea that sensuous imagination could do the job will be assessed and, secondly, the possible role played by conceptual background knowledge will be considered.

In order to figure out the sort of imaginative process that might be required by the metaphorical view, one can turn to *mental imagery*, a way to conceive of sensuous imagination that has been thoroughly explored in philosophy, cognitive sciences and neurosciences. Scholars tend to agree on mental imagery as consisting in a kind of imaginative state that is tightly connected to what we perceive (Richardson 1969; Ichikawa 2009; Gendler 2018). Let us stick to the visual case: we can visualize Pablo Picasso's *Les Demoiselles d'Avignon*, that is, we can close our eyes and imagine those perceptual properties that characterize the painting in quite a lot of detail, without being in perceptual contact with it. Notably, we can do the same without closing our eyes. Let us now extend to the auditory case: we can imagine a passage of Albinoni's *Adagio*, that is, we can bring to our minds those auditory properties that constitute the piece, without entertaining any actual perceptual relation with it. Granted, we can also perform analogous tasks involving other senses such as touch and smell (Bensafi 2013, Schmidt 2019). One reason why mental imagery is an appealing explanatory tool for various mental phenomena is its being a sort of blend of perception and imagination.[35] In a nutshell: unlike imagination and like perception it represents perceptual properties; like imagination and unlike perception it is about something with which the subject is *not* in direct contact.

This two-faced nature of mental imagery has been widely exploited by Bence Nanay in recent years. His particular view is worth introducing to see

---

35 The possibility to account for numerous mental phenomena by means of mental imagery is a matter of discussion. Among such phenomena are: perceptual attention (Fazekas & Nanay 2017, Moriya 2018), amodal perception (Nanay 2010; Briscoe 2011), hallucination (Nanay 2016b), perception of pain (Philips 2011, Nanay 2017), cognitive penetration of perceptual contents (Macpherson 2012).

whether it can integrate the picture provided by Peacocke. According to Nanay, the phenomenal character of mental imagery and that of perception are similar. Such a similarity is traditionally attested by the famous "Perky experiment" in which subjects took themselves to be visualising the objects, whereas they were in fact perceiving them (Perky 1910). Consistently, we can unconsciously undergo mental imaginings in such a way that they provide us with "quasi-perceptual" mental contents (Nanay 2015). Hence, Nanay grounds the similarity between the phenomenal characters of these mental states in terms of the attribution of properties, that is, the fact that both when we undergo mental imagery and perceptual states we ascribe properties to objects (Nanay 2010 and 2015, who finds support in Burge 2010 and in Peacocke 1985, 1992).

Since the phenomenal character of the two mental states is similar, Nanay argues that their intentional contents are similar as well. He attributes the responsibility for the differences in content to the different sources of determinacy of the two sorts of experience, that is, what makes the content of the two experiences more or less determinate (Nanay 2015, 2016a). Compare the experiences of seeing and visualising a natural scenario. If we are asked to focus on the perceivable details of that scenario, in the perceptual case we will *look more carefully* at what is in front of us, whereas in the latter case we will resort to those contents that we have, so to say, stored in mind. Whereas the determinacy of the content of perceptual experience is provided directly by the properties of the stimulus (it is bottom-up), the determinacy of the content of mental imagery is determined by top-down sources such as memories, beliefs, or expectations.

As a result, mental imagery turns out to be much closer to perception under many relevant respects, namely the phenomenal character, the intentional content and its functional role in our cognitive architecture. If this were right, then Peacocke's "empty box" could be filled in by mental imagery performing the mapping process – i.e. by a kind of mental state that is close to perception and therefore results in a perceptual-like phenomenal character, but is less constrained by worldly properties than perception.

This perspective is intriguing, yet two elements raise doubts when one tries to apply it to expressive experience. Firstly, if we take mental imagery to be ultimately responsible for the content of expressive experience, we have to look for its adequacy conditions precisely in those sources of determinacy Nanay refers to. Once again, the criterion for the ascription of expressive properties to objects would not reside in properties of the world (the perceptual structure of the musical gesture), but rather in our memory, beliefs, and expectations. Secondly, further specifications are required regarding the way in which mental imagery should perform the mapping from one domain to another, supposedly relating what is actually perceived to some storage we have in mind. Admittedly, these doubts are not enough to undermine the attempt to integrate the metaphorical stance with mental imagery, but they at least invite us to ask whether an analogous integration can be carried out by perception instead.

As Peacocke states: "the recognition of expression in a piece of music, and more generally identification of the content of the music, is fundamentally perceptual identification" (Peacocke 2010, p. 190). Focusing again on the mapping process and on the storage that makes it possible, one can consider this mapping as being a case of perceptual recognition that exploits some background knowledge. This intuition is supported by the idea of "mentally non-predicatively subsuming" something under a certain concept:

> The isomorphism involved in the perception of Zurbaran's painting of pots maps the concept of those pots to the concept *person*. So this explanation counts the perceiver of the painting as mentally non-predicatively subsuming the depicted pots under the concept *person*. (Peacocke 2010, p. 189)

In the light of this proposal, the aforementioned notion of recognitional concept proves useful. On this interpretation, the perceptual stimulus of a musical gesture would trigger in the subject the application of a concept that is stored in mind and that would appropriately apply in virtue of the underlying isomorphism. However, such an approach straightforwardly leads us back to the discussion about the background knowledge required for the recognition of expressive features. What kind of concept is actually required in order to perform the mapping? The risk of intellectualising expressive experience against phenomenal evidence is considerable, for also those who are neither expert in artistic creation, nor particularly skilled in emotion ascriptions can hear expressive music and see expressive landscapes.

In order to decide whether conceptual integration is required to represent certain perceptual properties as expressive, an assessment of *seeing-as* is helpful. It must be noticed that such scholars as Kivy, Davies, Levinson, Noordhof, and Peacocke are attracted by and sometimes overtly refer to seeing-as as an explanatorily powerful notion. The challenge is therefore to offer a quick overview of the various positions concerned with seeing-as experiences, questioning the role of conceptual intervention.

The battlefield immediately shows an important divide. On one side, one can think that seeing-as experience has a conceptual content (e.g. Fodor 2007; 2015). Accordingly, in order to undergo the experience, subjects need to possess those concepts necessary to specify what that content is. If this is correct, then concepts are part of the content of seeing-as experiences: the concept of "duck" is part of the experience of the Jastrow figure as representing a duck, whereas the concept of "rabbit" is part of the content of the experience of the same figure as representing a rabbit. On the other side of the barricade, there is the position according to which the content of seeing-as experiences is non-conceptual (e.g. Jagnow 2011; Peacocke 1992; Raftopoulos 2011), that is, one does not need to possess any relevant concept in order to undergo them.[36]

As shall be recalled, Peacocke appeals to the process of subsuming something under a concept, although he suggests that this process might occur "non-predicatively". The focus should therefore be on the role that conceptual abilities play in the recognition of expressive characters of objects. To this aim, one can rely on a Wittgenstenian distinction concerning bi-stable figures. The argument goes as follows: not all ambiguous figures that lend themselves to seeing-as experiences can be accounted for in the same way. We can, for instance, experience the shift from the black to the white cross in Figure 3 without appealing to the concept of 'cross'. Rather, it seems that such a phenomenal switch depends on properties of the visual pattern itself.

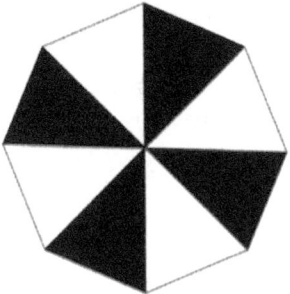

Figure 3: The Double Cross. Reproduced by the author.

As Wittgenstein writes:

> Those two aspects of the double cross (I shall call them the aspects A) might be reported simply by pointing alternately to an isolated white and an isolated black cross.

---

36 Whether Ludwig Wittgenstein, whose remarks on seeing-as are pivotal for the whole debate, spouses a conceptualist approach is controversial. Brian O'Shaughnessy (2012), favours this interpretation, whereas Alberto Voltolini (2013) argues for the opposite view. It has also been argued that concepts might be required in order to entertain an experience whose content is nevertheless non-conceptual (Tye 1995). However, Tye writes: "Where a figure has an ambiguous decomposition into spatial parts, concepts can influence which decomposition occurs. This is one way in which top-down processing can make a phenomenal difference" (Tye 1995, p. 140). I cannot discuss Tye's view in details, but for present purposes his admission that concepts can, in one way or another, make a phenomenal difference to some perceptual experiences of this sort is enough.

> One could quite well imagine this as a primitive reaction in a child even before it could talk. (Wittgenstein 1986, p. 207)

This kind of aspect perception might accordingly consist in the grasping of certain "grouping properties" which are responsible for both two-dimensional and three-dimensional organisation of patterns (Voltolini 2013, 2015). Grouping properties are "the different ways for the figure's elements of being arranged according to different orientations" (Voltolini 2013, p. 219), that is, *gestalten* responding to orientation rules. The grasping of such properties as being internally organised is something that does not require the intervention of concepts.

However, the case of the duck-rabbit – or, as suggested by Voltolini, of Arcimboldo's *Vertumnus* – is more complicated than this and it is likely to require some conceptual apparatus. Following the Wittgensteinian distinction, it is possible to claim that one must possess the concept of "duck" in order to see the Jastrow's figure as a duck, and the concept of "fruits" (of various types) in order to recognise them in Arcimboldo's famous portrait. In short, someone who was completely unaware of what a rabbit looks like, would be blind to the rabbit-aspect of the Jastrow's bi-stable figure, and someone who did not know what a fruit or a vegetable looks like, would not recognise the fruit-aspect – so to speak – of Arcimboldo's painting. In Wittgenstein's words:

> You only 'see the duck and rabbit aspects' if you are already conversant with the shapes of those two animals. There is no analogous condition for seeing the aspects A. (Wittgenstein 1986, p. 207)

The content of this latter kind of seeing-as is therefore two-layered. Experiencing the Jastrow's figure as a duck implies that one has grasped the grouping properties that are responsible for the specific perceptual organisation of the figure. Once this perceptual grasping has taken place, the conceptual intervention allows the viewer to see the configuration as being the depiction of a duck (or, alternatively, of a rabbit). The content is accordingly constituted by a recognitional conceptual level that presupposes a non-conceptual level of grasping grouping properties (Voltolini 2013, p. 229).

We can now look back at the case of the expressive musical gesture. The hypothesis is that it can be explained as a case of experiencing-as. The kind of experience that Peacocke's account captures is a recognitional experience whose content is perceptual and consists in the detection of the isomorphism between the perceptual properties of the gesture – its internal structure, or, to use the same vocabulary adopted by Voltolini, the grouping properties that are constitutive of it – and typical expressive behaviours, postures, tones, and so on. The fact that isomorphism is not phenomenally manifest does not imply that the experience does not involve conceptual abilities. On the contrary, metaphorical experience so conceived admittedly requires a mapping capacity that consists in a conceptual subsumption.

The metaphorical explanation, therefore, can be understood as a refined version of a resemblance theory that allows for a perceptual phenomenal character, but whose content represents perceptual properties by means of a conceptual intervention. As in the case of complex bi-stable figures, the experience consists in recognising something as something else thanks to conceptual capacities. To use a distinction sketched by Loar, this class of expressive experiences requires not only a recognitional *disposition*, i.e. "the disposition to classify objects (events, situations) together" (Loar 1990, p. 87), but also the recognitional *ability* to do that. We need to be able to apply concepts on the basis of a detectable isomorphism in order to undergo expressive experiences of this kind.

3.5.3 The Minor Chord

> The minor chord is nothing like a premusical human expression of sadness. There is no changing pitch contour of the music that in some way corresponds to the contour of a non-musical bodily or verbal expression of sadness over time. There is no changing contour of the single, isolated chord. If someone were to play the chord to indicate sadness, that will succeed only because the chord is already heard as expressing sadness.
> (Peacocke 2009, p. 262)

The case of the minor chord is probably one of the most mysterious in the philosophy and psychology of musical expressiveness (Hevner 1935a; Curtis and Bharucha 2010). As Peacocke notices, there is no contour in such a temporally limited and simply structured object that justifies the appeal to isomorphism or to resemblance. Even contour theorists are well aware of this challenge to their view. Peter Kivy, in particular, accounts for the experience of simple expressive features in terms of *conventions*. As we have already seen, this alleged difference is not such that it is mirrored by the phenomenal character of expressive experience. Indeed, it does not seem that the experience of an expressive musical gestures is phenomenally different from the experience of an expressive chord, as per its affective character.

Yet, one may insist that these two experiences have distinct types of contents that require different explanations. Kivy's proposal about convention goes in this direction, as it argues that we can represent something like a minor chord as sad in virtue of its occurring within a context (musical and, more widely, cultural) that makes it appear as sad. The minor chord *per se* would therefore be much too underdetermined to be experienced as expressive of an affective state. The same claim might be made for colours, given that cultural and contextual relativity of the affective value of colour shades is hard to deny.

There is no need to oppose this intuition, arguing against the idea that the expressive experience of shades of colour and of simple sounds is relevantly determined by contextual elements. However, accepting this relativity cannot amount to accepting that expressive experience of simple features consists in the expressive representation of such features – which are *per se* affectively neutral – being fully determined by our cultural habits, beliefs, and expectations. Indeed, this would amount to denying that expressive experience bears a significant relationship to the perceptual look of things. On this view, any simple property that does not resemble any expressive behaviour would be neutral, its expressive character being completely dependent on contextual variables.

One minimalist intuition is instead worth defending here: even when we ascribe some affective character to these sorts of properties, we tend to justify our ascriptions on the basis of their appearance. This is compatible with the idea that the affective value of this kind of features may vary from context to context. However, the explanatory effort should be to find out whether something in the perceptual appearance of these objects may justify, for instance, the aesthetic purposes for which they are selected (bright instead of dark tones, high instead of low pitches, smooth instead of pointy shapes, and so on), *before* resorting to conventionalist explanations. Once this effort has been pushed to its limit, arguments from contexts and cultural specificities can be taken back into account. In virtue of this intuition, it is worth making an attempt to explain the case of simple expressive properties. It consists in focusing on what something intuitively simple – like a colour or a sound – looks like when we experience it as affectively charged.

3.6 Dynamic Properties

Interestingly, Kivy refers to the property of being "static" to describe simple features such as colours and sounds. He writes that "A static event like the sounding of a chord cannot be similar to any expressive behaviour" (Kivy 1980, p. 80), meaning that the quality that simple features lack, to be explained by a contour theory, is some sort of *dynamism*. Indeed, dynamism supports the resemblances with human behaviours. Something similar is implied by Davies when he refers to the "dynamic topography" of music as being responsible for similarities between it and human "gaits, carriages, or comportments" (Davies 2005, p. 181). So, we need to clarify what exactly the invoked dynamism amounts to.

Dynamism is problematic not only for the philosophy of music, where it raises questions about what musical movement actually is, but also for philosophy of perception in general. It is indeed unclear what the experience of something dynamic consists in, above all when experiences are about static images. Consider the case of figurative paintings: in Giacomo Balla's famous *Dynamism of a Dog on a Leash* (1912) we tend to see the dog as if it were moving its legs fast. One may argue that this sort of perceived dynamism could be explained by reference to our knowledge about real dogs' behaviour. But the immediate counterexample would arise that not every dog represented as running gives the same impression of dynamism.

James Cutting (2002) proposes to sort the different ways to convey movement in representations into five categories: dynamic balance, also described as broken symmetry or instability, multiple or stroboscopic images, affine shear, blur, and vector-like lines superimposed on an image. Movement in Balla's dog is clearly represented by means of multiple images. All these techniques are used by painters and illustrators to represent moving objects. The use of dynamic balance makes represented things appear less static – think about the widely acknowledged difference between Classical and Hellenistic sculpture. Affine shear has been widely used by cartoonist to convey the idea of a fast movement towards – think about the ellipsoidal tire or the way that a train's smoke stack leans forward to emphasise its movement. A good example of blur that gives the impression of movement is that of pictures taken while the subject was actually moving, so that the edges of the figure appear increasingly transparent in the image, whereas vector-like lined are widely present in comic-book illustrations.

Thus, the possibility to convey and to perceive movement in static images is not mysterious. Yet the fact that objects can be represented as moving by manipulating certain pictorial techniques is just a minimal step towards the solution of our problem. What interests us is indeed the perceptual experience of dynamism of very simple features that cannot be explained through any reference to represented objects. When we see the depicted train as "moving" along the depicted rails, we must be perceiving some of the patterns that constitute the drawing as being dynamic. Depicted movement is likely to depend on the arrangement of these features plus their being applied to represented objects whose real referents usually move. Take instead abstract paintings. We happen to perceive them as being *dynamic* although not properly "moving", which suggests that some difference exists between perceiving movement and perceiving dynamism – although the latter experience is likely to make the former possible.

In the previous chapter, the perceptual phenomenal character of expressive experience was defended, along with its dynamic nature. The task is therefore to find out what properties must be mobilised by the content of a perceptual experience for it to be dynamic. Straightforward support can be found in the tradition of Gestalt psychology, which developed between the end of the nineteenth century and the first half of the twentieth century. The works by Max Wertheimer, Wolfgang Köhler, Kurt Koffka – the Berlin School – and, later, by Rudolf Arnheim, provided both a theoretical framework and experimental procedures to test human perception of dynamic visual and auditory patterns. They famously argued against the idea that we only perceive the atomic components of more complex patterns, insisting that we rather perceive "wholes" that cannot be reduced to the simple sum of their parts. According to this essentially phenomenological approach, they proposed a list of fundamental phenomenal rules that govern the perception of these units. Factors such as *similarity*, *continuation*, *closure*, *proximity*, *figure-ground*, *good-form*, and *pregnancy* were individuated as being responsible for our perception of gestaltic figures (Köhler 1929). Moreover, Gestalt psychology emphasised how these same factors are at work in spatial grouping as well as in temporal grouping: sequences of sounds can form temporal gestalt in a way that is isomorphic with that of visual structures. In addition, Gestalt theory has been fruitfully applied to arts, showing how dynamic effects can be created with simple oriented figures.

Mainly interested in paintings and pictorial techniques, Rudolf Arnheim developed a theory for the perceptual experience of visual art, focusing precisely on dynamism. Rejecting the view that perceived dynamism conveyed by static images is a perceptual illusion, he claims that dynamic forces ("oriented tensions") are inherent to images at a very elementary level and that painters and artists are supposed to address these forces in order to realise dynamic (and subsequently, on his view, valuable) works. Relying on a vast range of artistic examples, Arnheim claims that "Obliqueness is perceived spontaneously as a dynamic straining toward or away from the basic spatial framework of the vertical and horizontal" (Arnheim 1974, p. 425). For this purpose, artists should always try to break the symmetry, because "Broken symmetry introduces perceptual effects, often called dynamic balance" whereas "Perfect bilateral symmetry can have a perceptually stultifying effect" (Cutting 2002, p. 1170). Interestingly, this sort of rule applies not only to represented figures, but also to decorations and abstract patterns, both in painting and in architecture. For instance, Arnheim remarks that "Baroque architecture used the dynamics of curved shapes to increase tension" (Arnheim 1974, p. 428). And just to quote some more examples concerning compositional and formal features of paintings: distortion of shapes (ovals rather than circles, rectangles rather than squares), the interval between compositional

3.6 Dynamic Properties — 115

elements, the more or less symmetrical relation between them, up to the visual occlusion of certain portions of a figure can, if duly handled, create and enhance perceivable dynamism of static figures.

Importantly, the kind of dynamism at stake in these descriptions does not coincide with movement. In point of fact, the examples above do neither refer to those techniques and tools that artists can intentionally use to represent movement or to create the illusion of movements. Instead, very simple perceivable features are responsible for the fact that a pattern is experienced as crossed by tensions, rather than as static. Artists can (learn to) manipulate such features so as to obtain dynamic effects. Moreover, dynamism does not seem to depend on the complexity of the pattern at stake: Arnheim's examples range from the representation of human figure in paintings and sculptures, to the inclination of two orthogonal lines. So the question is, once again, what are the dynamic properties that are represented as expressive when we undergo expressive experience of such simple things? To be clear, the entity to look for must play a role in expressive experience that is analogous to that played by grouping properties in seeing-as experiences.

In Chapter 2 (especially in 2.4.2), we dealt with an enactivist approach to musical expressiveness that, it was argued, manages to account for those cases in which music is actually enacted, triggering in the listener movements that echo musical movements. In order to criticise that approach, Forlè borrows from Andrea Zhok (2012) the notion of *rythmos*. She suggests that *rythmos* could be what ultimately grounds the dynamic qualities of music. Let us attempt to clarify this notion that, elusive as it is, might nevertheless satisfy our need for a dynamic, percivable entity capable of grounding expressiveness.

As one might suspect, although it assumes a general meaning and covers a wider range of phenomena than the standard musical notion, *rythmos* has to do with rhythm. According to Giovanni Piana (1991) rhythm – although not explicitly used as a technical term – is not only one of the most pervasive components of music, especially for it triggers bodily (dancing) responses, but it also applies to a variety of items, particularly visual ones: pinnacles, colonnades, and architectural elements more generally can be said to display a certain rhythm. Once again, he notices how such manifoldness of rhythm weakens the relation one may think it has with temporality (Piana 1991, p. 169–70). As soon as rhythm acquires this cross-modal meaning, it lends itself to the characterisation of the intrinsic structure of perceptual (especially auditory and visual) patterns presenting regularities that are perceptually graspable.

Zhok goes as far as extending the notion of *rythmos* to any sort of pattern that is perceived as displaying regularities shaping our experiences of objects. Such regularities are experienced as dynamic, i.e. as involving movement directed towards some kind of end, realisation, or closure. Both Piana and Zhok remark that when we experience a perceptual pattern as having a certain internal oriented structure, we are confronted with the *discontinuity* between the lower-level components of the pattern, be they sounds or dots on a canvas. Such a discontinuity is constituted by the differences and similarities existing between such components, as well as (or above all) by the *pauses, intervals,* and the *voids* that separate them. The articulation of this discontinuity takes the shape of a *rythmos* whenever it lends itself to the recognition of a "minimal rule of development", i.e. to the possibility of forecasting *what will come next* (Zhok 2012, p. 130). In order for the internal articulation of the pattern to be in place, the time that the experience of this pattern requires is not a valid criterion. Indeed, *rythmos* is a feature of perceptual patterns and it is cross-modal, that is, it is not specific to one sense modality such as hearing or vision. It is therefore present in various – if not all – kinds of perceptual experiences, thereby leaving the door open to multimodal experiences.

Yet two conditions are needed for something to be experienced as having *rythmos*. Firstly, there is a minimal and a maximal limit of the intervals that can be experienced without two elements collapsing one onto the other or resulting in being completely disconnected from one another; secondly, a pattern has to present an *opening* and a *closure* (Zhok 2012, p. 132–133). These two conditions are responsible for making perceptual patterns liable to be experienced as dynamic. The theory clearly espouses a gestaltic approach to perception: claiming that regularities, discontinuities and other objective relations are ultimately responsible for the presence of *rythmos* is analogous to claiming that measurable rules such as continuity, similarity, or closure are responsible for the instantiation of gestalts.

This notion might seem more evocative than truly explanatory, it surely needs to be refined and possibly supported by reliable empirical evidence. It has nevertheless the virtue of grasping important aspects of expressive experiences that find correspondence in widely acknowledged features of perceived sounds and colours.

In the case of music, we describe melismatic gestures as rising and falling, jumping, and quietening, but it is also possible to zoom in and consider lower level musical constituents such as *harmonics*. These are "Sets of musical notes whose frequencies are related by simple whole-number ratios. A harmonic series is a set of frequencies which are successive integer multiples of the fundamental (or first harmonic)" (Oldham, Campbell, Greated 2001). In more trivial terms, harmonics are sounds whose frequency determines audible notes, timbre, and pitches. They are described as having "a complex pattern or waveform" whose components are hardly heard separately and are therefore perceived as a single sound. Instead, components of patterns that are only a close approximation to harmonics can be heard separately and do not give rise to a clear pitch. Even if this hypothesis should be enquired further, it seems legitimate to think that harmonics and their approximations are responsible for the dynamism of the resulting perceived sounds, i.e. for their *rythmos*.

In vision, we can describe visual patterns of static images as pointing or tending towards a direction, as more or less regularly alternating features, colours as exploding, slopes as descending or ascending. Certain shades of colours seem to *pour out* of the (e.g. pictorial) surface, whereas others seem to be *attracted toward* the centre of the surface – think about canvas painted in the "vibrating", "intense", "absorbing" Klein Blue. Perceived colours notoriously depend on a number of variables such as hue, saturation, brightness, and gloss (e.g. Palmer 1999). The combination of these (and possibly further) dimensions determines the visible outcome that is perceptually accessible. Colours are experienced, for instance, as tending more or less towards white or towards black, to be more or less nuanced, bright, saturated, that is, dynamic. They are perceived as having an internal – though minimal – structure, plausibly, something like *rythmos*.[37]

So, by focusing on this minimal level, it emerges that the dynamic structure of simple features so conceived enables us to undergo expressive experiences analogously to what happens when we see the white or the black cross of the Wittgesteinian example. The function of such a dynamic structure is functionally analogous to so-called grouping properties. In point of fact, the dynamic structure of perceptual patterns provides the adequacy conditions for the content of our experiences. Perceptual structures so conceived are not mere causal triggers of a phenomenally *sui generis* experience, but constitutive of the representational content in such a way that they justify our expressive ascriptions. In short, they can account for the objective side of expressive experience, limiting the range of possible expressive outcomes. Davies puts this same concept the following way:

> Even if our hearing of the musical features of slowness, etc. in a musical work does not entail that we will also hear sadness in that work, these features may be relevant to our experience of the music's sadness. They could not be used to support the mistaken claim that the music expresses happiness in the way they may be used to support the claim that the music expresses sadness. (Davies 2005, p. 143)

---

[37] The perceptual structure of colours deserves a much more thorough treatment that I am unable to consider here. The common knowledge about perceived colours being determined by the interaction of various dimensions suggests that colours – as well as sounds – are instantiated in our experience as dynamic structure rather than as atomic perceptual features.

This "objective" side of expressive experience is relevantly attested by the way in which properties are manipulated by artists and experts: creative expertise can be taken to consist – also – in the ability to employ materials characterised by certain perceptual properties to convey expressive outcomes. Designers know (or should know) how to make a place look welcoming or alienating, composers know how to make a music sound threatening,[38] painters know how to juxtapose colours so as to make a painting look mournful. The fact that such outcomes are relatively under our (or experts') control provides a good reason to believe that expressive properties are at least partly determined by their objective dynamic perceptual structure.

An account based on the notion of *rythmos* does not seem doomed to commit the heresy of the separable experiences. Rather, it justifies the experience by reference to features of its objects, namely perceptual dynamic properties. This understanding of dynamic properties accounts for a perceivable structure having a minimal and a maximal limit of experienceable intervals, openings and closures. In addition, it does so without appealing to time, bodily movement or comparisons with behaviours. As a consequence, it offers an alternative strategy to Kivy's characterisation of simple expressive features as "static", as opposed to dynamic musical gestures or melodies. Those features that Kivy accounts for in an *ad hoc*, highly context-dependent way can be characterised instead in terms of their dynamic structure.

So far, so good. But, the reader will argue, it is one thing to experience a dynamic pattern as being sad and another thing to experience it as dynamic. That is: there must be more to the experience of expressive features than the mere grasping of dynamism. A movement or a musical pattern may well be perceived as slow, without being experienced as sad. Analogously, a patch of grey may be seen as less bright than a patch of orange, but not necessarily sad. The instability and relativity of expressive properties must be accounted for by explaining what is required on behalf of the experiencing subjects. What is left to do after having anchored expressive experience to perceptual structures, is to provide an account of its response-dependency.

---

38 The numerous studies conducted by Patrik Juslin and colleagues go in this direction. They have claimed that expressive cues of music can be learnt and manipulated by musicians in order to produce expressive music (e.g. Juslin 2000; Juslin and Laukka 2003; Juslin and Timmers 2010).

Chapter 4
Metaphors and Resemblances

The present chapter deals with the role of concepts in recognitional expressive experiences. Firstly, questions about the conceptual intervention in expressive experience are reframed in the light of the distinction between recognitional and non-recognitional experiences (§ 4.1). The working hypothesis is that recognitional expressive experiences can be explained as cases of cognitive penetration occurring at the level of the phenomenal character. In § 4.2 I suggest that concepts of emotion apply to recognitional expressive experiences as metaphors. In order to clarify the status of metaphorical uses of concepts, the debate about aesthetic ascriptions will be recruited as a model (§ 4.3). In § 4.4 cognitive penetration will be presented as a plausible phenomenon that accounts for (certain cases of) expression recognition. In § 4.6 I will finally put the pieces of the puzzle together, offering a proposal for recognitional expressive experiences as weakly cognitively penetrated by metaphorically applied concepts.

4.1 An Important Distinction

In Chapter 3, the distinction between three sorts of expressive experiences has been introduced, namely the case of the weeping willow, the case of the musical gesture, and the case of the minor chord. Unlike the experience of the weeping willow – that can amount to the recognitional experiences of a resemblance – the other two cases seem to work differently, that is, they do not mobilise *manifest* resemblances. However, the case of the musical gesture has been treated as requiring the capacity to detect an isomorphism between an expressive gesture and the heard musical pattern, the outcome of this detection being the perception of the musical gesture as expressive. It is time to focus on the conceptual import of such a recognitional process.

Malcolm Budd argues against Peacocke's metaphorical approach, claiming that it does not do justice to an important distinction, namely that between perceiving the expressive character of a musical gesture, perceiving it *as having* a specific, namely expressive character. The latter experience is likely to require some knowledge of emotion, allegedly consisting in the capacity to apply concepts to experiences, whereas the former might occur without the intervention of such conceptual knowledge. According to Budd, a metaphorical stance like the one put forward by Peacocke does not *per se* account for this difference, since the metaphor – that is, the conceptual mapping relation from the emotion domain to the experienced object – is taken to be part of the content. As a consequence, it seems that all expressive experiences consist in the recognition of the expressive character as such, whereas it can never be the case that we experience the cheerfulness of music without *recognising it as* cheerfulness. What Peacocke considers a very specific relation to a content is, on Budd's view, the very same content which, on some occasions, triggers a conceptual response.

This divergence stems from an original disagreement between the two approaches. Peacocke believes that metaphorical recognition depends on the existence of an isomorphism that, although it need not be represented as such, is nonetheless ultimately responsible for this recognition. Budd, instead, thinks that the peculiarity of aesthetic experience (of which expressive experience is, for him, a sub-class) consists in the power that some non-conceptual perceptual contents have to trigger the application of certain concepts. Such an application is responsible for the distinction between a recognitional experience and a merely perceptual one.

In order to support his view, Budd invites us to imagine a situation in which we experience an artwork but we struggle to find the term to describe it. Then, someone comes up with a predicate that suddenly seems to us to perfectly match the artwork's aspect. Once we (or somebody else) come up with the emotion word that applies to that work or character of the work, our experience becomes the recognitional experience of a quality as falling under that concept:

> Now suppose a characterization in metaphorical terms is offered to someone who experiences difficulty in coming up with an adequate description of the aspect, and this characterization seems to them to fit the character of the work well [...] When they now look at, read or listen to the work, regarding this characterization as being well suited to convey the work's character, without anything else needing to happen, they thereby experience the work as having that character. Their experience of the work has changed: previously it was inchoate, the character being obscure, now it is distinct, the character apparent.
> (Budd 2008, p. 150)

Accordingly, conceptual abilities are required only in order "to understand and engage in the practice of musical analysis and criticism" (Budd 2008, p. 141), whereas:

> [...] neither the lack of a certain concept of a particular phenomenon nor the inability to recognize instances of the phenomenon as falling under the concept prevents a person from being sensitive to the presence of the phenomenon in a work of art and alive to the aesthetic or artistic function of the phenomenon in the work. (Budd 2008, p. 139)

4.1 An Important Distinction — 121

The point, here, is to find a convincing way to distinguish between those experiences that require concepts to take place and those that occur independently of the possession of such concepts.[39]

Michael Martin (1992) offered a thorough discussion about whether recognition requires the application of concepts. He argued against conceptualism about perceptual experience that the assumption that we have an experience only as long as we possess the concept required to appreciate it (i.e. recognising it as such), prevents from accounting for the difference between *experiencing* and *noticing*. Martin holds that a "belief-independent view of experience" is instead in the position to account for such a difference. Here is his argument in brief. According to the conceptualist, experience is to be reduced to *noticing*, that is, to recognitional experiences based on the capacity to apply concepts. The conceptualist would accordingly end up claiming that: "If one lacks the recognitional capacity, one will not be able to discriminate between the presence or absence of a certain feature in a perceived scene" (Martin 1992, p. 757). Martin's argument against this claim relies on memory, namely on the possibility that we do not notice the presence of a feature at a certain time, but that we may recall such a presence afterwards, in memory. If this is true, his argument goes, then there is a reason to insist that we neither need concepts nor the capacity to apply them in order to experience features of the environment.[40]

This argument is not knock-down, but it provides the basis for assessing the phenomenal difference between recognitional and non-recognitional expressive experience. If it is possible to distinguish between experiencing a sad character and realising afterwards that such a character was actually sad, expressive experience need not always be recognitional. It may well be the case that we do not recognise the atmosphere of a room painted in dark colours as being mournful, but this does not imply that we do not notice the difference

---

39 This controversy is not new and concerns the distinction between conceptual and non-conceptual contents of perceptual experiences in general. The debate is wide-ranging and cannot be assessed here. However, as it will become clear, I am sympathetic to views claiming that perceptual content is non-conceptual, despite allowing for cognitive interventions on some occasions.
40 In Martin's famous example, a dice player lacking the geometric concept of dodecahedron (in the example she is not able to count past five) is nevertheless capable of distinguishing, for the purpose of the game, an eight-faced from a twelve-faced dice, based on the differences they present, let's say, in spots and colours. If the player acquired the recognitional concept of dodecahedron, Martin supposes, she may recall past games and distinguish in memory whether they were performed using a twelve-faced dice or not. If this is possible, then it counts as evidence for the fact that the feature identified by the concept "dodecahedron" was already present in the content of the past, non-conceptualised experiences of the player (Martin 1992, p. 754).

between entering such a room, and entering a bright one. If asked to describe the two rooms, we may well use the words (and the related concepts) "mournful" and "bright" in case we possessed them, but this does not seem to imply that we were to apply them at the time of the experience. As Budd remarks, and as the distinction between different kinds of bi-stable figures provided above helps to clarify (§ 3.5.2), an account of expressive experience should also explain the case in which one undergoes an expressive experience without any recognitional disposition.

Importantly, the possible intervention of concepts that makes a recognitional experience out of a non-recognitional one applies both to the case of the musical gesture and to the one of the chord, that is, both when resemblances are involved and when they seem more difficult to work out. The task is now to find a plausible way to account for such a conceptual intervention.

4.2 Metaphorical Descriptions

One way to deal with the impact of concepts on expressive experiences consists in questioning the sort of concepts that are involved in it and in considering what in the experience content could justify their application. If the recognition of an expressive pattern like a musical gesture relies on the resemblance between it and affective expressions, then the involved concepts are probably emotion concepts. Yet, rather than being applied straightforwardly as when we ascribe emotions to humans, such concepts are applied in virtue of the detected resemblances. A sunset could accordingly trigger the application of the concept of melancholy in virtue of some resemblance that its perceptual look bears to common expressions of melancholy – tension towards the ground, decreasing energy or light, gradual passage from bright to sombre colours, suspended dynamic.

Now, concepts can be defined generically as:

> the building blocks of the kinds of thoughts expressed in sentences, which stand to whole thoughts as words stand to whole sentences. [...] we can think of concepts as components of the content of the thought expressed. (Gauker 2017)

The assumption behind the adoption of this definition is that, although the correspondence between descriptions of experiences (namely expressive ones) and recognitional concepts is not warranted, to employ the former mirrors to a relevant extent the application of the latter. The minimum requirement met by this definition of concepts is that the relation between the recognitional concepts that we use and the descriptions we provide of the corresponding experience is non-contingent.[41]

Given that emotion concepts find their natural field of application in emotion episodes and manifestations, it seems *prima facie* reasonable to think that their use in expressive experience is non-literal. In other words, concepts that are mobilised in recognitional expressive experiences, shaping their phenomenal character, could be used *metaphorically*. Importantly, this hypothesis is not considered to be outlandish and finds support in the aesthetics literature.

That of metaphor is admittedly a controversial notion and its role is especially debated by philosophers concerned with aesthetic properties. Nick Zangwill has repeatedly claimed that descriptions of music as expressive of emotions are obviously metaphorical (Zangwill 2007; 2011; 2013). This is maintained to be true also of other inanimate objects and artworks. Accordingly, if one refers to a piece of music as *joyful*, to a painting as *melancholy* or to a sculpture as *sombre*, one is providing metaphorical descriptions of those items. More specifically, Zangwill considers all (or at least most) aesthetic descriptions as non-literal descriptions and argues that we should not treat expressive attributions differently. For something to be *literally* "delicate" amounts to it being liable to break (Zangwill 2007, p. 394), which is not the case for something – such as a piece of music or a pictorial composition – that is merely *aesthetically* "delicate".

Things stand in the same way in the case of expressive attributions. In fact, within such a non-literalist approach, for a term to be used literally is for it to apply to something that possesses those properties that the term applies to. For the term "green" to apply literally, objects must be green (or have the property of "greenness"); for the term "white" to apply literally to the snow, the snow should possess the property of "whiteness", and so on. But whereas this correspondence between predicates and properties in the case of terms such as "green" and "white" is intuitively straightforward, things get more complicated with more complex predicates, such as emotion terms. That is: in order for something to be literally "sad" we should be able to say what the property of "sadness" consists in – which cannot be reduced to a trivial question. Actually, what Zangwill is interested in, is not to establish what a metaphorical or extended use of predicates consists in. Rather, he wants to argue that emotion words cannot be used literally when referring to inanimate objects and to music

---

[41] Concepts are a complex matter and the discussion about their role (provided that one can treat all concepts in the same way) in expressive experience would benefit from a more sophisticated account of what they are and how they operate within our cognitive architecture. I am hopeful that the adoption of a quite generic definition will not undermine the plausibility of the overall proposal.

in particular.[42] Therefore, the required distinction is between literal and non-literal applications of emotion terms.

However, considering metaphors as the application of a predicate to an object that is not *commonly* maintained to have the property to which such a predicate *usually* refers is, at best, vague. Claiming that attributions of expressiveness to objects imply a metaphorical use of emotion terms, requires a deeper insight into the nature of properties and that of metaphors. In order to avoid a trivialisation that would make Zangwill's view uninformative (at least in the case expressive attributions), one has to be sure about what affective properties consist in. And it is precisely for this reason that Zangwill endorses an overtly stipulative view according to which an emotion is a mental state with a certain qualitative character and distinctive rationalisation (Zangwill 2007, p. 393). Therefore, either something possesses at least one of these features, such as being a mental state with a certain phenomenology, or any application of emotion terms to describe it is to be considered "metaphorical or at least an extended use of the word" (Zangwill 2007, p. 393).

In *Languages of Art* (1968) Nelson Goodman provides an explanation for the case of expressive attributions that is to some extent consistent with Zangwill's proposal. In fact, also according to Goodman, when we apply an affective term to a work of art, we use the term metaphorically. Goodman famously faces this issue as follows:

> A picture literally possesses a gray color, really belongs to the class of gray things; but only metaphorically does it possess sadness or belong to the class of things that feel sad.
> (Goodman 1968, p. 51)

There are properties that artworks literally possess, such as their colours and shapes, and other properties that artworks possess in a special way. The idea of "metaphorical possession" is employed by Goodman to account for expressive things. For an object to be expressive amounts to metaphorically possessing the property that it is said to express. This means that a piece of music expresses sadness as long as it metaphorically possesses sadness.

---

42 Notice that Zangwill believes that aesthetic properties of music in general and expressive properties in particular are ineffable so that we can describe them only through metaphors: "I maintain that there is a reality that we can think about but cannot describe, except by means of metaphor (or other nonliteral devices). This is an "ineffabilist" view. In particular, the ineffabilist thesis holds of properties of sensations and music. Judgments about music are based on experiences with ineffable content; and we then think that music has ineffable aesthetic properties" (Zangwill 2011, p. 96).

Goodman's view can provide further arguments in favour of Zangwill's non-literalist view about expressive attributions. He believes that, say, a grey object is denoted by the label (predicate) "grey" and it possesses the property of greyness as long as such a predicate applies to it. This amounts to saying that what property the object possesses depends on the predicate that applies to it (Goodman 1968, p. 51–52). Expression is, on his view, a kind of possession and therefore of labelling, yet a special one. It is indeed a metaphorical possession, i.e. the application of a label to something that exemplifies a property. One can therefore say that a sad painting expresses sadness since it (somehow) exemplifies sadness, i.e. it is an instance of the domain of objects to which the label "sad" applies. It seems that this description of the expressive relation is true both of sad behaviours and of sad paintings. They both *express* insofar as they exemplify the label "sad", even though each in its own way (namely, literally vs. metaphorically).

In order to capture the distinction between metaphorical and literal applications, the focus of Goodman's account shifts to the way in which labels organise the logical space of linguistic uses. Labels apply to *realms* of objects and come networked in *schemas*. Labels and schemas apply literally to certain domains or realms of objects: anatomical labels apply to the domain of the body, botanical terms apply to plants, chromatic labels apply to colours, and so on. Thus, what happens with metaphorical applications is that schemas *move* from one realm to another, which is not their "native" one. Tactile labels are applied to the chromatic domain (warm colours), bodily labels to geography (a cape, a river's mouth), affective labels to the domain of inanimate things etc. (Goodman 1968, p. 70 ff.). According to Goodman, the metaphorical shift does not challenge the possession of the labelled property by the described object. There are warm colours and there are dark colours, and the fact that predicates can be applied metaphorically does not make the predication false.

If this moving of a schema of labels from one realm to another is what makes the application of a label metaphorical, then the distinction between literal and metaphorical attributions is to be sought for in the "novelty" of the application: "Briefly, a metaphor is an affair between a predicate with a past and an object that yields while protesting" (Goodman 1968, p. 69). Once the new, metaphorical application is performed, such a past (i.e. the usual, literal applications that stabilised over time) leads the new application, which indeed is not randomly realised, but rather depends on the intrinsic organisation of the schema to which the label originally belongs.

Famously, Max Black (1954) has offered an evocative (metaphorical) explanation of this mapping process of one domain over another:

> Suppose I look at the night sky through a piece of heavily smoked glass on which certain lines have been left clear. Then I shall see only the stars that can be made to lie on the lines previously prepared upon the screen, and the stars I do see will be seen as organized by the screen's structure. We can think of a metaphor as such a screen.
>
> (Black 1954, p. 288)

The organisation of the original or "past" application schema determines, at least to some extent, the application to the new domain. According to Goodman's nominalism, there exists several kinds of metaphoric transfers, among which are euphemisms, personifications, synecdoche, antonomasia, hyperboles, litotes, but what makes them metaphors is the "novelty" of application, rather than some intrinsic connection with the property of the world they apply to.

Goodman's lesson seems to provide some deeper insight in the possible role of metaphors in expressive attributions. In his theory, expression and metaphor overlap, and Goodman too can be taken to be a non-literalist about expressive attributions of affective properties to inanimate objects. Yet he does not manage to answer the question of *why* such shifts occur, especially within the aesthetic domain. Let us keep the focus on expressive experience: why are we allowed to use emotion terms to describe inanimate objects? Goodman does not take any explicit stance on the kind of properties that are responsible for a linguistic use to be born, or at least to be efficacious. He explicitly states that:

> The question why predicates apply as they do metaphorically is much the same as the question why they apply as they do literally [...] the general explanation why things have the properties, literal and metaphorical, that they do have [...] is a task I am content to leave to the cosmologist.
>
> (Goodman 1968, p. 78)

As Goodman's approach to properties is so dismissive and Zangwill's strategy is overtly stipulative (at least for what concerns emotions), the door remains open for further discussion. Namely, since Goodman does not provide any property-based criterion to distinguish between literal and transferred applications, and he rather lists several degrees of metaphorical shifts (giving birth to a wide range of figures of speech) he may in principle agree that, so to speak, metaphors come in degrees. And the same standpoint seems to be shared by Zangwill, who claims that a non-literal use of a predicate is metaphorical or at least an "extended use" of a word. This element, along with the widespread intuition that language and usage change over time, makes the distinction between literal and non-literal applications blurrier than Zangwill would like it to be.

On the one hand, Zangwill's strategy does not *per se* support the distinction between metaphorical and literal applications. On the other hand, Goodman's theory of metaphor gives convincing arguments about how metaphors work, but when it comes to the properties an object is expected to possess in order to be labelled as expressive, he passes the ball to the cosmologist. In particular, if one relies on current habits in order to establish the correspondence between domains and schemas and the subsequent shift's relevance, it is not obvious that this strategy applies to aesthetic attributions. Why should we buy into the idea that the label "balanced" finds, in our current practices, its literal application within the domain of mechanics instead of in the domain of pictorial composition rules? How can our linguistic habits tell us whether the adjective "graceful" is *mostly* used to describe artworks or people's attitudes?

4.3 Metaphorical Use of Concepts in Aesthetic Ascriptions

In order to explore this problem, it is helpful to draw on the traditional debate about metaphorical ascriptions of aesthetic properties. There seems to be at least two good reasons for making this move. Firstly, within the aesthetics domain, expressive properties are often listed among so-called aesthetic properties (De Clercq 2008) and, secondly, aesthetic descriptions are often maintained to be metaphorical descriptions. With respect to the first reason, it is important to note the following caveat. Most philosophers take for granted that expressive features such as melancholy or cheerfulness are aesthetic properties along with gracefulness or balance. In point of fact, aesthetic descriptions, frequently make use of affective terms: we experience lively paintings, sad pieces of music, cheerful ballads. However, this should not induce one to believe that expressive properties entertain an exceptional relationship with artistic objects.

Some basic taxonomy can help at this stage. Firstly, expressive properties can be distinguished from essentially aesthetic properties such as *beauty, ugliness, sublimity*, or *gracefulness*. Independently of the account that one adopts, these properties seem to be ultimately responsible for aesthetic experience, as long as they determine purely aesthetic judgements. Secondly, expressive properties can be distinguished from formal properties such as *balance, symmetry, dynamism*, and *staticity*, although, as we have already seen, there seems to be a strong connection between them and expressive features. Thirdly, expressive properties can be distinguished from arousal properties such as being *sexy, disgusting*, or *appealing*. Arousal properties bear a necessary relation to the elicitation of a reaction (sexual excitement, disgust, repulsion, attraction). As we have already seen, one can argue against arousal approaches by claiming that expressive properties ascribed to objects do not necessarily elicit our reactions. This being said, descriptions of expressive properties continue to pose problems that are analogous to the problems regarding other aesthetic ascriptions.

Expressive features are identified via emotion terms such as *sad, lively, cheerful, melancholy, serene, anguished, tense, desolate, prostrate*, that are also used in non-aesthetic contexts to indicate emotional expressions. As well as for other aesthetic terms, the issue is how to account for the relationship between their aesthetic and non-aesthetic (ordinary) use, based on the kind of properties to which they apply and that therefore justifies their application. At first sight, one may argue that the possibility to apply certain terms in different contexts makes these terms somehow ambiguous. Roger Scruton phrased this question nicely:

> To understand the word 'sad' is to know how to apply it to people in order to describe their emotional state. The criteria for the application of the term 'sad' concern the gestures, expressions and utterances of people on the basis of which I describe them as sad, and to grasp the concept of sadness is to know how to apply it on the basis of these criteria. When we apply the concept to art, however, it is arguable that these criteria are not, or need not be, present. Does this mean that the term 'sad' is ambiguous?
> (Scruton 1998, p. 38)

Roger Scruton, claims that metaphors – understood as transferred uses of words from one original domain to another (namely the aesthetic one) – are constitutive of our experience of music as moving through space. He argues that if we were not able to conceptualise features of music in terms of standard concepts describing physical movements, we would not be able to experience music as if it were moving across the musical space. If we lacked the capacity to apply metaphors of movement to melodies:

> We should then cease to hear orientation in music; tones would no longer move towards or away from each other; no phrase would mirror another, no leaps be bolder or larger than others, and so on. In short, the experience of music would involve neither melody nor counterpoint as we know them. (Scruton 1997, p. 92–93)

The same holds for metaphors using emotion terms and for aesthetic predicates more generally. According to Scruton, expressive experience is exhausted by the recognitional experience that consists in being prompted to subsume perceptual properties under aesthetic and especially emotion concepts:

> To see the sadness in the music and to know that the music is sad are one and the same thing. To agree in the judgement that the music is sad is not to agree in a belief, but in something more like a response or an experience; in a mental state that is – unlike belief – logically tied to the immediate circumstances of its arousal. 'The music is sad' is only superficially, therefore, of propositional form: what you know when you know that the music is sad cannot be elucidated by referring to the conditions for a proposition's truth.
> (Scruton 1998, p. 54)

4.3 Metaphorical Use of Concepts in Aesthetic Ascriptions — 129

Accordingly: "aesthetic descriptions are divorced from truth conditions in the epistemological sense: aesthetic features are not properties" (Scruton 1998, p. 53).

Scruton argues that aesthetic and expressive properties are not like standard perceptual properties, that is, they cannot justify our ascriptions. Rather, they are intrinsically conceptual and require that one possesses aesthetic and emotion concepts in order to be instantiated. Labelling is not a simple description of some property that is "out there" independently of our experience. Instead, it is constitutive of the experience that it is taken to label.

On this view, the application of metaphors to perceptual patterns shapes the resulting experience in such a way that it is conceived as fully response-dependent. Perceptual patterns that allegedly constitute the content of aesthetic experience of music cannot even be heard as being *melodies* or as *moving in space*, unless the concepts relating to movement are applied. Concepts turn out to be entirely responsible for the structure of the representational content, upon which aesthetic (expressive) experience supervenes. If we lack concepts, not only are we in a position where we cannot ascribe aesthetic qualities to a piece of music or to a painting, but we would basically hear successions of mere sounds, or mere juxtapositions of colours and shapes, lacking any aesthetic and expressive value.

Clearly, this way of conceiving the experience as being conceptually structured struggles to account for the difference between experiencing and recognising (or noticing). Moreover, making expressive experience fully response-dependent is problematic in that it does not account for the fact that "we cannot in general *choose* which experiences to have" (Boghossian 2010, p. 71).

Interestingly, Paul Boghossian (along with Budd) raises this same criticism against Peacocke. True, Peacocke's account diverges from Scruton's. It indeed assumes that isomorphisms between distinct domains exist, are responsible for metaphorical experiences and justify metaphorical descriptions of such experiences. As said, Peacocke holds that the detection of resemblances is not necessarily a conscious mechanism, but rather is something that takes place under the level of our awareness. On some occasions, we simply experience certain things as apt to be metaphorically identified, but this must necessarily happen in virtue of existing isomorphisms linking distant domains of properties. So-conceived isomorphism is causally responsible for metaphorical experiences to occur. Such a causal triggering, can be followed (or not) by the conscious subsumption under a metaphorical concept.

> Suppose, for example, one hears a piece of music as expressing a gradual transformation of suffering into joy. On my account, this hearing exploits (but does not explicitly represent) an isomorphism between the musical features in question and a domain of mental

states including suffering and joy. [...] It is essential to the theory that the isomorphism exploited in such perception of music is specified using the very same concepts as are employed outside the scope of metaphorical embeddings. (Peacocke 2010, p. 189)

Unlike Scruton, Peacocke vindicates the distinction between the conceptual (metaphorical) subsumption and metaphorical experience. He states: "We have metaphors in language only because we need a device for expressing these mental states whose content involves metaphor" (Peacocke 2009, p. 260). Accordingly, in Peacocke's view there is room for a non-conceptual content that, nevertheless, requires conceptual subsumption to be experienced as such.

Despite these differences, Boghossian casts doubts on the idea of metaphorical content so conceived. The problem with Peacocke's account is that, by appealing to a non-propositional (that is, non-judgemental) subsumption of a perceptual content under a concept, he ends up with an obscure notion of content. According to Boghossian's criticism, if the content of metaphorical experiences were non-conceptual, it would be unclear how concepts should (metaphorically) apply to it, making a metaphorical experience out of a standard non-conceptual one; if the content were conceptual, it would turn out that we could in principle *decide* what metaphorical experience to undergo – which is not the case.

This interpretation locates Peacocke's account in the vicinity of Scruton's. Namely, the metaphorical experience as Peacocke conceives of it is doomed either to have an inherently conceptual content – going against the intuition that we cannot *choose* our experiences – or to commit the heresy of the separable experience. In point of fact, if isomorphisms merely *cause* metaphorical experiences, it is not clear how we should account for the correctness of metaphorical ascriptions. Sure, as Peacocke insists, since resemblances are not always manifest, we may "have to think hard about, and work out, what exactly the correspondence in question is if someone raises the issue" (Peacocke 2009, p. 260), but from the perspective provided by his account, the intentional role of correspondences is fundamentally unwarranted. On the one hand, we would have an experience – that of music sounding sad – and on the other hand a conceptual subsumption leading to a judgement that, nevertheless, could not find any confirmation or disconfirmation in the experience itself. Therefore, any ascription would apply equally well to any experience whatsoever.[43] This is where the notion of resemblance comes back into play.

---

[43] Peacocke's account could possibly benefit from an approach to experience that takes metaphors to structure the way in which we *standardly* perceive objects and properties. According to George Lakoff and Mark Johnson's *Metaphors We Live By* (1980), we are provided with some very basic concepts that are strongly related to our sensory motor system, which allow us to explore the world. Instead of a sharp divide, this view entails a continuum between literal and

4.3 Metaphorical Use of Concepts in Aesthetic Ascriptions — 131

In his famous article about metaphors entitled "What Metaphors Mean", Donald Davidson argues in favour of a resemblance account of metaphors. His claim that "metaphors mean what the words, in their most literal interpretation, mean, and nothing more" (Davidson 1978, p. 32) relies on the idea that metaphors simply direct our attention to some resemblances that hold between the source and the target domain:

> A metaphor makes us attend to some likeness, often a novel or surprising likeness, between two or more things. [...] Ordinary similarity depends on groupings established by the ordinary meanings of words. Such similarity is natural and unsurprising to the extent that familiar ways of grouping objects are tied to usual meanings of usual words.
> (Davidson 1978, p. 33–34)

Regardless of the stance one takes on Davidson's theory, resemblances provide a natural way to account for metaphorical descriptions. They seem indeed to preserve the link between literal and metaphorical uses of the words in terms of the similarities that can in principle be grasped between properties in different domains. One can therefore argue that the recognitional concepts involved in expressive (and more generally aesthetic) experiences are used metaphorically in virtue of the alleged resemblances between expressive (or aesthetic) properties of things and human expressions. The exact role played by similarities between aesthetic and standard perceptual properties is thus at stake:

> There is, of course, a question as to how exactly this idea of a perceived resemblance is to be understood, and whether there are any aesthetic qualities – and if so which – for which the idea of perceived resemblance figures in the specification of the intrinsic nature of the canonical basis of a judgement that a certain item possesses that aesthetic quality.
> (Budd 2008, p. 138)

We must accordingly establish whether aesthetic ascriptions involving the metaphorical use of concepts rely on resemblances and to what extent. What is it for a concept to apply metaphorically in such a way that the resulting experience is a recognitional experience of aesthetic or expressive properties? What

---

metaphorical applications in virtue of the existing continuum among various domains of properties and experience modalities. If such a strategy were viable, we would have reasons to think that the content of – at least some of – our experiences is inherently metaphorical and offers the required justification to metaphorical ascriptions. In particular, such a proposal may substantiate the notion of metaphorical content by introducing a view of metaphors that blurs the distinction between experiences and conceptual categorisation. However, an adequate exploration of this strategy would entail an exaggerated detour. Let us just add this to the list of further endeavours that are worth engaging with.

happens when concepts that we possess about a domain of objects or features apply to another domain in virtue of the similarities that link the two?

Discussing Frank Sibley's work on aesthetic properties, Budd writes:

> [...] for at least some aesthetic qualities commonly ascribed by an expression used metaphorically (or quasi-metaphorically) nothing more, but nothing less, is needed for someone to perceive an item as possessing that quality than for the person, in perceiving the item, and triggered or confirmed by that perception, to regard that expression (or some synonymous expression) as being well-suited to capture an aspect of the item's character.
> (Budd 2008, p. 149)

This seems to attest once again that concepts borrowed from other domains play a major role in aesthetic and expressive experiences. Budd holds that there is an interplay between what we perceive in an item and the concept that we are prompted to apply. Moreover, he believes that the use of such a concept influences the overall experience, making the difference – for instance – between expert and non-expert listeners:

> [...] the acquisition of a musical vocabulary, especially if it includes the ability to recognize by ear the phenomena that the terms designate, is likely to involve an enhancement of the understanding of music: the sensitivity of the ear to musical patterns and relationships can be increased.
> (Budd 2008, p. 141)

Concepts provide enhancements to the extent that they increase our sensitivity to patterns. This approach is consistent with the phenomenology of our experiences. Indeed, it takes conceptual intervention to modify the "way it is like" to undergo an experiences by leaving its content unspoilt and still able to justify conceptual labelling. Now we are in the position to speculate about the mental processes that might explain such a phenomenology. What we actually need is an explanation of how concepts of emotions can intervene in expressive experience. Such an explanation will have to take into account the role of resemblances between patterns perceived as expressive and actual emotional expressions. In addition, the explanation will need to deal with the distinction between recognitional and non-recognitional experiences.

4.4 Cognitive Penetration and Expression Recognition

A plausible strategy that promises to meet the abovementioned requirements appeals to the notion of "cognitive penetrability", that is, the possibility that concepts intervene and to some extent modify our perceptions. As one can easily imagine, this is not an undisputed notion, but I suspect that a sufficiently liberal version can be exploited in order to account for some instances of expressive experience.

A widely accepted definition of cognitive penetrability states that perception is cognitively penetrable if it is possible for two subjects (or one subject at different times) to have two different experiences on account of a difference in their cognitive systems that makes this difference intelligible when certain facts are held fixed, namely, the nature of the proximal stimulus on the sensory organ, the state of the sensory organ, and the location of the attentional focus of the subject (Macpherson 2012; 2015; Stokes 2013).[44] It has been argued that cognitive penetration can help to explain a number of experiences, from aesthetic expertise (Stokes 2014), to differences in perception of chromatic cues (Macpherson 2012), to the perception of bi-stable figures (Voltolini 2013). It is indeed taken to explain one of the ways in which, in spite of being functionally and phenomenally distinct, perception and cognition can interact, accounting for differences in the phenomenology of our experiences (Stokes 2013). Here is Dustin Stokes' definition of cognitive penetrability of perception:

> A perceptual experience E is cognitively penetrated if and only if (1) E is causally dependent upon some cognitive state C and (2) the causal link between E and C is internal and mental.[45] (Stokes 2013, p. 650)

Traditionally, cognitive penetration differs from (a) the difference in judgement about the same perceptual experience; (b) changes in spatial attention (Macpherson 2012) and (c) merely causal effects of beliefs on perceptual experiences that are not semantically consistent with the experience itself (Pylyshyn 1999; Macpherson 2012).[46]

---

[44] The notion of cognitive penetrability of perception was originally introduced and discussed by Zenon Pylyshyn (1980, 1984, 1999). Pylyshyn's aim was to distinguish between high cognitive functions and encapsulated functions such as early vision (understood as a biological mechanism) that cannot be influenced by the former. Therefore, Macpherson points out, what he had in mind were the sub-personal representational outputs of brain processing mechanisms (Macpherson 2012). However, also owing to Pylyshyn's alleged ambiguity in defining his target, philosophy and psychology took on the notion of cognitive (im)penetrability of perception as regarding perceptual experience, rather than its biological implementation.
[45] Stokes is aware that his definition is not immune to counterexamples. Yet, duly integrated by the listed requirements, it is sufficient for the present purpose.
[46] That of semantic coherence is another controversial aspect of cognitive penetrability. Various versions of this requirement have been proposed. Whereas Stokes is happy with the connection between contents being "internal" and "mental", Macpherson insists that the kind of link that is needed for a cognitive content to penetrate a perceptual one is semantic coherence. This amounts to the cognitive content being not only the *cause* of the perceptual change,

On the top of this definition, a distinction can be added between the possibility that concepts intervene in such a way that they structure the content of the experience, and the possibility that they modify its phenomenal character. The former type of cognitive penetrability is usually taken to be "strong", for it influences a level of experiences that has been traditionally maintained to be "encapsulated", i.e. impermeable to conceptual influences (e.g. by Fodor 1983). In the widely explored case of vision, strong cognitive penetration would have an impact on so-called *early vision*, representing shapes, size, and colours.[47] In the latter kind of cognitive penetration, concepts intervene at the level of the phenomenal character, so as to influence the way it is like to have a certain perceptual experience, leaving its underlying content intact. In relation to visual experiences, this cognitive intervention is taken to occur at the level of *late-vision*, which is held to enable the subject to recognise an object as belonging to a certain kind, i.e. to be classified and recognised as such. Therefore, although one can legitimately insist that the content of perceptual experiences is non-conceptual and cannot be modified by concepts, the possibility that the phenomenal character is cognitively influenced remains plausible.

If, as it seems, cognitive penetrability of the phenomenal character is a way to conceive of a range of interactions between cognitive and perceptual components of our experiences, what is now needed is a reliable connection between cognitive penetrability and the recognition and ascription of emotional expression.

When introducing and discussing contour theory, I have already pointed out that it can rely on evolution in order to account for the human tendency to detect expressive features. All theories of emotions nowadays share a broad evolutionary assumption about the perceptual recognition of facial – and, more generally, behavioural – emotional expressions. In short, they accept that, given the evolutionary importance of emotions ascriptions, human and (some) non-human animals developed some mechanism for the immediate perceptual detection of affective expressions.[48]

---

but also providing *reasons* for it. This is in line with Pylyshyn's worries about a merely causal influence that would not preserve the distinction between higher-level and lower-level functions. I will propose an account of expressive experience as a perceptual experience that is cognitively penetrated in such a way that satisfies the semantic requirement.

47 Importantly, Fodor admits for top-down influences that take place *within* modules, determining changes at the level of *late vision*. Modularism is accordingly worried that allowing for cognitive penetration of early vision would ultimately cancel the distinction between these levels (see also Marr 1982).

48 The discussion about the exact mechanisms allowing for this sort of recognition is far from settled. As it is well-known, Paul Ekman conducted extensive and cross-cultural empirical research on the detection of emotional expressions (1972; 1992). More recently, Simon Baron-

Given the plausibility of such a general assumption, philosophers have elaborated on the functional structure of a perception-based ascription of emotions via the recognition of emotional expressions. To mention three recent examples, Ned Block (2014) claims that expression recognition is a case of perceptual recognition of patterns that does not require any conceptual intervention. A diverging path is taken by Newen *et al.* (2015), who affirm that the recognition of emotional expressions is akin to objects recognition and consists in the integration by means of the relevant concepts of multi-sensory perceptual inputs.[49] In a more compatibilist fashion, Marchi and Newen (2015) have developed an account for the perceptual recognition of emotions expressed by human faces that appeals to cognitive penetration. Theirs is a two-stage argument. Firstly, they can rely on the fully perceptual explanation provided by Block to claim that the integration of facial cues does not require conceptual integration. Secondly, they claim that the perceptual integration of sensory cues leading to the recognition of facial expressions is influenced by contextual background knowledge in such a way that it can be explained by appealing to cognitive penetration. It is worth dwelling on their account, since their strategy can be taken as a model for explaining the case of objects' expressiveness.

Based on a well-known experiment carried out by James Carroll and James Russell (1996),[50] the authors can claim that faces provide information that is relevant to the recognition of emotions, but do not signal any specific emotion. Low-level sensory cues impose constraints on the range of emotions that can be ascribed to the corresponding facial expressions. For instance, the same facial patterns can be recognised as an expression of joy or of surprise, depending on contextual information, but not as an expression of fear. However, these cues are not specific enough to identify an exact emotion from within the range (e.g. to allow for a discrimination between anger and fear on the basis of the same pattern). This discriminatory job is, on Marchi and Newen's view, performed by

---

Cohen (2005) postulated the existence of *The Emotion Detector* (TED), a computational mechanism responsible for the detection and ascription of basic emotional expressions, consistently with what Dennett has named the inherently human *intentional stance* (Dennett 1987). However, I will not take any relevant stance on this matter here.
49 Their explanation relies on the model of object recognition put forward by Ernst and Bülthoff (2004).
50 In the experiment, participants were asked to ascribe emotions to stereotyped facial expressions after a story had been told them about the situation in which ambiguous facial expressions were displayed. Such information was supposed to influence the way in which presented facial expressions were perceived. The experiment had been explicitly designed to undermine the idea that facial expressions can *per se* be recognised as expressive of a specific emotion, but they rather require contextual information to be processed.

background conceptual knowledge. The authors take the fact that previous beliefs influence our responses to ambiguous facial expressions to be evidence that facial recognition is sensitive also to higher-level conceptual knowledge.[51] In a nutshell, they claim that since certain facial expressions are too vague to be experienced as expressive of one emotion rather than another, then their recognition requires that some background knowledge shape the percept.[52]

Given these general premises, the account offered by Marchi and Newen for expression recognition entails weak cognitive penetration. The phenomenal character of the perceptual experience we have of certain facial patterns can be modified by our background knowledge concerning typical expressions and contextual information. The intervention of concepts is maintained to have an impact on the phenomenal character of the perceptual experience, that is, it is maintained to make the difference between the perceptual experience of an object before we are able to recognise it (i.e. to discriminate it from others with a certain degree of accuracy), and the perceptual experience of an object once recognised as such. Yet their claim is compatible with the idea that low-level cues that constitute the content of the recognitional experience – on which the phenomenal character depends – are not modified by conceptual interventions.[53]

---

51 It must be said that Marchi and Newen endorse a view of conceptual knowledge as corresponding generically to *top-down* inferences from the cognitive system to the perceptual system. They therefore seem to blur the distinction between concepts, perceptions, and mental imagery, although they assume that a "minimally clear separation between *perceptual experience* (be it conceptual or non-conceptual) and the *judgement* based on this perceptual experience" must be preserved (Marchi and Newen 2015, p. 4).
52 Notice that what they are interested in arguing against is the view according to which the same phenomenon can be fully accounted for as a change in judgement, rather than in perception.
53 Notably, this is not the only way to account for *emotion* recognition. Even narrowing it down to those theories that assign a key role to perception in the ascription of emotions, there is no agreement about the role of cognitive penetration. For instance, theories of direct perception of emotion take it that others' emotions are directly perceived in the absence of concepts (Gallagher 2008; Zahavi 2011; Krueger 2012). According to this phenomenological approach, the perceptual process that would enable us to ascribe emotions would not be mediated by the perception of behavioural manifestations; rather, it would consist in the direct perception of a mental state (see Jacob [2011] for a criticism and Smortchkova [2017] for an account of emotion recognition that manages to save the idea of emotions as perceivable, from the contradictions pointed out by Jacob).

4.5 Recognitional Expressive Experiences Shaped by Metaphorical Concepts

Let us now take stock. As already noticed, the recognitional process involved in expressive experience is analogous to processes of *seeing-as* in that they involve perceptual patterns that are perceived as relevantly related to emotional expressions. This is in line with contour theories and with the intuitions shared for instance by Levinson, Noordhof, and Peacocke, i.e., with the idea that expressive experience is a fundamentally perceptual experience that, nevertheless, mobilises some cognitive background. The discussion in the previous chapter brought to light a disagreement within the seeing-as debate concerning the role played by concepts. However, many authors seem disposed to accept that concepts can intervene and modify perceptual experiences, although they disagree on the way in which this intervention takes place.

It has been suggested that top-down modifications of perceptual experience, that is, interventions from high-level cognitive and especially conceptual functions can occur in the form of cognitive penetration. In the case of recognitional expressive experiences, for example the experience of a musical gesture as being expressive of an emotion, such a conceptual intervention plausibly mobilises one's knowledge about emotions and especially emotional expressions. If one agrees that conceptual intervention can make the difference in the phenomenal character of an experience, and if cognitive penetration is a plausible explanatory strategy to account for (some) recognitional experiences, then such a difference could be explained in two ways, mirroring the above mentioned distinction between strong and weak cognitive penetration. The first consists in arguing that emotion concepts influence the *content* of expressive experience whereas the second amounts to denying that concepts play such a constitutive role, arguing instead that they intervene at the level of the *phenomenal character*.

We have seen that the idea of a conceptually structured content of expressive experience – *à la* Scruton – fails to account for the phenomenological distinction between recognitional and perceptual experiences. In other words, if we claim that the content of expressive experience that instantiates dynamic patterns is shaped by emotion concepts, then we end up without a clear distinction between those cases in which one simply hears an expressive musical gesture or a sound (possibly because she or he does not possess or master any suitable emotion concept) and those cases in which one recognises it as such. Therefore, it seems that the intervention of conceptual knowledge in expressive experience must be explained in a way that preserves the non-conceptual nature of its content.

Cognitive penetrability of the phenomenal character of perceptual experiences may provide an explanation. By (i) introducing the view that conceptual abilities are responsible for recognitional processes of ambiguous facial expressions, and (ii) endorsing the idea that the recognition of patterns such as musical gestures as being expressive may require the detection of underlying resemblances to expressive behaviours, it can be argued that recognitional expressive experiences consist in the perceptual experience of dynamic patterns involving the intervention of emotion concepts. Such an intervention takes place in virtue of (and applies to) detected similarities between patterns and typical expressive manifestations that one has learnt to discriminate in humans.

Recalling the debate about the role of concepts in aesthetic ascriptions, it can be suggested that concepts involved in this process apply metaphorically, that is, in virtue of those resemblances that potentially justify the ascription of expressive qualities. Such resemblances allow for the use of concepts that find their literal application in the domain of emotions, within the domain of perceptual experiences of inanimate objects. Regardless of the aesthetic relevance of expressive properties, the parallel with the problem of aesthetic concepts is well-suited. In point of fact, emotion concepts that standardly apply to actual emotional expressions – and possibly play a role in processes of discrimination – intervene in the discrimination of patterns that, although cannot *literally express* emotions, result *expressive of* those emotions.

This description of the recognitional mechanism satisfies the requirements for something to be an instance of cognitive penetration. In point of fact, the phenomenal character of expressive experience so conceived is causally dependent on the emotion concept that modifies it. To put it counterfactually, if one were not able to apply metaphorically the concept of, say, melancholy to a landscape, one would not be able to *recognise* that landscape as being melancholy. This seems to be a plausible consequence of this account.[54]

In addition, this mechanism satisfies the requirement that the causal chain relating the cognitive and the perceptual content be internal and mental, for the described chain does not refer to any non-mental function. Moreover, the link between the emotion concept and the phenomenal character resulting from cognitive penetration is semantically coherent. As noticed above, the way to interpret the semantic constraint is not undisputed. Yet, the basic worry from

---

54 Whether attention counts as cognitive penetration is a debatable issue. Steven Gross recently addressed it, arguing for a pluralist answer (2017). Since my aim is not to establish what cognitive penetration actually is, I will rather follow Macpherson (2012), Voltolini (2013) and Lupyan (2017) allowing for certain attentional mechanisms – namely those that do not overtly involve spatial attention – counting as instances of cognitive penetration.

4.5 Recognitional Expressive Experiences Shaped by Metaphorical Concepts — 139

which it stems is to avoid merely causal relationships, which would not do justice to the epistemological function that cognitive penetrability is held to accomplish. The resulting requirement is that the cognitive content that pervades the phenomenal character also provides *reasons* for the resulting experience (Gross 2017). If this is so, then the intervention of an emotion concept that applies in virtue of the resemblances between a component of emotions (namely expressive behaviours) and a perceivable pattern can provide a rational justification for the resulting phenomenal character, which is therefore experienced as semantically connected to emotions.[55]

This overall account can be taken as a version of resemblance theory that nevertheless has some advantages over others. The first is that the account does not imply that expressive experience is necessarily a recognitional experience, for it holds that the content of the experience is non-conceptual and is not cognitively penetrated. As a consequence, it leaves room for non-recognitional experiences of expressive features. Moreover, its explanatory claim is limited to cases in which resemblances can be detected (either personally or sub-personally), leaving the door open for an explanation of cases in which resemblances are lacking. Moreover – despite preserving the idea of a perceptual phenomenal character – by allowing for cognitive intervention, it is compatible with accounts that take imagination to be at work in expressive experiences. In point of fact, given the recognitional step, one may well explain the imaginative engagement in terms of those imaginings that rely on resemblances. Imagination, be it sensuous or propositional, can be legitimately deemed responsible for expressive experiences that draw sophisticated connections between perceptual patterns and complex emotions – and psychological states more broadly.

Unlike ascriptions of emotion to living beings, the ascription of expressiveness relies entirely on the possibility of ranging over the perceptual aspect of things, relating it to background knowledge and imaginings about emotions, preventing the subject from the ascription of emotional states. Once recognised as sad, a musical gesture may well be imagined as the expression of a sad fictional persona, or as the outcome of a sadness-driven creative process. Additionally, natural objects may be imagined as being the result of an intentional creative gesture and included within a wider network of imaginings that can be plausibly captured by creative usage of language.

---

[55] The semantic link between the cognitive content and the perceptual content will be articulated more clearly in the next chapter, where I will clarify the kind of concepts that are in play when we talk about (and recognise) emotions.

Finally, endorsing a view that makes conceptual intervention at least partly responsible for the resulting expressive experience, and that therefore takes expressive properties to be relatively response-dependent properties, one must take into account the risk represented by the heresy of the separable experience. As seen, Peacocke's account faces this risk, as long as it takes resemblances to be merely causal triggers of those concepts that should shape the phenomenal character of expressive experience. At the same time, his account cannot say that expressive experience represents resemblances, for this is not always the case according to the phenomenology. However, I should insist that the appeal to cognitive penetration can mitigate the risks entailed by response-dependence. In point of fact, those concepts that intervene in perceptual experiences are meant to make salient those dynamic perceptual properties that the experience is about and that constitute its perceptual content. Rhythmic, dynamic, and gestaltic properties are in fact constitutive of the content of expressive experience and the conceptual intervention is meant to – so to speak – cast light on their connections with emotional expressions. This makes expressive properties *weakly* response-dependent properties. The instantiation of such properties depends on the way in which we conceptualise them only as long as (i) they are represented in a recognitional experience and (ii) emotions concepts apply in virtue of detectable resemblances between dynamic patterns and patterns typical of human expressions. Importantly, as we will see, this is not the case for all expressive experiences. Granted, a further step forward must be taken to illuminate cases in which, lacking resemblances, recognitional experiences by means of metaphorical application of concepts cannot take place.

Chapter 5
Secondary Meaning and Core Affect

This last chapter focuses on the expressive experience of simple expressive features. Their simplicity intuitively amounts to the fact that they are expressive even though they do not resemble any emotional expression. In § 5.1, the problem is framed by addressing the sort of knowledge that one is expected to have in order to recognise a chord or a shade of colour as expressive of an affective state. In § 5.2 emotions are treated as multi-componential items adequately captured by cluster-concepts. Besides offering further support to the metaphorical account previously given of conceptual intervention in the case of the expressive musical gesture, this view of emotion concepts allows for one further step. Namely, it paves the way for the notion of *secondary meaning* that, I contend, accounts for how concepts apply within simple expressive experiences (§ 5.3). Subsequently, § 5.4 introduces the notion of *core affect* as it is put forward by James Russell's constructivist theory of emotions. Following the distinction between emotions and meta-emotions, I can suggest that even the recognition of simple affective features may consist in the application of conceptual knowledge to a non-conceptual content, and that this conceptual intervention can be accounted for as weak cognitive penetration involving secondary meaning (§ 5.5). In § 5.6 the hypothesis is introduced and supported by empirical evidence that expressive experiences are not necessarily recognitional experiences. This is still treated as an open question.

5.1 What if Resemblances Lack?

When we recognise musical gestures as expressive one may argue that resemblances, although not manifest, play a role such that some comparison is triggered, possibly involving top-down conceptual interventions, but the cases of expressive chords is more difficult to explain this way. When we hear a mournful chord, not only are we not aware of what makes it similar to typical expressive behaviours, but it is also difficult to justify *ex post* such an experience referring to some kind of isomorphism. According to Peacocke:

> The relation of the perceived minor to its (unheard) major is perceived metaphorically-as an instance of the relation an emotion of sadness, a subdued emotion experienced from the inside, bears to a non-sad ordinary state of mind that is not subdued. The isomorphism in question is a mapping from the domain of moods (a normal non-sad mood, and sadness in this case) to the modes of major and minor. One of the literal relations of

sadness to a normal mood is that of the former being more subdued than the latter. Under the isomorphism, this relation is mapped onto the relation of being the minor of the corresponding (unheard) major. (Peacocke 2009, p. 262–263)

On his view, the detectable isomorphism does not consist, as in the case of the musical gesture, in the resemblance between the pattern and some expressive behaviour. Rather, it has to do with the "position" that the perceptual pattern occupies within the network of related features. In the case of the minor chord, its being "subdued" compared to the major offers the appeal for a comparison with subdued affective states, such as sadness, compared to other, more lively ones. The dynamic tension provided by this relationship is sufficient for a comparison with some component of an affective state.

An analogous argument can be made for colours. Let us consider chromatic shades used to paint internal walls of public buildings. Trivial as it may sound, this example gets to the point: the choice of light, pastel shades of grey rather than lively shades of orange provides the overall environment with an affective tone. Interior designers are well aware of this minimal expressive power of colours, that is, they are aware of the perceptual space in which shades of colours are located and can interact with one another. Grey will therefore present itself to the observer as more subdued than red, for example, thus entertaining a relationship analogous to the major–minor relationship between chords. On this perspective, simple expressive features are perceived as being related to other features, and if we follow Peacocke, it is thanks to these more or less manifest relations that they can be mapped onto the domain of affective states.

It must be added that we rarely see isolated colours or hear isolated sounds, that is, they seldom are instantiated in our experiences devoid of a minimal context. This point is vividly assessed by Martin Lindauer:

First note that more than just "red" is experienced [...]. The color could be crimson, scarlet, ruby, burgundy, or cherry – as well as dark, deep, exciting, and "fire" red. (Similarly, the family of blues originating in the sky includes azure, beryl, cerulean, cobalt, indigo, navy, royal, sapphire, teal, turquoise, and ultramarine – and "electric" and "sky" blue.) Within the family of reds, one particular shade "stands out" as the most representative (prototypical) and memorable (codable). A flood of color names, like cerise, fuchsia, mauve, and "Weekend in the Country" are invented by paint manufacturers, decorators, and interior designers in an attempt to capture subtle physiognomic nuances [...]. The perception of a color is also affected by the circumstances under which it is seen, its surround. Viewed without distance cues, devoid of surface properties, and without a context, like the sky overhead, colors are called "aperture colors." When seen under even more restricted circumstances, "film color" describes a color viewed in isolation, not tied to any object, as when looked at through a peephole that restricts our view to the object itself without any of its surrounding area. (Lindauer 2013, p. 87)

Colours hardly ever present themselves as being segregated from further shades, shapes, surfaces, and textures; similarly, sounds are rarely heard in isolation. Therefore, when considering expressive experience of simple properties, one should always be aware that they tend to present themselves in context. Thus, one may insist that, also given our standard encounters with these sorts of features, it is likely that we experience them and learn to recognise them as being related to other features, such as their surroundings or in overt or covert comparison with other shades or sounds.

Yet it is not clear why recognising something as being subdued should lead us to experience it as sad rather than, simply, as toned-down. Peacocke focuses on a specific sort of knowledge one is expected to possess in order to hear a chord as sad. Namely, he argues that, to this aim, one has to know how emotions feel "from within". He explains the relationship between the perceptual experience of a minor chord as subdued and the emotion of sadness in terms of the knowledge one has about what sadness is like subjectively: "The perception of the chord as expressing sadness is possible only for someone who has some idea of what sadness is like from the inside" (Peacocke 2009, p. 263).

The power of such an intuition is attested by accounts that we have already encountered and discussed. Along the line of Carroll Pratt, we have seen that Budd claims that we perceive the resemblance between music and the first-person experience of emotions "from within" (Budd 1985). Aaron Ridley (1995) retorts against contour theory that we cannot reduce expressive experience to the simple detection of perceptual patterns and their resemblances to expressions, claiming instead that some knowledge of those feelings connected to emotions is required by an explanation of expressive experience. And the same worry can be found in Wollheim (1993), where it takes the shape of an anti-reductionism of expressive properties to standard perceptual ones, and appeals to the intervention of associative mechanisms of projections.

Two aspects of this intuition are problematic however. Firstly, as Trivedi (2001) rightly remarks, such a recognitional process does not amount to ascribe anything like an expression to the chord, because it mobilises subjective feelings rather than expressions of those feelings as an element of comparison. Instead, it provides us with some causal story that is not *per se* sufficient to explain expressive experience. Secondly, it is difficult to understand how the capacity to recognise something as a *felt* feeling could translate into the ascription of a property to an object. An intervention of knowledge can be hypothesised in order to answer this question. A plausible answer is that having some knowledge about emotions makes it so that a subdued chord is conceptually categorised as bearing some relation to emotions. Emotion concepts would therefore shape the experience we have of the chord making such a relation salient, allowing us to label its content (the perceivable structure of the chord) as *sad*.

5.2 Cluster-Concepts and Emotions as Patterns

Given what I have been arguing about recognitional experiences of expressive properties as involving the possession of emotion concepts, a consistent view about what emotion concepts are is urgently needed at this stage. Authors, such as Zangwill, who assume that emotions amount to one feature – usually an internally felt state – or to a limited set of necessary components, derive from this assumption the idea that the kind of concept that has to be mastered in order to perform the recognition of certain perceptual aspects as connected to emotions, is the concept that applies to such a feature (or set of components). This narrow view of what emotions are and of what kind of concept identifies them is overtly contradicted by many theories of emotions. Arguably, the kind of concept in play depends on the kind of emotion theory one is disposed to endorse: if one holds that emotions are to be identified by means of their intentional object (e.g. Stecker 1984), then one would probably think that possessing the concept of sadness is to possess the concept of what we can be sorrowful about; if one holds that emotions are identified by the typical appraisal (Scherer 2009), then one will consider the concept of sadness to correctly apply to that typical appraisal; if one thinks that emotions are identified by the "gut reaction" we undergo when feeling sad (Prinz 2004), then the concept of sadness will correctly apply only to those cases in which one undergoes the gut reaction, and so on.

Nowadays, most authors agree that emotions are better identified as complex patterns of heterogeneous components rather than by a unique necessary feature. The occurrence of an emotion is hardly identifiable as the instantiation of a single kind of property such as the presence of its intentional object, the evaluative attitude of the subject, the activation of some physiological, measurable reaction or the external manifestation of a feeling. Moreover, many philosophers and psychologists maintain that emotions consist in dynamic processes that involve a number of components, rather than in temporally and functionally limited episodes (e.g. Izard *et al.* 2000; Scherer 2009; Newen *et al.* 2015; Barrett *et al.* 2015. See also Robinson 2005 for an insightful overview).

Appraisal theories, for instance, tend to consider emotions as adaptive processes that detect and assess the significance of the environment for wellbeing. Appraisal is precisely such a detection process. Accordingly, emotions consist in the recognition of what features of the environment (and how) can satisfy or prevent the satisfaction of our needs, attachments, values, goals, and beliefs (Smith and Ellsworth 1985; Lazarus 1991; Frijda 2007; Scherer 2004, 2009; Ellsworth 2013). They thereby establish interactive connections with objects and events. In order to describe and explain these processes, Klaus Scherer put forward the so-called Component Process Model that accounts for the architecture of emotions as dynamic processes involving a number of variables, reactions, and organismic systems and subsystems (Scherer 2009). Among these components are physiological reactions, motivational components, evaluative (cognitive) components, tendencies to action, motor activations, bodily and facial expressions, feeling components, the neural systems and subsystems that implement all these factors, and the social and normative variables that can affect the emotional process. Moreover, emotions are usually said to possess intentional objects, towards which they are directed with axiological attitudes. In principle, the list of components is not limited to such features, nonetheless this should be sufficient to realise that the most adequate way to conceive of emotions is as patterns of components that relate to one another (the dynamic model proposed by Scherer offers an insight into these relations), but do not necessarily occur all together in every emotional episode.

Although appraisal theories exemplify a multi-componential approach to emotions (see Moors *et al.* 2013 for a review of their common assumptions and specificities), they take appraisal process to be essential for the occurrence of an emotional episode. In a motto: no appraisal, no emotion. Therefore, even if their account of how emotion work is extremely convincing, such a remains of essentialism makes appraisal theories a weak candidate for the present purpose. What I am indeed looking for is a theory of emotions that allows for an application of emotion concepts that is, so to speak, as liberal as possible. The envisaged achievement is a view that does justice to a liberal way of talking about emotions.

Constructivist theories stress a multi-factorial view of emotions and of affectivity more in general. As it has been noticed, constructivism is an approach to psychology whose history has not been reconstructed as a unitary tradition so far (Barrett and Russell 2015). Nevertheless, it can be understood as assuming an anti-essentialist perspective on affective phenomena (Barrett 2013). On this count, constructivism radicalises the multi-componential approach that I have introduced referring to appraisal theories by rejecting the essential role of appraisals too.

Constructivism of emotions stems from the consideration that there is no agreement about what emotions are, that is, about the paradigmatic concept of emotion that should be adopted, neither in the field of psychology and philosophy, nor in the field of neurosciences. According to a constructivist approach, an unwarranted essentialist assumption is responsible for such a disagreement:

> [...] there are a variety of meanings employed for emotion, but scientific inquiry seems unable to settle the matter. The reason for this conundrum can be found in what these unanswered questions (What are the classes of emotion? How many? Definition? What is it?) have in common: an assumption that the components (nonverbal expressions, physiological changes, etc.) in an emotional episode are caused by and therefore explained by a common agent behind them, the essence of each emotion. (Barrett and Russell 2015, p. 4)

Supporters of constructivism hold the view that emotion concepts apply to many of the listed components, none of which are essential to those emotional episodes that psychology and cognitive sciences should account for. Not all components will appear in all emotional episodes and they need not occur in a fixed order. Both according to constructivism and to appraisal theories, these components are mostly processes, unfolding over time and interacting with one another and with further psychological and physiological processes (Russell 2015, p. 201; Scherer 2009; Newen *et al.* 2015). Let us consider the example of sadness. The concept of sadness is taken by constructivist approaches to apply not only to those cases in which all the components of the pattern of sadness are present (also because establishing a fixed amount of components does not seem possible beyond approximation), but even in cases in which a subset of such components is instantiated, such as behavioural expressions.

Constructivism makes it even harder to find an exhaustive definition for a phenomenon that seems to be constitutively multi-faceted. Importantly, it denies that emotions are natural kinds (Russell 2003, p. 163), but rather insists that they are "unified events or episodes that have physiological, cognitive/perceptual, and social elements" (Barrett and Russell 2015, p. 9). Too many different things fall under the broad category of emotion, leading us to the point where something that was originally employed as a folk notion requires progressive expansion in order to cover all those factors and components that scientific research brings about.

> The instances within the category named emotion are qualitatively different: occurrent events and dispositions, intentional and nonintentional states, automatic and controlled processes, motives and lack of motivation, reflexes and cognitive states, and so forth. The implications of this heterogeneity are vast. Heterogeneity undermines the seemingly endless search for a precise definition of emotion. It undermines categorical statements purporting to be laws of emotion. (Russell 2015, p. 187)

Therefore, the search for a definition of emotion (and for sub-definition of every type of emotion) seems doomed to fail, unless a strategy is adopted that looks for "family resemblances" instead of "common cores".

5.2 Cluster-Concepts and Emotions as Patterns

> The everyday, ordinary words emotion, fear, anger, love, and the like name categories that have proven to be vague and heterogeneous. Instances that fall within each of these categories share a family resemblance rather than a common core. [...] What do all and only emotional episodes have in common? They bear a family resemblance to one another, but what they and only they have in common is that our language community calls them emotional. (Russell 2015, p. 186–201)

This is the case in our everyday use of emotion words: we employ the adjective "anxious" to describe ourselves on the basis of the feeling of anxiety that we experience from a first-person perspective, but also to describe someone moving incessantly or speaking frenetically, and also somebody whose gaze conveys anxiety, lacking any sort of more explicit behavioural manifestation. Moreover, we may imagine being neuroscientists in the business of finding out what neural mechanisms implement anxiety, in which case our description would correctly apply to a specific neural activation that is intended to relate to the emotion of anxiety. It is therefore difficult to identify the component of an affective pattern that adequately justifies, once and for all, the use of an emotion term.

Based on these considerations about common ascriptions of emotional states, constructivism holds that the meaning of emotion concepts should be found by looking at their everyday uses in our language games. In point of fact, it seems that concepts such as "sadness", "happiness", "fear", "frustration", "nostalgia", "jealousy" can only be meaningfully applied in their folk, everyday use. Interestingly, Russell notes that only as everyday concepts do "they play an actual role as in, for example, emotional meta-experience and the perception of emotion in others, which in turn play a role in social interactions" (Russell 2015, p. 204).

If, firstly, we agree that emotions are not reducible to one or to a limited set of components, but that they are rather multi-componential entities, and, secondly, we agree that emotion concepts are only effective in their everyday use, then I suggest that the kind of concept that better captures emotions as complex patterns is a "cluster-concept". Cluster-concepts are generally characterised by a sufficient amount of characteristic features, none of which are necessary to possess that concept (Newen *et al.* 2015). The notion explicitly refers to Wittgenstein's remarks about "family resemblances" according to which we are wrong in thinking that there must be something common to all the instantiations of a category to which we apply the same term. Instead, those things that fall under the same definition share family resemblances. Russell seems to have precisely this approach in mind when he writes: "There are no necessary and sufficient features to be found, no border separating emotion from not-emotion" (Russell 2015, p. 188).

Admittedly, this approach to concepts raises problems when it comes to scientific definitions. As Kathryn Parsons insists, if cluster-concepts are understood as "family resemblance clusters", then we lack the criteria to establish what is relevant and what is not for something to fall under a certain concept:

> any term may show family resemblance cluster features if the similarities among instances are inappropriately chosen. To make his position plausible, the philosopher holding a "family resemblance view" must make tenable the claim that the characteristics he has chosen are those which are genuinely relevant to being a thing of the kind in question.
> (Parsons 1973, p. 519)

Therefore, scientific concepts should be better intended as "cluster-*law* concepts". According for instance to Hilary Putnam's account which originally brought about this label, the reference of cluster-law concepts is determined by a cluster of law-like statements that contain the term, rather than by the simple appeal to the way in which language games happen to work (Putnam 1975). According to Parsons, this normally allows for explanations of borderline cases to which we apply scientific concepts: in cases of controversial applications one can appeal to such law-like statements that define cluster-law concepts in order to verify whether the application is justified.

Now, it is not entirely clear whether psychology should be treated as, say, physics when it comes to establishing the justified employment of its technical terms. In the light of Parsons' remarks, when examining the criteria for the correct application of a term that refers to a mental state as it is treated by psychology (broadly conceived), one would be tempted to appeal to cluster-law concepts, rather than to everyday use of terms such as "belief", "thought", "intuition", "desire", and so on. This would entail that applications of these terms within the scientific domain is justified as long as the cluster definition appeals to the use of those terms within the scientific discourse. Yet, it is admittedly difficult for psychology and related disciplines to establish the technical meaning of such terms when employed within the scientific domain, owing to the fact that they are borrowed from everyday discourses.

This is especially problematic in the case of emotions and the related emotion terms. On the one hand, the references of emotion concepts (i.e. those objects or features to which they apply) are better identified as patterns; on the other hand, adopting a cluster notion of emotion concepts in terms of family resemblances attested by their common use in everyday talk might lead to the impossibility of establishing whether borderline cases qualify as emotions (Newen et al. 2015, p. 191). Would one be justified in applying the concept "sad" to the mere behavioural expression of sadness? And what about the application of such a term to cases in which one is not fully aware of one's own feeling, but realises to have been sad only afterwards?

Parsons seems to endorse a solution for this problematic case that lies in between that of law-like clusters for scientific terms and family resemblances for everyday terms. What is interesting is that her view is compatible with the constructivist approach to emotions and emotion concepts. According to Parsons, cluster-concepts of psychological phenomena should be modelled on the kind of "cluster-law concept", taking into account the fact that the "theories" in which psychological terms appear also include common-sense rational discourses about psychological phenomena (Parsons 1973, p. 522). Therefore, explanations of why certain phenomena (especially borderline ones) are correctly defined by a psychological everyday term (such as "sadness") or not, will be given in terms of reasons, everyday practices and all those contexts in which – as Russell affirms – such terms play an "active role". Importantly, this is not to say that psychologists must limit their inquiries about affective states to those that are identified by folk notions of emotions. On the contrary, while we should preserve a cluster notion of emotions based on family resemblances attested by the common use of words, psychological research about emotions needs to employ technical terms that do not necessarily coincide with the folk ones. We can see this in the following analogy:

> [...] consider the scientific status of the concept of a house. All houses (whether palace, mansion, shack, toy house, birdhouse, or houseboat) conform to the laws of physics, and the builder of houses does well to take those laws into account. Houses are real, but, all the same, house is not a technical term in physics. [...] Emotional episodes are simply an especially interesting and important subset of human episodes, much as houses are an interesting and important subset of physical systems. (Russell 2015, p. 205)

In the light of cluster-concepts so conceived, the application of emotion terms to mere manifestations of emotions sounds justified. The use of the term "sad" to describe a shabby posture is not only justified by the fact that this is the way our language games commonly work (as it would be in a rough application of the Wittgensteinian stance), but by the composite nature of emotions that gathers together an indefinite amount of components. One does not need to look for such a justification in the presence of a mental state or of a typically felt feeling. Expressive behaviours are constitutive (although not necessary) components of emotion patterns and, therefore, are adequately captured by cluster-concepts.

This latter point offers further support to Stephen Davies' theory of emotion-characteristic-in-appearance, according to which certain perceptual patterns share certain perceivable characteristics with human expressive gestures. By endorsing an anti-essentialist view about what emotions are and an account of psychological concepts modelled on a – partially amended – version of the notion of family resemblances, we can conceive of emotion terms as being cluster-concepts. The possession of emotion concepts might therefore amount to the capacity to apply emotion terms to some of the features that are commonly taken to be part of emotion patterns, rather than to allegedly essential features such as internal mental states.

This approach promises to ferry us beyond the resemblance-based account that relies on emotion-characteristic-in-appearance. For, if emotion concepts apply to an indefinite number of heterogeneous features in virtue of their cluster nature, it is reasonable to extend the range of recognitional experiences to which they apply beyond those justified by similarities. Similarities holding between references are one of the conditions at which cluster-concepts apply, but they are not the sole condition.

5.3 Metaphorical, Quasi-Metaphorical, and Secondary Meaning

In the previous chapter, I have argued that metaphorical uses of concepts are well suited to explain those experiences of perceptual patterns that bear resemblances to expressive gestures. More specifically, concepts intervene and modify the experience thanks to resemblances, allowing for the use of those same concepts involved in the recognition of expressions. Notably, metaphors can, in principle, be analysed by direct reference to underlying resemblances. Let us exemplify this point by referring to a lively musical gesture: instead of describing it as simply "cheerful", one could refer to the similarities that link it to a human tone of voice and describe it as sounding like a cheerful tone of voice normally sounds. Another way to tell the same story is to say that when metaphors are understood in this way they can, in principle, be reduced to *similes*. According to the accounts of metaphors previously introduced, this seems uncontroversial. For this reason, the explanatory power of a metaphorical account is limited. Namely, it is in trouble when it comes to explaining recognitional expressive experiences whose contents do not mobilise resemblances.

Malcolm Budd (2008) has thoroughly discussed Frank Sibley's approach to aesthetic descriptions. In a nutshell, Sibley accounts for the attribution of aesthetic qualities introducing the notion of "quasi-metaphors" (Sibley 2001). Sibley claims that most concepts that we use in the aesthetic discourse are used metaphorically, that is, their original and literal use is derived from some domain other than the aesthetic one. He also distinguishes between those concepts that are used metaphorically and concepts that, although they have been borrowed

5.3 Metaphorical, Quasi-Metaphorical, and Secondary Meaning — 151

from other domains of the experience, "*have come* to be aesthetic terms by some kind of metaphorical transference" (Sibley 2001, p. 2). This latter case is that of quasi-metaphors, i.e. of metaphors that gradually lose their metaphorical status and become part of the standard vocabulary of art criticism.

The problem with this view is obviously the relationship between (quasi) metaphorical and literal uses of words. As Budd rightly remarks, the problem is not that sometimes metaphors "die". Rather, it is the way in which the use of words is related to the properties to which they apply literally, metaphorically, or "quasi-metaphorically".

Sibley argues that the metaphorical and quasi-metaphorical use of words to capture aesthetic properties is such that the terms we employ seem to us perfectly suitable.

> There is nothing unnatural about using words like 'forceful', 'dynamic', or 'tightly-knit' in criticism; they do their work perfectly and are exactly the words needed for the purposes they serve. We do not want or need to replace them by words which lack the metaphorical element. In using them to describe works of art, the very point is that we are noticing aesthetic qualities related to their literal or common meanings. [...] Aesthetic concepts, all of them, carry with them attachments and in one way or another are tethered to or parasitic upon non-aesthetic features. (Sibley 2001, p. 17)

Thus, on one hand, Sibley believes that metaphorical and quasi-metaphorical descriptions of aesthetic properties are perfectly appropriate and that alternative literal expressions (if some were available) would not serve the same purpose; on the other hand, he maintains that those words that we use to refer to aesthetic properties are indissolubly linked to non-aesthetic properties that they literally and originally refer to. Yet, the nature of such a link is unclear. On Budd's view, appealing to resemblances when trying to explain the ascription of aesthetic properties does not properly account for their nature. He claims that Sibley coins the term "quasi-metaphors" precisely in order to explain those ascriptions that cannot be justified in terms of resemblances. It seems, indeed, that certain aesthetic properties (expressive properties among them) are captured by those concepts that we use to identify them in such a way that is not mediated by their similarity to non-aesthetic properties. And in point of fact, these features cannot be characterised in other words, nor reduced to similes.

According to Budd, in order to preserve the idea that quasi-metaphorical ascriptions are such that the same property could not be characterised in other words, the concept expressed by the term must figure in the experience of the property: the concept of "dynamism" should accordingly figure in the content of the experience we have of, say, a dynamic picture, so that we could not find any adjective that were more appropriate than "dynamic" (or of its synonyms) to describe it. Yet, suggesting that a concept can be part of an experience falls short of an explanation.

In order to cast light on this intuition, Budd refers to the Wittgensteinian notion of secondary meaning. Secondary meaning (or sense) is something in between literal and metaphorical meaning: on the one hand, it applies in such a way that one cannot substitute the word with any other – precisely as Sibley observes is the case for aesthetic predicates; while on the other hand, it is not a paradigmatic use of a term, because in order to grasp it, one needs to understand the primary (literal) use of the term in question. Let us delve into this notion.

As it is well known, according to the latter Wittgenstein, meaning is the way in which we use the words within our "language games":

> § 43. For a large class of cases – although not all cases – in which we use it, the word "meaning" can be defined as follows: The meaning of a word is its use in language.

However, in the second part of the *Philosophical Investigations*, Wittgenstein puts forward some remarks that are apparently difficult to reconcile with his views on meaning.

> Given the two ideas 'fat' and 'lean', would you be rather inclined to say that Wednesday was fat and Tuesday lean, or *vice versa?* (I incline decisively towards the former.) Now have "fat" and "lean" some different meaning here from their usual one? – They have a different use. – ought I really to have used different words? Certainly not that. – want to use *these* words (with their familiar meanings) *here*.
>
> [...]
> Asked "What do you really mean here by 'fat' and 'lean'?" – I could only explain the meanings in the usual way. I could *not* point to the examples of Tuesday and Wednesday.
>
> Here one might speak of a 'primary' and 'secondary' sense of a word. It is only if the word has the primary sense for you that you use it in the secondary one.
>
> (Wittgenstein 1986, p. 216)

In this passage, Wittgenstein envisages the case where we use certain terms whose meaning is already known to us – i.e. that we use literally in the appropriate language games – to refer to objects or use in contexts where these terms do not seem to apply literally, at least not as smoothly as in their literal applications. Well, he wonders, does the very fact that they are being used in an uncommon way change the meaning of such words? This would seem to be a logical consequence of the hypothesis that meaning consists in the use of words in language games. Yet Wittgenstein's answer is negative: their meaning remains the same and, in cases like this, words preserve the meaning we are familiar with.[56]

The problem can be formulated as follows: if the meaning of a word should be understood as its use in language, then how can a word be used in different ways and nevertheless preserve the same meaning? And if the meaning remains the same, although the word is used in different games and applied within different realms, what accounts for the difference between primary and secondary meaning? The reply to this question would help to explain the case in which an emotion term whose meaning is standardly determined by language games concerning emotions as mental states is applied to something that neither is nor has a mental state, nor – more importantly – resembles an expression. Following Sibley and Budd, this might be something slightly different from a metaphor.

If we admit that secondary meaning is not a special sort of meaning that must be explained as the result of specific psychological mechanisms, then its metaphorical nature can be assessed.[57] Wittgenstein explicitly denies that secondary meaning amounts to metaphorical application:

> The secondary sense is not a 'metaphorical' sense. If I say "For me the vowel *e* is yellow" I do not mean: 'yellow' in a metaphorical sense, – for I could not express what I want to say in any other way than by means of the idea 'yellow'.   (Wittgenstein 1986, p. 216)

---

56 Here are two remarks from the *Philosophical Investigations* which the problem stems:

§ 558. What does it mean to say that the "is" in "The rose is red" has a different meaning from the "is" in "twice two is four"? If it is answered that it means that different rules are valid for these two words, we can say that we have only *one* word here. – And if all I am attending to is grammatical rules, these do allow the use of the word "is" in both connexions. – But the rule which shows that the word "is" has different meanings in these sentences is the one allowing us to replace the word "is" in the second sentence by the sign of equality, and forbidding this substitution in the first sentence.

§ 561. Now isn't it queer that I say that the word "is" is used with two different meanings (as the copula and as the sign of equality), and should not care to say that its meaning is its use; its use, that is, as the copula and the sign of equality?

One would like to say that these two kinds of use do not yield a *single* meaning; the union under one head is an accident, a mere inessential.

57 Wittgenstein introduces the problem of secondary meaning in order to deal with the hypothesis that the understanding of certain words could amount to the experience they trigger in us and that we take as being attached to the words as a sort of physiognomy. Without denying that this kind of experiences takes place, I contend that secondary meaning is better accounted for in accordance with Wittgenstein's view of meaning as use. This being said, my primary concern here is that secondary meaning is neither replaceable like a fully-fledged metaphor nor paradigmatically literal.

However, Wittgenstein does not have an explicit theory of metaphors, so that what is actually interesting about his view is that the notion of "secondary meaning" is introduced as a further category, partially different from that of literal use and from that of metaphorical use. Accordingly, there are literal (primary) meanings, secondary meanings, and metaphorical uses. Notably, Sibley's account of aesthetic predicates also implies that there are literal, quasi-metaphorical, and metaphorical meanings. On this view, we sometimes use words in a way that, although not literal, does not admit for any substitution (or at best the substitution by a synonym) nor paraphrase.[58]

While metaphors are characterised by their translatability, the distinctive feature of primary meanings is that they are paradigmatic uses. Paradigmatic uses are those exemplar uses that we can employ when we want to teach or explain to someone the meaning of a word. They are those uses that rely on the features of the world that make the statements containing those words true. If I want to explain to someone the meaning of the world "yellow", I will point at something yellow in the environment or, lacking the concrete example, I will probably formulate sentences referring to something yellow in the actual world. Analogously, if I had to explain to someone the meaning of "fat" I would offer examples where the word fat refers to something – or someone – actually fat. Things work differently in the case of secondary meanings. On the one hand, secondary meanings cannot be used as paradigmatic examples in order to explain the meaning of words, (like metaphors) whereas, on the other hand, they cannot be paraphrased (like literal uses) – remember Wittgenstein saying: "I want to use these words (with their familiar meanings)".

If the opposite poles are paradigmatic uses (used to establish literal meanings) and metaphorical uses, then secondary meanings are placed halfway between them. Secondary meanings can be considered "literal" in the sense that we cannot replace them with any other word, but, like metaphors, they cannot

---

[58] The latter quotation from Wittgenstein implies that the distinctive feature of metaphors is that they can be paraphrased, that is, expressed by means of other words (arguably, by means of similes). As Budd notices: "[...] Wittgenstein declares that the secondary use is not a "metaphorical" use, understanding by metaphorical use of an expression a use which is such that you could say what you want to say without using that expression" (Budd 2008, p. 148). The question of whether metaphors can actually be paraphrased is extremely controversial. Further discussion of this matter here would lead us astray. For the present purpose, I have assumed an affirmative answer consistent with what has been previously said about metaphorical uses and resemblances.

be used to explain the literal meaning of words (Diamond 1967, p. 192).[59] For instance, we will not refer to days of the week to explain the meaning of "lean" and "fat", nor will we refer to "Nature" in the first place to explain the meaning of the word "Temple". In the case of expressive ascriptions, we would not explain the meaning of the word "melancholy" using the example of a melancholy landscape; analogously, if we were to explain the meaning of "cheerful" we would not appeal to the example of a cheerful piece of music. In both cases we would rather point at some typical behaviours or feelings whose descriptions as "melancholy" or "cheerful" are paradigmatic. As a consequence, we would not fully understand the application of an emotion term to an artwork if we were not capable of understanding the meaning it has in cases of paradigmatic applications to inner feelings or to people's expressions.

In a similar vein, Roger Scruton suggests that we distinguish between two possible ways in which the application of a term can extend to domains that are not their original ones. The first is via "analogy", that is, owing to the recognition of resemblances, whereas the second is via "paronymy": "A paronymous use is a derivative use, and can be understood only by someone who has first understood the primary employment of the term" (Scruton 1998, p. 46. See also Barwell 1986). As with secondary meaning and quasi-metaphor, the understanding of a paronymic use is parasitic on the literal or paradigmatic use of a word. Indeed, according to Scruton, one is not able to use the word "sad" to describe something inanimate if one does not possess the concept "sad", i.e. if one is not able to apply it literally. However, unlike the case of analogy, being able to apply the term literally does not depend on the capacity one has to detect resemblances.

Many seem to acknowledge the distinction between metaphors and quasi-metaphors (or paronymies), and Wittgenstein's notion of secondary meaning is well suited to account for this distinction. In order to grasp a secondary meaning of a term, one has to master its primary uses; however, the use of secondary meaning is not based on the recognition of similarities, unlike in the case of metaphorical applications. As an outcome, detectable similarities between

---

[59] Clearly, once it is established that this is what ultimately distinguishes secondary meaning from fully-fledged metaphors, one can be more liberal than Wittgenstein and allow for a more continuist approach between paradigmatically metaphorical expressions and paradigmatically literal expressions. For instance, although he also appeals to secondary meaning, Malcolm Budd is satisfied with the inclusion of secondary uses among the metaphorical ones and deems Wittgenstein's notion of metaphors too restrictive.

standard perceptual properties and aesthetic properties do not account for secondary meaning. This is why Wittgenstein can affirm that words applied in their secondary sense keep their familiar meaning, the one that we have learnt by learning their primary use. In addition, this is why they can argue that, unlike fully-fledged metaphors rooted in similarities, secondary uses cannot be paraphrased.

In the light of all these converging perspectives we can agree on that (at least certain) concepts can be used in ways that are neither paradigmatic, nor metaphorical – at least in the sense in which metaphorical application requires resemblances. Therefore, recognitional expressive experiences where resemblances to emotional expressions are not available might exploit secondary or quasi-metaphorical uses of emotion terms, independently of resemblances and therefore in such a way that they cannot in principle be substituted nor analysed into similes.

Although this way to conceive of the application of emotion concepts when similarities are not available is convincing, a tile is still missing. Namely, given that the link between this kind of expressive experience and emotions is not provided by expressions (through resemblances) we need to understand what ingredient of emotions – if any – is responsible for expressive experiences of, say, a minor chord. To this aim, a stance must be taken within the realm of emotion theories.

5.4 Emotions as Core Affect and Meta-Emotions as Conceptual Recognition

When it comes to emotions in theories of expressive experience, it is not always clear what theory of emotions we should refer to. So far, emotions have been examined only in terms of their phenomenal character, without discussing nor endorsing any specific account. However, constructivist theories of emotions seem to occupy a privileged position to account for the role of emotion concepts in expressive experiences.[60] They indeed offer an original approach to what emotions consist in and to what knowledge about emotions is. Moreover, they take these two components (emotions and the related knowledge) to interact, giving rise to emotion episodes. Interestingly, the way in which affective experience is related

---

[60] This is not an endorsement of constructivism as the best available theory of emotions. It should rather be considered as an attempt to pick up those interesting aspects of a constructivist account that help to assess the overall topic of expressive experience in a consistent way. As the reader will notice, some of these aspects are present in other accounts of emotions as well.

to its recognition (self-ascription) parallels the relation that can be thought to exist between non-recognitional and recognitional expressive experiences.

A brief introduction of a version of constructivism – the one that seems to satisfy the theoretical needs that have emerged from the discussion above – is now in order. According to this view, emotion episodes consist in the combination of somatosensory perceptions relating to some intentional object that can be represented in a conscious intentional state that requires some emotion concept to be instantiated (Russell 2015, p. 195).[61] Besides constituting the knowledge one has about emotions, this conscious, conceptual representation is itself part of the emotional episode, but can be analysed in terms of an *emotional meta-experience* that, importantly, need not be present at every occurrence of an emotion. Russell conceives of the content of these meta-emotions as the appraisal of what in the world may alter our wellbeing. Emotional meta-experiences are therefore self-ascriptions of affective states that require discriminatory capacities, but – although such conceptual self-ascriptions can be considered legitimate components of emotion episodes – they do not exhaust the emotional episode.

This conception of emotions' self-ascription offers a palatable view on what it is to have knowledge of emotions from within, that is, of Peacocke's intuition about the expressive minor chord: it consists in being able to apply concepts such as "fear", "sadness", and "joy" to the perceptions that we have of the way in which things in the world, as well as our own thoughts or beliefs, may alter our wellbeing. Russell takes the core of such appraisals to be what he names "core affect". As I will try to show, this notion provides a thought-provoking bridge between the domain of perception and that of emotions, thereby promising to link expressive experience and emotions bypassing expressions.

Here is how Russell introduces core affect:

> Core affect is a part of what are commonly called emotions, feelings, and moods, but it is not synonymous with any of these [...] whereas emotional episodes are said to begin and then, after a short time, end, one is always in some state of core affect, which simply varies over time (sometimes slowly, sometimes rapidly) without beginning or end. Emotional episodes are typically directed at something (one is angry with, afraid of, or sad about something). In contrast, core affect is not necessarily directed at anything. Like mood, core affect per se can be free-floating (as in feeling down but not about anything and without knowing why), but it can come to be directed at something.
>
> (Russell 2015, p. 195–196)

---

[61] See Kringelbach and Berridge (2015) for an overview of the neural underpinnings of core affect as basic component of emotions.

The notion of core affect proves to be a useful heuristic tool in psychology and neuroscience. In point of fact, according to Russell's seminal formulation:

> Core affect is a neurophysiological state that is consciously accessible as a simple, non-reflective feeling that is an integral blend of hedonic (pleasure–displeasure) and arousal (sleepy–activated) values. (Russell 2003, p. 147)

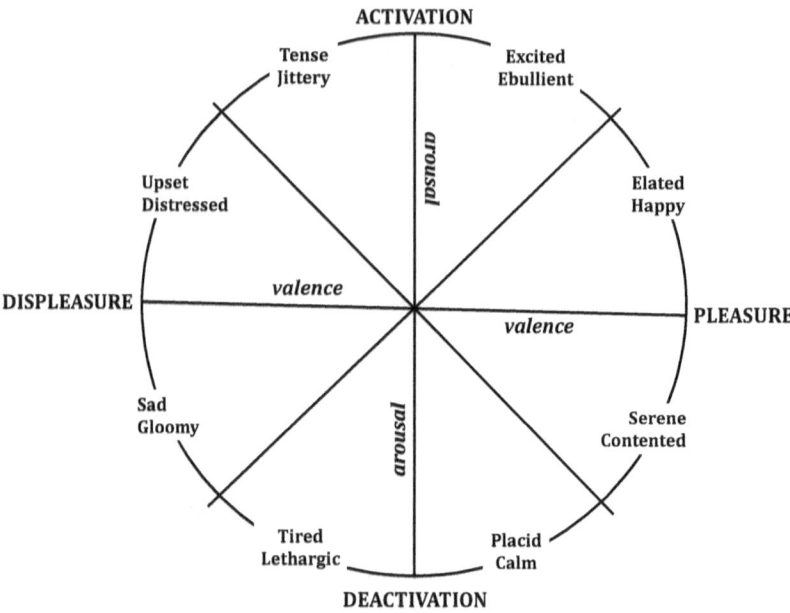

Figure 4: Core Affect. Reproduced by the author.

Core affect is standardly represented as the combination of these two dimensions, so that they consist in an assessment of one's condition at a certain time, determined by the degree of pleasure (ranging from agony to ecstasy) combined with that of arousal (ranging from sleep to frenetic excitement) (Russell and Barrett 1999; Russell 2003; Russell 2015). Core affect can be activated by and/or directed towards "affective qualities", the perception of which is "a 'cold' process, made hot by being combined with a change in core affect" (Russell 2003, p. 148).

So, two fundamental components of emotional episodes (whose conceptual categorisation may or may not take place) are individuated: core affect on the one hand and affective qualities on the other. Whereas the former can be intuitively understood as moods or feelings, the latter are dispositional properties that are perceived according to the same dimensional criteria (pleasure – or valence – and arousal) as that which can potentially alter one's core affect. Such dispositions are, on this view, perceptually appraised without the need for conceptual interventions. Moreover, such an appraisal of affective qualities does not require that any modification of core affect occurs:

> Phenomenologically, core affect is a feeling inside oneself, whereas an affective quality is a property of the thing perceived. [...] in principle, perception of affective quality can occur with no change at all in core affect. (Russell 2003, p. 157)

This way of conceiving affective qualities maintains that there are properties of the world that can be experienced as inherently connected to our affective dimension, requiring neither the activation of background knowledge on one hand, nor the arousal of emotions on the other. Such a perspective supports the claim that the experience of expressive properties is inherently perceptual. Moreover, it is in the position to rule out arousal as a necessary condition for expressive experience. Yet it maintains that a fundamental connection exists between what happens "inside" as a feeling and what is recognised "outside" as a property of the world.

In some sense, the isomorphism invoked by Peacocke is preserved by this view. It amounts to qualities of the environment and qualities of feelings being classifiable according to the same dimensions, namely arousal and valence. But what is crucial for the present proposal is that, if this is how things stand, we do not need to assume that the recognition of any inner modification of core affect occurs prior to recognition of affective qualities in the environment. Moreover, the conceptual intervention resulting in the self-ascription of an affective state is not considered a necessary condition for the emotional episode to take place.

Recently, Céspedes-Guevara and Eerola (2018) argued that constructivist approaches to emotions based on core affect are better suited than traditional theories of basic emotions to account for what they call the "emotional meaning" of music – that is, its expressiveness. They extensively review the available psychological literature about music and emotions, contending that empirical results both regarding adults and children are best interpreted through the constructivist dimensional lens. Among their claims is the idea that core affect can account for cross-cultural and cross-age differences and convergences. Grounded in a biological and evolutionarily consistent kernel, constructivism so conceived accommodates cultural and, more generally, cognitive integrations. The dimensional approach accounts for the basic layer of emotion and expressive perception appealing to biological functions such as the preservation of wellbeing; however, it considers this level of emotional experience as interacting with high-level (conceptual) cognitive functions.

Let me summarise the salient aspects of this dimensional approach. Firstly, the notion of affective qualities as being dispositionally related to core affect can explain the relationship between felt emotions and perceived affect without appealing to arousalism. The claim is therefore that certain properties of the world are experienced as expressive as long as they are recognised as being capable of modifying one's core affect. What Russell calls affective qualities can be interpreted as corresponding to those low-level perceivable items (chords, sounds, colours, lines) that we tend to perceive as affectively loaded and therefore to recognise as being minimally expressive of emotions. Additionally, this view should satisfy Ridley's concern about formalist and perceptualist explanations of expressive experience that – he maintains – do not account for the difference between sentient beings and computers that undergo expressive experiences (Ridley 1995). The perception of affective qualities in the environment is, according to Russell, intrinsically connected to the possibility that such features alter the balance of inner wellbeing – something that, allegedly, is not available to computing machines. This connection is granted by the dimensional field that core affect shares with affective qualities.

Secondly, the theory of core affect combined with affective qualities avoids the limitation to traditional "basic emotions" of the range of expressions that can be perceptually recognised. Therefore, applied to a theory of expressive properties, this dimensional model allows extending such a range to as many emotional expressions as the concepts of emotions that one possesses. Accordingly, depending on contextual elements and also on one's background knowledge, white can be peaceful, inhuman, still, devoid of life, promising, or boring.[62] Yet, all these possible descriptions based on a recognitional experience are grounded in the dimensional space of core affect that is purportedly our basic affective equipment. The conceptual categorisation occurs once the modification of core affect is felt, or the affective quality is perceived, or once the combination of the two is in play.

If this kind of appraisal applies to expressive experience, then the expressive experience that can eventually be shaped by conceptual categorisation is anchored to very low-level features that we do not need to conceptualise in order to apprehend as emotionally loaded. These features can be vague and coarse-grained, for they range along the vectors of pleasantness and arousal. Therefore, it is likely that, lacking more fine-grained concepts, one can only

---

[62] Herman Melville devotes a paragraph of *Moby-Dick* to the inhumanity of white, whereas Paul Klee speaks of its lack of life. I owe these examples to Paolo Spinicci's illuminating course of theoretical philosophy at the University of Milan, 2014.

experience simple expressive qualities such as being more or less agitated, static, potentially pleasant, or potentially unpleasant. Instead, the expressive experience of white as being "inhuman" is something that requires more refined emotion concepts in order to take place (and, allegedly, some imaginative context that justifies the conceptual application).[63]

Thirdly, accounting for expressive experience by referring to the dimensional structure proposed above and to the possibility of cognitive integrations allows for an explanation of the differences between distinct levels of expertise in the affective domain on the one hand and in the aesthetic field on the other. By endorsing a theory of core affect, a perceptualist theory of expressive experience can easily claim that the expert musician and the novice listener will entertain distinct expressive experiences of the same auditory feature (the minor chord, once again), owing to their conceptual capacities being more or less fine-grained. Analogously, such a theory can explain why children are very skilled from a very early age in discriminating between positive and negative affective values of music (Giomo 1993;[64] Trehub, Hannon, and Schachner 2010). This type of theory can indeed insist that the experience is based on the same perceptual appraisal of low-level affective qualities that comes prior to the conceptual categorisation of the chord as being, say, simply "subdued" or "sad". Conceptual categorisations can intervene and refine the overall experience, allowing for subsequent ascriptions.[65] Therefore, although conceptual intervention can enhance expressive experience, such an experience will not be fully response-dependent. Instead, it will consist in the perception of those worldly low-level features that are inherently connected to core affect. This specific advantage will be discussed in the last paragraph, and it will finally allow me to suggest that not only is the content of expressive experience non-conceptual, but also its phenomenal character can be understood without appealing to the intervention of emotion concepts.

---

[63] This is probably one of the aspects of my account of expressiveness that should be developed further. The idea that the sort of context that allows for the application and the recognitional experience of properties as expressive of complex emotions is put forward and elaborated by Spinicci (2017). This seems to me the right direction to take, for it reintroduces imagination in expressive experience by capturing its inherent capacity to establish relationships between what is actually perceived and higher-level sorts of representations.

[64] It is interesting to note that Giomo found scarce correlation between musical training and capacity to ascribe affective value to music.

[65] An analogous dimensional approach to emotions is fruitfully exploited by Juslin and Timmers (2010), where it is explicitly related to experimental results concerning musical fruition and evaluation. Emotions ascribed to music are accordingly located along the two orthogonal axes of valence and arousal.

Finally, as we have seen, constructivism generally endorses an anti-essentialist view of emotions as psychological episodes in conjunction with a theory of emotion concepts as family-resemblance concepts. As a result, this view takes emotion knowledge that can intervene in emotional episodes to be grounded in common language and everyday experiences. This means that the criteria for the justified use of emotion concepts is not rigidly fixed, neither by the presence of a mental state, nor by the presence of gestures, behaviours, or the like.

5.5 Recognitional Experiences of Chords and Colours

In the previous chapter, cognitive penetration has been taken to explain the phenomenal character of experiences in which we recognise certain perceivable patterns as expressive of emotions. On the assumption that some perceivable patterns resemble certain genuine expressions, the literature about expression recognition provided support to this hypothesis. Moreover, in spite of the distinction between the case of the musical gesture and the case of isolated chords and colours (addressing an admittedly problematic distinction for resemblance theories), I have argued that the phenomenology of these experiences does not justify Peter Kivy's conventionalist account of the latter. I am hopeful that the introduction on the stage of core affect and affective qualities, along with the idea of emotion concepts as cluster-concepts and the notion of secondary meaning, provide the necessary tools for such an endeavour.

What sort of work do emotion concepts perform when it comes to the recognition of, say, a chromatic shade as being lively? More extensively: does the concept of "liveliness" enter and shape the phenomenal character of this sort of expressive experience as I argued happens for more complex perceptual patterns? A positive reply to this question relies on the cognitive penetration of phenomenal character and on the conceptual intervention of secondary meanings.

As we have seen, the ability to apply a concept is standardly acquired by means of paradigmatic uses. Accordingly, one's capacity to use the concept of liveliness consists in one's capacity to use that concept to refer to one's own and others' affective states, tempers, moods, gestures, and behaviours. One may also be able to use this concept to refer to items that are relevantly similar to the listed ones, in which case one would be using it metaphorically. Although it presupposes such a mastery in the paradigmatic (and allegedly metaphorical) cases, secondary meaning is held to work differently. Remarkably, in Wittgenstein's observations on secondary meaning, the subject is referred to as having a certain "inclination" or being "willing" to use the terms in this way, or to do so "spontaneously". Secondary uses are neither the result of a learning process, nor the outcome of a perceptual recognition of similarities, but consist in the willingness to use words spontaneously in new contexts. What is more, there is a sense in which Wittgenstein's subject feels forced to use those words, not having the possibility of using any other one.

Budd puts forward some remarks that are consistent with this aspect of secondary uses. Criticising Peacocke's metaphorical stance, he argues that:

> the cognition is just the suitability of the alignment of the concept of sadness (rather than joy) with that character: the property revealed by the metaphorical-as perception is this suitability and nothing more. (Budd 2009, p. 292)

Budd is claiming that – at least for those aesthetic ascriptions that Peacocke calls metaphorical – all that happens is that we perceive features as apt to be described by a certain term. A certain concept is just well suited to capture a particular character and our recognition consists in such a feeling of aptness that, however, we would not be able to justify otherwise by appealing to the look of the object.

Contrary to what I intend to claim, Budd seems to deny that this kind of perceptual intervention *modifies* our perception:

> If the right concept springs to mind, is our perceptual experience thereby different from what it was when we were puzzled about the work's character? If my own experience counts for anything, when I find a characterization that for me hits off the expression of some aspect of one of Debussy's *Préludes*, the only change I am aware of as I experience the work is my readiness to come up with this characterization (much as, when looking at a colour and wondering what it is, the sudden realization that it is cinnamon leaves my perception unchanged). (Budd 2009, p. 291)

I am not entirely sure that this amounts to a strong denial of cognitive penetrability though. For, as we have already seen, Budd also admits that of concepts can enhance our overall musical experience (e.g. Budd 2008, p. 141). A compatibilist approach to Budd's statement can be hypothesised, interpreting his denial as targeting possible conceptual modifications of the *content* of our perception, rather than of the phenomenal character. Once one feels prompted to apply a concept, then such a concept can modify the way in which the object appears, i.e. the phenomenal character of the corresponding experience: when I apply the concept of liveliness to the shade of orange, the shade will seem to me especially apt for such an expressive characterisation. Emotion concepts can thus modify the phenomenal character of recognitional expressive experiences of simple features in a way that seems compatible with Wittgenstein's remarks on secondary meaning.

There is nonetheless one count on which this conclusion sounds a bit unsatisfactory. Wittgenstein observes, commenting on the possible causes of this sort of use of concepts: "Now, I say nothing about the causes of this phenomenon. They *might* be associations from my childhood. But that is a hypothesis. Whatever the explanation, – the inclination is there" (Wittgenstein 1986, p. 216). His target here is the way in which language usages function, regardless of the underlying psychological mechanisms. A hypothesis worth exploring is, instead, that the secondary use of emotion concepts in expressive experience of simple perceptual features finds its psychological explanation in something like core affect. I suggest that we deal with what Wittgenstein calls the associations by appealing to the notion of core affect as that which provides a map to navigate affective qualities.

To consider core components of emotions as primarily located on a dimensional field makes the conceptual triggering much less coincidental and idiosyncratic than one may think, and much more rooted in our shared and developing affective life. I suggest that we recognise the expressive character of simple features that lack resemblance relations with expressive gestures, as long as we are prompted to use emotion concepts to identify them. Such triggering is due to the fact that certain low-level perceptual features share with core affect a dimensional space, which is plausibly structured along the dimensions of dynamism and value, mirroring the dimensions of arousal and pleasantness. The perceptual grasping of these properties as what may alter core affect allows for the intervention of those concepts that are paradigmatically used for self-ascriptions of affective states. However, in such cases, those concepts are used with their secondary meaning.

One may rightly argue that this proposal reintroduces isomorphism as long as core affect and the corresponding affective qualities share, so to speak, a common location on a map. The affective quality of a lively shade of orange would occupy a location on the dimensional space of affective qualities based on its capacity to trigger a modification of core affect. Such a modification would occupy the corresponding location on the dimensional space defined by arousal and pleasantness. Nevertheless, I am sceptical about the idea that a recognitional experience of this sort can be justified in terms of resemblances or isomorphism. This is why Peacocke's intuition about the minor chord as being subdued obtains only to a limited extent. True, being "subdued" is a relational property that the minor chord shares with certain felt emotions, but in order for this resemblance to justify the ascription of sadness rather than of, say, lowness, something more must be said.

Peacocke is right in thinking that the kind of knowledge that is required concerns felt emotions, but he does not put forward any account of the way in which such a knowledge applies. If we take core affect seriously and we pair it with secondary meaning as that which explains conceptual interventions, then we can get rid of resemblances, since what we actually recognise when we ascribe affective qualities to simple perceptual features is their aptness to fall under a certain concept. The coupling of affective qualities with possible corresponding modifications in core affect is not a recognisable resemblance, but rather the underlying mechanism that triggers such a conceptual application. Importantly, however, the mechanism is not an arousalistic one, that is, it does not actually elicit the feeling component of emotions (the actual modification of core affect and the entailed phenomenology), but it can admittedly consist of a "cold" perceptual appraisal of worldly features, dispositionally connected to such a component.

This hypothesis is highly speculative. However, one can empirically test the affective resonances of certain low-level features, that is, the commonality and differences of reactions among subjects in front of colours, simple shapes, and chords. This has been done, for instance, for the minor third, showing that "The Minor Third Communicates Sadness in Speech, Mirroring Its Use in Music" (Curtis and Bharucha 2010). The title of this article serves as a prelude to an interesting approach. In short, the authors tested the hypothesis that vocal expressions of negative emotions and the minor third share some audible structure, and found that the relationship between the salient pitches of the sad speech samples tended to approximate a minor third. What is especially interesting about this study is that the authors do not imply the priority of vocal expression over musical expression. Instead, they vindicate the plausibility of both an evolutionary and developmental perspective according to which:

> a communicative system comprising acoustic elements common to both language and music was an evolutionary predecessor to language and music and that the two domains evolved divergently from this common origin.[66]   (Curtis and Bharucha 2010, p. 347)

Although I find it especially fascinating, I will not commit to this view, nor am I in the position to evaluate the reliability of the experimental results provided by Meagan Curtis and Jamshed Bharucha.[67] Rather, I retain of their proposal the idea

---

66 Steven Brown calls this hypothesis the "musilanguage", according to which "the many structural features shared between music and language are the result of their emergence from a joint evolutionary precursor rather than from fortuitous parallelism or from one function begetting the other" (Brown 2000, p. 271). However, the main interest of Brown's view concerns the compositional and syntactic nature of both music and language, rather than their emotional value.

67 Although he has overtly criticized contemporary attempts to address the cross-cultural nature of musical expressiveness, Stephen Davies pleads in favour of a psychological research endeavour to establish the extent to which (at least some) musical features are perceived as

that the progressive refinement of discriminatory capacities for emotions and for expressive qualities, may rely on low-level features that lend themselves to be conceptually integrated without requiring the detection of similarities to behavioural expressions. This can be stressed to the extent that musical and vocal features share the very same affective and perceptual components.[68]

With respect to the visual field, psychologists and psycholinguists have elaborated on the possibility that very simple shapes and colours convey expressive characters that are cross-culturally captured by emotion words. Relying on Charles Osgood's differential scale model (Osgood et al. 1957), for instance, Takahashi (1995) and Stamatopoulou (2008) show that there is cross-cultural matching in the ascription of certain emotional values to non-representational, extremely simple drawings. Analogously, Adams and Osgood (1973) insist on the cross-cultural tendency to ascribe affective values to colours.[69]

Admittedly, these results are far from conclusive and I cannot take them to corroborate my view. Yet, they are compatible with what I am suggesting about core affect. Namely, they provide minimal ground to insist on the viability of treating low-level perceptual features according to a dimensional scale where they occupy a place depending on their degree of dynamism and of valence. Moreover, they are consistent with the view that occupying similar positions on such dimensional fields does not entail that the recognition of low-level expressive features entails the identification of resemblances. Rather, certain low-level features are originally experienced as expressive, that is, as affectively loaded, in virtue of their perceptual structure. Such a structure is what I have tentatively described as *rythmos*, i.e. a gestalt-like cross-modal structure that can be located along the vectors of dynamism-stasis and of potentially positive–negative valence.

Arguably, recognitional expressive experiences of this kind are less fine-grained than expressive experiences of the kind relying on perceptual resemblances. It is limited to simple features and to their vague affective load. The isolated minor chord can be perceived as having a negative dynamic value, but

---

expressive across different cultures. Such a research, however, should be carried out along the lines drawn by philosophers (Davies 2011).

[68] María José Alcaraz León has argued for an analogous view for music in a Wittgensteinian vein, namely that expressive qualities "should not be understood as being strongly dependent on our prior grasp of ordinary expression – be it linguistic or behavioural – but as contributing to our more expanded expressive repertoire" (Alcaraz León 2013, p. 282).

[69] A similar experimental interest in the affective value of colours and lines can be found in much earlier studies such as Lundholm (1921), Poffenberger and Barrows (1924), Hevner (1935b), Wexner (1954), Murray and Deabler (1957), Wright & Rainwater (1962).

it is hardly experienced as "dramatic" or "desperate" – as a musical gesture can be. Nevertheless, this kind of low-level expressive property establishes – so to speak – the lower constraint of expressive ascriptions. More clearly, it is such that the same perceptual feature is hardly experienced both as positive *and* negative, static *and* dynamic – at least in ideal conditions where it appears isolated from the context. Black will hardly be perceived as lively, orange will hardly be perceived as sad.[70] Descriptions of this sort of expressive experience are not metaphorical in the sense that they rely on the detection of similarities. Rather, they are described in terms of secondary meanings that are plausibly rooted in the way in which humans tend to experience simple patterns of visual and auditory features as being *inherently* affectively loaded.

5.6 Expressive Experience Without Concepts?

I hope the argument presented so far succeeded in showing that in expressive experience of simple features: (i) emotion concepts turn merely perceptual experiences into recognitional expressive experiences; and (ii) this recognitional process is not mobilised by resemblances to which concepts apply metaphorically, but rather is grounded in core affect and compatible with secondary uses of concepts. The last step of this proposal assesses the possibility that we experience expressive properties without possessing – or without using – the relevant emotion concepts to identify them.

As anticipated, we should recall Budd's claim that not every perception is also a recognition. The intuition is that, in order for a subject to undergo an expressive experience there might be no need for conceptual intervention, not even in the form of weak cognitive penetration. Although we happen to conceptually categorise a shade of colour in terms of its affective character, the recognitional experience that I have accounted for in terms of cognitive penetrability of the phenomenal character does not seem to exhaust expressive experience.

For this purpose, it is first useful to refer once more to the theory of expression recognition that I have already explored in the previous chapter. As we

---

[70] These tendencies revealed by psychological inquiries are of the kind of the notorious *takete–maluma* effect introduced by Wolfgang Köhler (1929). As is well known, most people associate the word "takete" with a jagged shape and the word "maluma" with a more rounded shape. Importantly, it is not impossible that someone could ascribe the labels the other way round. Analogously, I would say, it is not *impossible* that someone experiences a minor chord as gay and a major chord as sad. Yet, there is a relevant tendency to describe minor chords as sad and major chords as gay.

have seen, Marchi and Newen claim that conceptual intervention takes place as long as the perceptual stimulus is not clearly expressive *per se*. Indeed, they consider ambiguous facial displays, taking cognitive penetration to determine the phenomenal character of their recognitional (meaning discriminatory) perception. Yet, they do not deny that perceptual patterns displayed by faces are already expressive of (vague or ambiguous) emotions *before* or *in the absence* of conceptual intervention.

Block (2014) is more radical. He argues – and shows evidence for the fact – that even the recognition of ambiguous expressions is fundamentally perceptual and does not require that one possesses particular conceptual abilities. This implies that, according to both views, there exists a level of expression perception and recognition that does not require concepts of emotions. In passing, this is especially compatible with the idea that expressions of emotions need be processed quickly for evolutionary reasons and invites us to consider the mechanism of expression recognition as preceding high-level cognitive interventions.

Following the idea that low-level features can be experienced as being minimally expressive without conceptual interventions, correlations have been observed between the attribution of intensity to (stereotyped) facial expressions and the co-instantiation of very low-level perceptual features such as inclination, simple geometric figures, and speed (Kamachi *et al.* 2001; Pavlova *et al.* 2005). Moreover, findings about inner structures that allow young children to perceive objects, fruitfully enhances this view (Spelke 1995, 2000, 2007). In her theory of "core knowledge", Elizabeth Spelke claims that we are equipped from a very early age so as to perceptually discriminate object boundaries, cohesion of shapes, intentional or self-propelled movements, that is, to discriminate perceptual dynamic features all around our environment.[71] If this were the case, then it may well be that perception of simple features as affectively loaded were linked to this sort of primitive discriminatory devices that we use to navigate the environment.

In addition, just to mention a widely cited study concerning discriminatory capacities of very young children for low-level features of music, Perani *et al.* (2010) used functional magnetic resonance imaging to measure brain activity in 1-to-3-day-old newborns hearing excerpts of Western tonal music and altered versions of the same excerpts. They provided evidence that the infant brain has a hemispheric specialisation for processing music that are already functional in

---

[71] To do justice to Spelke's view, I must mention that she interprets her data as showing that infants possess the innate concept of object (conceived in terms of core knowledge). However, it has been argued that these data fit better with a perceptualist interpretation, rather than with a conceptualist one (Smortchkova 2017).

the first postnatal hours. They concluded that the neural architecture underlying music processing in newborns is sensitive to changes in tonal key and also to differences in consonance and dissonance.

I argued that the properties instantiated by the content of expressive experiences are dynamic low-level features, nicely captured by the phenomenological notion of *rythmos*. Far from being conclusive, these empirical results seem at least compatible with the claim that low-level dynamic features (in particular those of music) are discriminated from a very early age when conceptual abilities plausibly lack. These same features are among those that constitute the content of expressive experience.

Certain low-level perceptual properties could consistently be experienced as expressive without the subject possessing emotion concepts. Rather, what could be required are elementary discriminatory capacities for core affect on the one hand and for low-level perceptual properties (such as consonance and dissonance) on the other. The resulting perceptual processes would amount to the possibility of *feeling* those modifications that environmental stimuli can have on our wellbeing in terms of pleasure and arousal, and to the capacity of *perceiving* properties in terms of their intrinsically dynamic structure. Neither of these capacities requires concepts. The content of this expressive experience is accordingly non-conceptual and its phenomenal character is not influenced by high-level cognitive interventions. However, it fixes the lower limit for enhanced, more fine-grained expressive experiences. In short: it limits response-dependence of expressive experiences, imposing some minimal constraints on it.

This last stage of my proposal is aimed at showing that we can undergo expressive experience without mobilising conceptual capacities. This is especially clear when simple perceptual features such as sounds and colours are involved. Cognitive interventions can modify the phenomenal character of these sorts of experiences, so that they become recognitional. However, even if we lack conceptual abilities we may perceive minor chords as sad and orange shades as lively. This is plausibly what happens to very young children presented with simple stimuli.

Moreover, one can think that the same holds for more complex patterns, such as musical gestures. Experiencing a sad musical gesture is not necessarily a recognitional experience – as Budd has repeatedly claimed – but can occasionally amount to perception of low-level dynamic properties. These can be conceived as gestalten that bear a relation to core affect, namely share the same dimensional space. If this were true, the appeal to conceptual subsumption based on resemblance would hold only for recognitional cases, whereas expressive experience of patterns would be possible even in the absence of conceptual recognitional abilities.[72]

If duly developed and supported by further evidences, this view would manage to do justice both to the idea that expressive experience is a perceptual experience whose content can in principle justify expressive ascriptions, and to the view that it relates in an interesting way to our affective life. Moreover, it is liberal enough to include a wide range of complex conceptually and culturally related ascriptions, and compatible enough with many psychological views about emotions and perceptions. What I take low-level perceptual properties to do, is limit the ways in which the same pattern can be perceived as being expressive. These properties can be simply perceived in the aforementioned way, or even categorised and related to one's background knowledge about emotions, expressions, and – especially in aesthetic experiences – art and creative techniques. The same account might extend to more complex patterns that, in the present inquiry, have been assessed only limited to their recognitional version, shaped by concepts. An adequate exploration of this possibility requires a more systematic empirical assessment that hopefully will be the subject of future research.

---

[72] Inquiries about autistic spectrum disorders seem to support the idea that affective sensitivity to musical patterns is not relevantly different in autistic children compared with non-autistic children (Heaton *et al.* 1999). Rather, differences emerge when it comes to ascribing musical affective value, that is, to conceptualize it (Goerlich *et al.* 2011; Allen *et al.* 2013). It is worth noting that studies conducted by substituting linguistic labels with stereotypical facial expressions showed that young (Giomo 1993) and autistic children (Heaton *et al.* 1999) perform equally well when making affective ascriptions to music. This suggests that conceptual inability does not *per se* prevent from experiencing the affective value of things.

Conclusions

The fundamental aims of this research were to cast some light on the debate about expressive experience and to provide an outline for a satisfactory philosophical approach to this phenomenon. As to the first aim, I hope that I succeeded by showing how the analytic debate has produced misunderstandings and disagreements that can nevertheless be smoothed out, such as regard the kind of phenomenology of expressive experience that is worth taking into account. Also, the scrutiny of various claims about the content and kind of properties mobilised by expressive experience should have presented a philosophically intriguing – though also messy – landscape.

Among the range of available solutions for the questions raised by expressive experience, I have endorsed a perceptualist account from the beginning of this inquiry. Nevertheless, I tried to concede as much as possible to alternative theories, highlighting their merits. In particular, I exploited Sartre's phenomenological theory of emotions in order to focus the attention on the perceptual appearance of inanimate objects; then I acknowledged that projectivism *à la* Wollheim has the advantage of discriminating between projection of occurrent emotions and more complex ones – those that are actually philosophically interesting. In the overall economy of this work, arousalism served mostly as a target, but was also useful for keeping in mind the importance of emotions, whose role in expressive experience cannot be easily discarded – as formalist approaches tend to do. Moreover, I devoted much room to the discussion of imaginativist theories, for I find them particularly appealing, especially when they rely on sensuous imagination.

In point of fact, my account is, for the most part, a compatibilist account. Indeed, it stands by perceptualism, taking the phenomenal character of expressive experience to be perceptual, and its content to be constituted by low-level dynamic properties. Yet, it also allows for cognitive interventions that make the resulting experience partly response-dependent. In so doing, the account opens the door to top-down contributions from imagination, both sensuous and propositional. So conceived, expressive experience can be enriched and integrated.

Furthermore, this account distinguishes between cases of recognition and cases of simple perception, especially when isomorphism between perceptual patterns and human expression is not available. Although I conceded that even in these latter cases, cognitive penetration is responsible for recognitional experiences, I preserved the non-conceptual nature of elementary expressive experiences by endorsing emotion constructivism based on core affect. On this basis, I am able to suggest that expressive experience at its basic level is rooted in our core affect dimensional system.

Finally, the hypothesis that cognitive intervention is not required in order to undergo the expressive experience of the minor chord extends to the previously discussed case of the musical gesture, where expressive experience was meant to rely on resemblances. I envisage the possibility that, even in these cases, it is possible to undergo expressive experience in the absence of recognitional capacities, simply owing to the dynamic patterns mobilised by the content and perceived as occupying a position in the dimensional space provided by core affect.

References

Adams, Francis M./Osgood, Charles E. (1973): "A cross-cultural study of the affective meaning of color". In: *Journal of Cross-Cultural Psychology* 4/2, pp. 135–157.
Alcaraz-León, María José (2013): "Ordinary expression and musical expressiveness". In: *Aisthesis* 3, pp. 267–284.
Allen, Rory/Davis Rob/Hill, Elisabeth (2013): "The effects of autism and alexithymia on physiological and verbal responsiveness to music". In: *Journal of Autism and Developmental Disorders* 43/2, pp. 432–44.
Arnheim, Rudolf (1974): *Art and Visual Perception: A Psychology of the Creative Eye*. Berkeley: University of California Press.
Barlassina, Luca/Newen, Albert (2014): "The role of bodily perception in emotion: In defense of an impure somatic theory". In: *Philosophy and Phenomenological Research* 89, pp. 637–678.
Baron-Cohen, Simon (2005): "The empathizing system: A revision of the 1994 model of the mindreading system". In: Ellis, Bruce/Bjorklund, David (Eds.) *Origins of the Social Mind: Evolutionary Psychology and Child Development*. New York: The Guilford Press, pp. 468–492.
Barrett, Lisa Feldman (2013): "Psychological construction: A Darwinian approach to the science of emotion". In: *Emotion Review* 5, pp. 379–389.
Barrett, Lisa Feldman/Russell, James A. (2015): *The Psychological Construction of Emotions*. New York: The Guilford Press.
Barrett, Lisa Feldman/Wilson-Mendenhall, Christine/Barsalou, Lawrence (2015): "The conceptual act theory: A roadmap". In: Barrett, Lisa Feldman/Russell, James A. (Eds.) *The Psychological Construction of Emotions*. New York: The Guilford Press, pp. 83–110.
Barwell, Ismay (1986): "How does art express emotion?". In: *Journal of Aesthetics and Art Criticism* 45/2, pp. 175–181.
Bavelas, Janet/Black, Alex/Lemery, Charles/Mullett, Jennifer (1987): "Motor mimicry as primitive empathy". In: Eisenberg, Nancy/Strayer, Janet (Eds.) *Empathy and Its Development*. Cambridge: Cambridge University Press, pp. 317–338.
Benenti, Marta/Fazzuoli, Giovanna (2018): "Experiencing the making. Paintings by Paolo Cotani, Marcia Hafif and Robert Ryman". In: *Proceedings of the European Society for Aesthetics* 10, pp. 35–54.
Benenti, Marta/Meini, Cristina (2017): "The recognition of emotions in music and landscapes: Extending contour theory". In: *Philosophia* 46/3, pp. 647–664.
Bensafi, Moustafa/Tillmann, Barbara/Poncelet, Johan/Przybylski, Laurianne/Rouby, Catherine (2013): "Olfactory and gustatory mental imagery: Modulation by sensory experience and comparison to auditory mental imagery". In: Lacey Simon/Lawson Rebecca (Eds.) *Multisensory Imagery*. New York: Springer, pp. 77–91.
Black, Max (1954): "Metaphor". In: *Proceedings of the Aristotelian Society, New Series* 55, pp. 273–294.
Block, Ned (2014): "Seeing-as in the light of vision science". In: *Philosophy and Phenomenological Research*, 89/3, pp. 560–572.
Boghossian, Paul/Velleman, David (1989): "Colour as a secondary quality". In: *Mind* 98, pp. 81–103.

Boghossian, Paul (2007): "Explaining musical experience". In: Stock, Kathleen (Ed.) *Philosophers on Music. Experience, Meaning, and Work*. Oxford University Press, pp. 117–129.
Boghossian, Paul (2010): "The perception of music: Comments on Peacocke". In: *British Journal of Aesthetics* 50/1, pp. 71–76.
Böhme, Gernot (1995): *Atmosphäre. Essays zur neuen Ästhetik*. Frankfurt a. M.: Suhrkamp.
Bozzi, Paolo (1990): *Fisica ingenua*. Milano: Garzanti.
Briscoe, Robert (2011): "Mental imagery and the varieties of amodal perception". In: *Pacific Philosophical Quarterly* 92/2, pp. 153–173.
Brown, Steven (2000): "The 'musilanguage' model of musical evolution". In: Wallin, Nils/Merker, Björn/Brown, Steven (Eds.) *The origins of music*. Cambridge (MA): The MIT Press, pp. 271–300.
Budd, Malcolm (1985). *Music and The Emotions. The Philosophical Theories*. London: Routledge.
Budd, Malcolm (1995): *Values of Art*, London: Allen Lane.
Budd, Malcolm (2008): *Aesthetic Essays*. Oxford: Oxford University Press.
Budd, Malcolm (2009): "Response to Christopher Peacocke's 'The perception of music: Sources of significance'". In: *British Journal of Aesthetics* 49/3, pp. 289–292.
Burge, Tyler (2010): *Origins of Objectivity*. Oxford: Clarendon Press.
Calabi, Clotilde (2014): "The blurred hen". In: Reboul, Anne (Ed.) *Mind, Values, and Metaphysics. Philosophical Essays in Honor of Kevin Mulligan*. Springer International, pp. 209–220.
Carroll, James M./Russell, James A. (1996): "Do facial expressions signal specific emotions? Judging emotion from the face in context". In: *Journal of Personality and Social Psychology* 70/2, pp. 205–218.
Casati, Roberto/Pignocchi, Alessandro (2007): "Mirror and canonical neurons are not constitutive of aesthetic response". In: *Trends in the Cognitive Sciences* 11/10. DOI: https://doi.org/10.1016/j.tics.2007.07.007.
Céspedes-Guevara, Julian/Eerola, Tuomas (2018): "Music communicates affects, not basic emotions – A constructionist account of attribution of emotional meanings to music". In: *Frontiers in Psychology* 9, 215. DOI: https://doi.org/10.3389/fpsyg.2018.00215.
Cochrane, Tom (2008): "Expression and extended cognition". In: *The Journal of Aesthetics and Art Criticism* 66/4, pp. 329–340.
Cochrane, Tom (2010): "Using the persona to express complex emotions in music". In: *Music Analysis*, 29/1–3, pp. 264–275.
Collingwood, Roger G. (1938): *The Principles of Art*. Oxford: Clarendon Press.
Cross Ian/Morley Iain (2009): "The evolution of music: theories, definitions and the nature of evidence". In: Malloch, Stephen/Trevarthen, Colwyn (Eds.) *Communicative musicality: Exploring the basis of human companionship*. Oxford: Oxford University Press, pp. 61–81.
Currie, Gregory (2011): "Empathy for objects". In: Coplan, Amy/Goldie, Peter (Eds.) *Empathy: Philosophical and Psychological Perspectives*. Oxford: Oxford University Press, pp. 82–95.
Curtis, Meagan E./Bharucha, Jamshed J. (2010) "Minor third communicates sadness in speech mirroring its use in music". In: *Emotions* 10/3, pp. 335–348.
Cutting, James E. (2002): "Representing motion in a static image: constraints and parallels in art, science, and popular culture". In: *Perception* 31, pp. 1165–1193.

Damasio, Antonio R. (2000): *The Feeling of What Happens: Body and Emotion in the Making of Consciousness*. New York: Hartcourt Brace.
Darwin, Charles (1871): *The Descent of Man, and Selection in Relation to Sex*. London: John Murray.
Davidson, Donald (1978): "What metaphors mean". In: *Critical Inquiry* 5/1, pp. 31–47.
Davies, Stephen (1994): *Musical Meaning and Expression*. Ithaca (NY): Cornell University Press.
Davies, Stephen (1997): "Contra the hypothetical persona in music". In: Hjort, Mette/Laver, Sue (Eds.) *Emotion and the Arts*. Oxford: Oxford University Press, pp. 95–109.
Davies, Stephen (2005): *Themes in the Philosophy of Music*. New York: Oxford University Press.
Davies, Stephen (2010): "Emotions expressed and aroused by music: Philosophical perspectives". In: Juslin, Patrik/Sloboda, John (Eds.) *Oxford Handbook of Music and Emotion: Theory, Research, Applications, II edition*. New York: Oxford University Press, pp. 15–43.
Davies, Stephen (2011): "Cross-cultural musical expressiveness: theory and the empirical programme". In: Schellekens, Elisabeth/Goldie, Pieter (Eds.) *The Aesthetic Mind: Philosophy and Psychology*. Oxford: Oxford University Press, pp. 376–388.
De Clercq, Rafael (2008): "The structure of aestehtic properties". In: *Philosophy Compass* 3/5, pp. 894–909.
De Sousa, Ronald (1987): *The Rationality of Emotion*. Cambridge (MA): The MIT Press.
Dennett, Daniel (1987): *The Intentional Stance*. Cambridge (MA): The MIT Press.
Deonna, Julien/Teroni, Fabrice (2012): *The Emotions. A Philosophical Introduction*. London and New York: Routledge.
Dewey, John (1934): *Art as Experience*. New York: Minton, Balch & Co.
Diamond, Cora (1967): "Secondary sense". In: *Proceedings of the Aristotelian Society*, New Series, 67, pp. 189–208.
Dorsch, Fabian (2012): *The Unity of Imagining*. Berlin: De Gruyter.
Dorsch, Fabian (2016): "Seeing-in as aspect perception". In: Kemp, Gary/Mras, Gabriele (Eds.) *Wollheim, Wittgenstein, and Pictorial Representation*. London: Routledge, pp. 205–238.
Drake, Carolyn/Penel, Amandine/Bigand, Emmanuel (2000): "Tapping in time with mechanically and expressively performed music". In: *Music Perception: An Interdisciplinary Journal* 18/1, pp. 1–23.
Ducasse, Curt (1944): *Art, the Critics, and You*. New York: Oskar Piest.
Ekman, Paul (1972): "Universal and cultural differences in facial expression of emotion". In: Cole, James (Ed.) *Nebraska Symposium on Motivation 19*, Lincoln: Lincoln University of Nebraska Press, pp. 207–82.
Ekman, Paul (1992): "Are there basic emotions?". In: *Psychological Review* 99/3, pp. 550–553.
Ellsworth, Phoebe C. (2013): "Appraisal theory: Old and new questions". In: *Emotion Review* 5, pp. 125–131.
Ernst, Marc. O., & Bülthoff, Heinrich H. (2004): "Merging the senses into a robust percept". In: *Trends in Cognitive Sciences*, 8/4, pp. 162–169.
Fazekas, Peter/Nanay, Bence (2017): "Pre-cueing effects: Attention or mental imagery?" In *Frontiers in Psychology* 8, 10.3389/fpsyg.2017.00222.
Fodor, Jerry (1983): *The Modularity of Mind*. Cambridge (MA): The MIT Press.

Fodor, Jerry (2007): "The revenge of the given". In: McLaughlin Brian P./Cohen, Jonathan (Eds.) *Contemporary Debates in Philosophy of Mind*. Oxford: Blackwell, pp. 105–117.

Fodor, Jerry (2015): "Burge on perception". In: Margolis Eric/Laurence Stephen (Eds.) *The Conceptual Mind: New Directions in the Study of Concepts*. Cambridge, MA: The MIT Press, pp. 203–222.

Forlè, Francesca (2016): "Movement in music. An enactive account of the dynamic qualities of music". In: *Humana.Mente Journal of Philosophical Studies* 31, pp.169–185.

Freedberg, David/Gallese Vittorio (2007): "Motion, emotion and empathy in esthetic experience". In: *Trends in the Cognitive Sciences* 11/5, pp. 197–203.

Frijda, Nico H. (2007): *The Laws of Emotion*. Mahwah (N.J.): Erlbaum.

Gallagher, Shaun. (2008): "Direct perception in the intersubjective context". In: *Consciousness and Cognition* 17/2, pp. 535–543.

Gardner, Sebastian (1993): *Irrationality and the Philosophy of Psychoanalysis*. Cambridge: Cambridge University Press.

Gauker, Christopher (2017): "Three kinds of nonconceptual seeing-as". In: *Review of Philosophy and Psychology* 8/4, pp. 763–779.

Geiger, Moritz (1911/2015): "On the essence and meaning of empathy". In: *Dialogues in Philosophy, Mental and Neuro Sciences* 8, pp. 19–31/75–86.

Gendler, Tamar (2018): "Imagination". In: Zalta, Edward N. (Ed.) *Stanford Encyclopedia of Philosophy*.

Gibson, James J. (1979): *An Ecological Approach to Visual Perception*. Boston: Houghton Mifflin.

Giomo, Carla J. (1993): "Experimental study of children's sensitivity to mood in music". In: *Psychology of Music* 21/2, pp. 141–162.

Goerlich, Katharina S./Witteman, Jurriaan/Aleman, André/Martens, Sander (2011): "Hearing feelings: affective categorization of music and speech in alexithymia, an ERP study". In: *PloS One* 6/5, e19501. DOI: https://doi.org/10.1371/journal.pone.0019501.

Goldman, Alvin I. (2006): *Simulating Minds: The Philosophy, Psychology, and Neuroscience of Mindreading*. Oxford: Oxford University Press.

Gombrich, Ernst H. (1960): *Art and Illusion. A Study in the Psychology of Pictorial Representation*. London: Phaidon.

Goodman, Nelson (1968): *Languages of Art. An Approach to a Theory of Symbols*. Indianapolis: The Bobbs-Merril Company.

Griffero, Tonino (2010): *Atmosferologia. Estetica degli spazi emozionali*. Roma-Bari: Laterza.

Griffero, Tonino (2013): *Quasi-cose. La realtà dei sentimenti*. Milano: Bruno Mondadori.

Gross, Steven (2017): "Cognitive Penetration and Attention". In: *Frontiers in Cognitive Sciences* 8, 221. DOI: https://doi.org/10.3389/fpsyg.2017.00221.

Heal, Jane (1986): "Replication and functionalism". In: Butterfield, Jeremy (Ed.) *Language, Mind and Logic*. Cambridge: Cambridge University Press.

Heaton, Pamela/Hermelin, Beate/Pring, Linda (1999): "Can children with autistic spectrum disorders perceive affect in music? An experimental investigation". In: *Psychological Medicine* 29, pp.1405–1410.

Hevner, Kate (1935a): "Expression in music: a discussion of experimental studies and theories". *Psychological Review* 42/2, pp. 186–204.

Hevner, Kate (1935b): "Experimental studies of the affective value of colors and lines". *Journal of Applied Psychology* 19/4, pp. 385–398.

Ichikawa, Jonathan J. (2009): "Dreaming and Imagination". In: *Mind & Language* 24, pp. 103–121.
Izard, Carroll E./Ackerman, Brian P./Schoff, Kristen. M./Fine Sarah E. (2000): "Self-organization of discrete emotions, emotion patterns, and emotion-cognition relations". In: Lewis, Marc E./Granic Isabela (Eds.) *Emotion, Development, and Self-Organization: Dynamic Systems Approaches to Emotional Development*. New York: Cambridge University Press, pp. 15–36.
Jacob, Pierre (2011): "The direct-perception model of empathy: a critique". In: *Review of Philosophy and Psychology* 2/3, pp. 519–540.
Jagnow, René (2011): "Ambiguous figures and the spatial contents of perceptual experience: a defense of representationalism". In: *Phenomenology and the Cognitive Sciences* 10, pp. 325–346.
James, William (1884): "What is an Emotion?". In: *Mind* 9, pp. 188–205.
James, William (1890): *The Principles of Psychology*. New York: Dover.
Juslin, Patrik N. (2000): "Cue utilization in communication of emotion in music performance: Relating performance to perception". In: *Journal of Experimental Psychology: Human Perception and Performance* 26, pp. 1797–1813.
Juslin, Patrik N./Laukka, Petri (2003): "Communication of emotion in vocal expression and music performance: Different channels, same code?". In: *Psychological Bulletin* 129/5, pp. 770–814.
Juslin, Patrik N./Timmers, Renee. (2010): "Expression and communication of emotion in music performance". In: Juslin, Patrik N./Sloboda John A. (Eds.) *Handbook of Music and Emotion, II edition*. Oxford University Press, New York, pp. 453–489.
Kandinsky, Wassily (1912/1977): *Concerning the Spiritual in Art*. New York: Dover Publications.
Kamachi, Miyuki/Bruce, Vicki/Mukaida, Shigeru/Gyoba, Jiro/Yoshikawa, Sakiko/Akamatsu, Shigeru (2001): "Dynamic properties influence the perception of facial expressions". In: *Perception* 30, pp. 875–887.
Kivy, Peter (1980): *The Corded Shell: Reflections on Musical Expression*. Princeton (N.J.): Princeton University Press.
Kivy, Peter (1989): *Sound Sentiment: An Essay on Musical Emotions*. Philadelphia: Temple University Press.
Kivy, Peter (1990): *Music Alone: Philosophical Reflections on the Purely Musical Experience*. Ithaca (NY): Cornell University Press.
Kivy, Peter (2002): *Introduction to a Philosophy of Music*. Oxford: Oxford University Press.
Koffka, Kurt (1935/2013): *Principles of Gestalt psychology*. London: Routledge & Kegan Paul.
Köhler, Wolfgang (1929). *Gestalt Psychology*. New York: Liveright.
Köhler, Wolfgang (1938): *The Place of Value in a World of Facts*. London: Kegan Paul, Trench, Trubner & Co.
Kriegel, Uriah (2002): "Phenomenal content". In: *Erkenntnis* 57, pp. 175–198.
Kringelbach, Morten L./Berridge, Kent C. (2015): "Brain mechanisms of pleasure: The core affect component of emotion". In: Barrett, Lisa Feldman/Russell, James A. (Eds.) *The Psychological Construction of Emotions*, New York: The Guilford Press, pp. 229–248.
Krueger, Joel (2009) "Enacting musical experience". In: *Journal of Consciousness Studies*, 16/2–3, pp. 98–123.
Krueger, Joel (2011): "Enacting musical content". In: Manzotti, Riccardo (Eds.) *Situated Aesthetics: Art beyond the Skin*. Exeter: Imprint Academic, pp. 63–85.

Krueger, Joel (2012): "Seeing mind in action". In *Phenomenology and the Cognitive Sciences* 11, pp. 149–173.
Lakoff, George/Johnson, Mark (1980): *Metaphors We Live By*. Chicago: University of Chicago Press.
Lazarus, Richard S. (1991): *Emotion and Adaptation*. New York: Oxford University Press.
Levinson, Jerrold (1996): "Musical expressiveness". In *The Pleasures of Aesthetics*. Ithaca (NY): Cornell University Press, pp. 90–126.
Levinson, Jerrold (2006): *Contemplating Art*. Oxford: Oxford University Press.
Levinson, Jerrold (2009): "The aesthetic appreciation of music". In: *British Journal of Aesthetics* 49/4, pp. 415–425.
Lindauer, Martin (2013): *The Expressiveness of Perceptual Experience*. Amsterdam: John Benjamins Publishing.
Lipps, Theodor (1903): *Grundlagen der Aesthetic*. Leipzig-Hamburg: Voss.
Loar, Brian (1990): "Phenomenal states". In: *Philosophical Perspectives* 4, pp. 81–108.
Lopes, Dominic (2005): *Sight and Sensibility: Evaluating Pictures*. Oxford: Oxford University Press.
Lundholm, Helge (1921): "The affective tone of lines: experimental researches". In: *Psychoogical Review* 28, pp. 43–60.
Lupyan, Gary (2017): "Objective effects of knowledge on visual perception". In: *Journal of Experimental Psychology: Human Perception and Performance* 43/4, pp. 794–806.
Lutz, Anika (2015): "The phenomenal character of emotional experience: A look at perception theory". In: *Dialectica* 69/3, pp. 313–334.
Macpherson, Fiona (2012): "Cognitive penetration of colour experience: Rethinking the issue in light of an indirect mechanism". In: *Philosophy and Phenomenological Research* 84, pp. 24–62.
Macpherson, Fiona (2015): "Cognitive penetration and nonconceptual content". In: Zeimbekis, John/Raftopoulos, Athanassios (Eds.) *The Cognitive Penetrability of Perception: New Philosophical Perspectives*. Oxford: Oxford University Press.
Macpherson, Fiona/Batty, Clare (2016): "Redefining illusion and hallucination in light of new cases". In: *Philosophical Issues*, 26/1, pp. 263–296.
Marchi Francesco/Newen, Albert (2015): "Cognitive penetrability and emotion recognition in human facial expression". In: *Frontiers in Psychology* 6, 828. DOI: https://doi.org/10.3389/fpsyg.2015.00828.
Marr, David (1982): *Vision. A Computational Investigation into the Human Representation and Processing of Visual Information*, San Francisco (CA): W.H. Freeman.
Martin, Michael G. F. (1992): "Perception, concepts, and memory". In: *The Philosophical Review*, 101/4, pp. 745–763.
Matravers, Derek (1998): *Art and Emotion*. Oxford: Oxford University Press.
Matravers, Derek (2007): "Musical expressiveness". In: *Philosophy Compass* 2/3, pp. 373–379.
Meltzoff, Andrew N./Gopnik, Alison (1993): "The role of imitation in understanding persons and developing a theory of mind". In: Baron-Cohen, Simon/Tager-Flusberg, Helen/Cohen, Donald J. (Eds.) *Understanding Other Minds. Perspectives from Autism*. Oxford: Oxford University Press, pp. 335–366.
Meltzoff, Andrew N./Moore, Keith (1977): "Imitation of facial and manual expressions by human neonates". In: *Science* 198, pp. 75–78.

Meltzoff, Andrew N./Moore, Keith (1983): "Newborn infants imitate adult facial gestures". In: *Child Development* 541, pp. 702–709.
Meltzoff, Andrew N./Moore, Keith (1989): "Imitation in newborn infants: exploring the range of gestures imitated and the underlying mechanism". In: *Developmental Psychology* 25, pp. 954–962.
Mendelovici, Angela (2014): "Pure intentionalism about moods and emotions". In: Kriegel, Uriah (Ed.) *Current Controversies in the Philosophy of Mind*. New York: Routledge, pp. 135–157.
Moriya, Jun (2018): "Visual mental imagery influences attentional guidance in a visual-search task". In: *Attention, Perception, & Psychophysics* 80, pp. 1127–1142.
Moors, Agnes/Ellsworth, Phoebe C./Scherer, Klaus R./Frijda, Nico H. (2013): "Appraisal theories of emotion: State of the art and future development". In: *Emotion Review* 5/2, pp. 119–124.
Murray, David C./Deabler, Herdis L. (1957): "Colors and mood-tones". In: *Journal of Applied Psychology* 41, pp. 279–183.
Nanay, Bence (2010): "Perception and imagination: amodal perception as mental imagery". In: *Philosophical Studies* 150, pp. 239–254.
Nanay, Bence (2015): "Perceptual content and the content of mental imagery". In: *Philosophical Studies* 172, pp. 1723–1736.
Nanay, Bence (2016a): "Imagination and perception". In: Kind, Amy (Ed.) *Routledge Handbook of Philosophy of Imagination*. London: Routledge, pp. 124–134.
Nanay, Bence (2016a): "Hallucination as mental imagery". In: *Journal of Consciousness Studies* 23/7–8, pp. 65–81.
Nanay, Bence (2017): "Pain and mental imagery". In: *The Monist* 100/4, pp. 485–500.
Newen, Albert/Welpinghus Anna/Juckel, Georg (2015): "Emotion recognition as pattern recognition. the relevance of perception". In: *Mind and Language* 30/2, pp. 187–208.
Noë, Alva (2004): *Action in Perception*. Cambridge, MA: The MIT Press.
Noordhof, Paul (2002): "Imagining objects and imagining experiences". In: *Mind and Language* 17/4, pp. 426–455.
Noordhof, Paul (2008): "Expressive perception as projective imagining". In: *Mind and Language* 23/3, pp. 329–358.
O'Shaughnessy, Brian (2012): "Seeing an aspect and seeing under an aspect". In: Ellis, Jonathan/Guevara, Daniel (Eds.) *Wittgenstein and the Philosophy of Mind*. Oxford: Oxford University Press, pp. 37–60.
Oldham, Guy/Campbell Murray/Greated, Clive (2001): "Harmonics". *Grove Music Online*. DOI: https://doi.org/10.1093/gmo/9781561592630.article.50023.
Osgood, Charles E./Suci, George/Tannenbaum, Percy (1957): *The Measurement of Meaning*. Urbana, (IL): University of Illinois Press.
Palmer, Stephen (1999): *Vision Science: From Photons to Phenomenology*. Cambridge (MA): The MIT Press.
Papoušek, Harmš (1996): "Musicality in infancy research: Biological and cultural origins of early musicality". In: Deliège, Irene/Sloboda, John A. (Eds.) *Musical beginnings*. Oxford: Oxford University Press, pp. 37–55.
Parovel, Giulia (2012): *Le qualità espressive*, Milano: Mimesis.
Parsons, Kathryn P. (1973): "Three concepts of clusters". In: *Phenomenological Research* 33/4, pp. 514–523.

Pavlova, Marina/Sokolov, Arseny A./Sokolov Alexander (2005): "Perceived dynamics of static images enables emotional attribution". In: *Perception* 34, pp. 1107–1116.
Peacocke, Christopher (1985): "Imagination, experience, and possibility: A Berkeleyan view defended". In: Foster, John/Robinson, Howard (Eds.) *Essays on Berkeley*. Oxford: Clarendon Press, pp. 19–35.
Peacocke, Christopher (1987): "Depiction". *Philosophical Review* 96/3, pp. 383–410.
Peacocke, Christopher (1992): *A Study of Concepts*. Cambridge (MA): The MIT Press.
Peacocke, Christopher (2009): "The perception of music: sources of significance". In: *British Journal of Aesthetics* 49/3, pp. 257–275.
Peacocke, Christopher (2010): "Music and experiencing metaphorically-as: Further delineation". In: *British Journal of Aesthetics* 50/2, pp. 189–191.
Perky, Cheves W. (1910): "An experimental study of imagination". In: *American Journal of Psychology* 21, pp. 422–452.
Perani, Daniela/Saccuman, Maria Cristina/Scifo, Paola/Spada, Danilo/Andreolli, Guido/Rovelli, Rosanna/Baldoli, Cristina/Koelsch, Stefan (2010): "Functional specializations for music processing in the human newborn brain". In: *Proceedings of the National Academy of Sciences of the United States of America* 107/10, pp. 4758–4763. DOI: https://doi.org/10.1073/pnas.0909074107.
Pérez Carreño, Francisca (2017): "La percezione espressiva della natura e dell'arte". In: Beneti Marta/Ravasio Matteo (Eds.) *Espressività. Un dibattito contemporaneo*. Milano: Mimesis.
Philips, H. Clare (2011). "Imagery and pain: The prevalence, characteristics, and potency of imagery associated with pain", *Behavioural and Cognitive Psychotherapy* 39/5, pp. 523–540.
Piana, Giovanni (1991): *Filosofia della musica*. Milano: Guerini e Associati.
Poffenberger Albert, Barrows B. (1924): "The feeling value of lines". In: *Journal of Applied Psychology* 8, pp. 187–205.
Pratt, Carroll (1931): *The Meaning of Music*. New York: McGraw-Hill.
Prinz, Jesse (2004): *Gut Reactions. A Perceptual Theory of Emotion*. Oxford: Oxford University Press.
Putnam, Hilary (1975): "The meaning of 'Meaning'". In: *Language, Mind and Knowledge* 7, pp. 131–193.
Pylyshyn, Zenon (1980): "Computation and cognition: Issues in the foundations of cognitive science". In: *Behavioral and Brain Sciences* 3, pp. 111–132.
Pylyshyn, Zenon (1984): *Computation and Cognition. Toward a Foundation for Cognitive Science*. Cambridge (MA): The MIT Press.
Pylyshyn, Zenon (1999): "Is vision continuous with cognition? The case for cognitive impenetrability of visual perception". In: *Behavioral and Brain Sciences* 22, pp. 341–365.
Raftopoulos, Athanassios (2011): "Ambiguous figures and representationalism". In: *Synthese* 181, pp. 489–514.
Ravasio, Matteo (2018): "On evolutionary explanations of musical expressiveness". In: *Evental Aesthetics* 7/1, pp.6–29.
Ridley, Aaron (1995): "Musical sympathies: the experience of expressive music". In: *The Journal of Aesthetics and Art Criticism* 53/1, pp. 49–57.
Robinson, Jenefer (2005): *Deeper than Reason. Emotion and its Role in Literature, Music and Art*. Oxford: Oxford University Press.

Robinson, Jenefer (2007): "Expression and expressiveness in art". In: *Postgraduate Journal of Aesthetics* 4/2, pp.19–41.
Roth, Phillip (1997 [2016]): *American Pastoral*. New York: Penguin Random House.
Richardson, Alan (1969): *Mental Imagery*. London: Routledge & Kegan Paul.
Roederer, Juan G. (1984). "The search for a survival value of music". In: *Music Perception*, 1/3, pp. 350–356.
Ruskin, John (1843): *Modern Painters*. New York: John Wiley and Sons.
Russell, James A. (2003): "Core affect and the psychological construction of emotion". In: *Psychological Review* 110, pp. 145–172.
Russell, James A. (2015): "My psychological constructionist perspective". In: Barrett, Lisa Feldman/Russell, James A. (Eds.) *The Psychological Construction of Emotions*, New York: The Guilford Press, pp. 183–208.
Russell, James A./Barrett, Lisa Feldman (1999): "Core affect, prototypical emotional episodes, and other things called emotion: Dissecting the elephant". In: *Journal of Personality and Social Psychology*, 76: 805–819.
Santayana, George (1905/2011): *The Life of Reason* (vol. I). New York: Charles Scribner's Sons.
Sartre, Jean Paul (1939/1993): *The Emotions. Outline of a Theory*. New York: Carol Publishing.
Scherer, Klaus R. (2004): "Feelings integrate the central representation of appraisal-driven response organization in emotion". In: Manstead, Antony S. R./Frijda, Nico H./Fischer, Agneta H. (Eds.) *Feelings and Emotions: The Amsterdam Symposium*. Cambridge, UK: Cambridge University Press, pp. 136–157.
Scherer, Klaus R. (2009): "The dynamic architecture of emotion: Evidence for the component process model". In: *Cognition and Emotion* 23/7, pp. 1307–1351.
Schmidt, Timo T./Felix Blankenburg (2019): "The somatotopy of mental tactile imagery". In: *Frontiers in Human Neuroscience* 13/10. doi:10.3389/fnhum.2019.00010.
Schmitz, Hermann (2014): *Atmosphären*. Freiburg-München: Alber.
Schiavio, Andrea/van der Schyff, Dylan/Céspedes-Guevara, Julian/Reybrouck, Mark (2017): "Enacting musical emotions. Sense-making, dynamic systems, and the embodied mind". In: *Phenomenology and the Cognitive Sciences* 16/5, pp. 785–809.
Scruton, Roger (1997): *The Aesthetics of Music*. Oxford: Oxford University Press.
Scruton, Roger (1998): *Art and Imagination: A Study in the Philosophy of Mind*. South Bend (IN): St. Augustine's Press.
Sibley, Frank (2001): *Approach to Aesthetics: Collected Papers on Philosophical Aesthetics*. Oxford: Oxford University Press.
Siegel, Susanna (2010): *The Contents of Visual Experience*. Oxford: Oxford University Press.
Simmel, Georg (1913/2007): "Philosophy of landscape". In: *Theory, Culture, and Society* 24/7–8, pp. 20–29.
Smith, Craig A./Ellsworth, Phoebe C. (1985): "Patterns of cognitive appraisal in emotion". In: *Journal of Personality and Social Psychology* 48, pp. 813–838.
Smortchkova, Joulia (2017): "Seeing emotions without mindreading them". In: *Phenomenology and the Cognitive Sciences* 16/3, pp. 525–543.
Solomon, Robert C. (2004): "Emotions, thoughts, and feelings. emotions as engagements with the world". In: Solomon, Robert C. (Ed.) *Thinking about Feeling*. Oxford: Oxford University Press, pp. 76–90.
Spelke, Elizabeth S./Phillips, Ann/Woodward, Amand L. (1995): "Infants' knowledge of object motion and human action". In: Sperber, Dan/Premack, David/Premack Ann

James (Eds.) *Causal cognition: A multidisciplinary debate*. Oxford: Clarendon Press, pp. 44–78.
Spelke, Elizabeth S. (2000): "Core knowledge". In: *American Psychologist* 55/11, pp. 1233–1243.
Spelke, Elizabeth S./Kinzler, Katherine D. (2007): "Core knowledge". In: *Developmental Science* 10, pp. 89–96.
Spinicci, Paolo (2017): "Fenomeni e manifestazioni espressive". In: Benenti, Marta/Ravasio, Matteo (Eds.) *Espressività. Un dibattito contemporaneo*. Milano: Mimesis.
Stamatopoulou, Despina (2008): "Perception of emotional expression in line-drawings created by artists". In: *Hellenic Journal of Psychology* 5, pp.17–46.
Stecker, Robert (1984): "Expression of emotion in (some of) the arts". In: *The Journal of Aesthetics and Art Criticism* 42/4, pp. 409–418.
Stefanucci, Jeanine K./Gagnon, Kyle T./Lessard, David A. (2011): "Follow your heart: Emotion adaptively influences perception". In: *Social and Personality Psychology Compass* 5/6, pp. 296–308.
Stokes, Dustin (2013): "Cognitive penetrability of perception". In: *Philosophy Compass* 8/7, pp. 646–663.
Stokes, Dustin (2014): "Cognitive penetration and the perception of art". In: *Dialectica* 68/1, pp.1–34.
Takahashi, Shigeko (1995): "Aesthetic properties of pictorial perception". In: *Psychological Review* 102/4, pp. 671–683.
Tormey, Alan (1971): *The Concept of Expression*. Princeton (N.J.): Princeton University Press.
Trehub, Sandra E./Hannon, Erin E./Schachner, Adena (2010): "Perspectives on music and affect in the early years". In: Juslin, Patrik N./Sloboda John A. (Eds.) *Handbook of Music and Emotion, II edition*. Oxford University Press, New York, pp. 645–668.
Trivedi, Saam (2001): "Expressiveness as a property of the music itself". In: *The Journal of Aesthetics and Art Criticism* 59, pp. 411–420.
Tye, Michael (1995): *Ten Problems of Consciousness. A Representational Theory of the Phenomenal Mind*, Cambridge (MA): The MIT Press.
Tye, Michael (2003): "Blurry image, double vision and other oddities: New problems for representationalism?". In: Smith, Quentin/Jokic, Aleksandar (Eds.) *Consciousness: New Philosophical Perspectives*. Oxford: Oxford University Press, pp. 7–32.
Umiltà, Alessandra M./Berchio, Cristina/Sestito, Mariateresa/Freedberg, David/Gallese, Vittorio (2012): "Abstract art and cortical motor activation: an EEG study". In: *Frontiers in Human Neuroscience* 6, 311.
Voltolini, Alberto (2013): "The content of a seeing-as experience". In: *Aisthesis* 6/1, pp. 215–237.
Voltolini, Alberto (2015): *A Syncretistic Theory of Depiction*. London: Palgrave Macmillan.
Von Ehrenfels, Christian (1890/1988): *On Gestalt Qualities*. In: Smith, Barry (Ed.) *Foundations of Gestalt Theory*. Munich and Vienna: Philosophia, pp. 82–117.
Walton, Kendall L. (1999): "Projectivism, empathy, and musical tension". In: *Philosophical Topics*. 26/1–2, pp. 407–440.
Walton, Kendall L. (2008): "Style and the products and processes of art". In *Marvellous Images*. Oxford: Oxford University Press.
Wexner, Lois B. (1954): "The degree to which colors (hues) are associated with mood-tones". In: *The Journal of Applied Psychology* 28/6, pp. 432–435.
Williams, Bernard (1973): *Problems of the Self*. Cambridge: Cambridge University Press.

Wittgenstein, Ludwig (1980): *Remarks on the Philosophy of Psychology*. Oxford: Blackwell.
Wittgenstein, Ludwig (1986): *Philosophical Investigations*. Oxford: Blackwell.
Wollheim, Richard (1986): "From voices to values: The growth o f moral sense". In *The Thread of Life*. Cambridge: Cambridge University Press, pp. 197–225.
Wollheim, Richard (1993): "Correspondence, projective properties, and expression". In *The Mind and Its Depths*. Harvard: Harvard University Press, pp. 144–158.
Wollheim, Richard (2003): "In defense of seeing-in". In: Hecht Heiko/Schwartz Robert/Atherton Margaret (Eds.) *Looking into Pictures*. Cambridge (MA): The MIT Press, pp. 3–15.
Wright, Benjamin/Rainwater, Lee (1962): "The meanings of color". In: *The Journal of General Psychology* 67/1, pp. 89–99.
Zahavi, Dan (2011): "Empathy and direct social perception: a phenomenological proposal". In: *Review of Philosophy and Psychology* 2/3, pp. 541–558.
Zangwill, Nick (2007): "Music, metaphor, and emotion". In: *The Journal of Aesthetics and Art Criticism* 65/4, pp. 391–400.
Zangwill, Nick (2011): "Music, essential metaphors and private language". In: *American Philosophical Quarterly* 48/1, pp. 1–16.
Zangwill, Nick. (2013): "Music, autism, and emotion". In: *Frontiers in Psychology* 4, pp. 1–3.
Zhok, Andrea (2012): *La realtà e i suoi sensi. La costituzione fenomenologica della percezione e l'orizzonte del naturalism*. Pisa: Edizioni ETS.

Index

Adams, Francis 166
Aesthetics
– Aesthetic ascriptions 119, 127–132, 138, 163
– Aesthetic descriptions 123, 127, 129, 150
– Aesthetic properties 63, 123, 124, 127, 131, 132, 151, 156
Affective features 15, 29, 35, 64, 141
Affective qualities 2, 10, 14, 158–162, 164–165
Affective states 1, 6, 7, 9, 11, 13–16, 18, 20, 21, 23–26, 29, 30, 32, 37, 46, 47, 51, 60, 63, 64, 66–68, 70, 90, 92, 94, 102, 105, 112, 141, 142, 149, 157, 159, 162, 164
Affective value 66, 112, 161, 166, 170
Affordances 2, 78
Albinoni, adagio 106
Alcaraz-León, María José 166
Allen, Rory 170
Ambiguous facial expressions 135, 136, 138
Ambiguous figures 109
Animated beings 7, 20, 47
Appearances 1, 4, 9, 11, 12, 14, 16, 20, 23, 25, 26, 29, 30, 33, 34, 36, 41, 42, 57, 74, 89, 101, 102, 112, 149, 150, 171
Appraisal 144–146, 157, 159, 160, 161, 165
Arnheim, Rudolf 2, 114, 115
Arousal
– Arousalism 4, 7, 31–37, 53, 56, 70, 71, 73, 78, 98, 160, 171
– Arousalistic theory, account, perspective 31
Artist 1, 9, 10, 16–19, 31, 75, 92, 93, 108, 114, 115, 118, 120, 127
Artistic creation 93, 108
Artworks 1, 8, 12, 16–19, 31, 41, 51, 58, 80, 83, 89, 90, 93–95, 120, 123, 124, 127, 155
Associations 29, 30, 66, 81, 82, 91, 92, 164
Atmosphere 1–3, 121
Attention
– Perceptual attention 61, 76, 106
– Spatial attention 133, 138
Awareness 24, 25, 71, 82, 129

Background knowledge 29, 67, 87, 91, 92, 94, 106, 108, 135, 136, 139, 159, 160, 170
Barlassina, Luca 68, 72
Baron-Cohen, Simon 134–135
Barrett Lisa, Feldman 144–146, 158
Baudelaire, Charles 26
Behavioural manifestations 43, 54, 136, 147
Beliefs 11–15, 24, 26, 31–35, 67, 101, 102, 107, 112, 121, 128, 133, 136, 145, 148, 157
Bensafi, Moustafa 106
"Black box" 96, 97, 99
Black, Max 125, 126
Block, Ned 135, 168
Bodily feelings 67–72
Boghossian, Paul 60, 97, 98, 129, 130
Böhme, Gernot 3
Bozzi, Paolo 2
Briscoe, Robert 106
Brown, Steven 135
Brute facts 27, 30, 95, 97
Budd, Malcolm 5, 28, 29, 33, 39, 40, 85, 90, 92, 93, 98, 99, 119, 120, 122, 129, 131, 132, 143, 150–155, 163, 167, 169
Burge, Tyler 107

Calabi, Clotilde 60
Casati, Roberto 80
causal relation, link 34, 95, 139
causal triggers 63, 85, 95–97, 100, 117, 129, 140
Céspedes-Guevara, Julian 159
Chords 5, 6, 39, 45, 51, 54, 62, 74, 81–83, 85, 101, 111, 112, 119, 122, 141–144, 156, 157, 160–167, 169, 172
– Minor chord 5, 6, 85, 101, 111, 112, 119, 142, 143, 156, 157, 161, 164, 166, 167, 169, 172
Cochrane, Tom 47, 78
Cognitive penetration
– Strong cognitive penetration 134
– Weak cognitive penetration 6, 136, 137, 141, 167

Collingwood, Robin George 16
Colours 1, 2, 5, 6, 7, 13, 15, 24, 31, 49, 50, 54, 56, 58, 59, 61–63, 69, 71, 80–82, 86, 92, 103, 112, 116–118, 121, 122, 124, 125, 129, 134, 141–143, 160, 162–167, 169
Complexity (of the phenomenology) 2, 5, 34, 55, 62, 74, 82, 83, 115
Concepts
– Cluster-concepts 6, 141, 144–150, 162
– Conceptual intervention 6, 108, 110, 111, 119, 122, 132, 135–137, 140, 141, 159, 161, 162, 165, 167, 168
– Conceptual knowledge 94, 119, 136, 137, 141
– Conceptual subsumption 111, 130, 169
– Emotion concepts 6, 66, 122, 123, 128, 129, 137–139, 141, 143–150, 156, 157, 161–164, 167, 169
– Recognitional concepts 92, 108, 110, 121, 122, 131
Consciousness 64, 71, 94, 96
Constructivism 145–147, 156, 157, 159, 162, 171
Content
– Conceptual content 108, 121, 130, 141
– Non-conceptual content 130, 141
– Perceptual content 45, 46, 106, 120, 121, 130, 138–140
– Representational 4, 59, 60, 85, 88, 89, 117, 129
– Thought content 28, 92
Contour theory 4, 5, 7, 38, 39, 41–44, 48, 53–57, 65, 66, 77, 78, 82, 90, 96, 99–101, 112, 134, 143
Contours 4, 5, 7, 38–44, 48, 53–57, 65, 66, 74, 77, 78, 81–83, 90, 96, 99–101, 111, 112, 134, 137, 143
Core affect 6, 141–172
Correspondence 25, 26, 28, 30, 91, 92, 104, 105, 116, 122, 123, 127, 130
Creative process 16, 51–53, 80, 88, 89–95, 139
Cross, Ian 43, 76
Curtis, Meagan 111, 165
Cutting, James 113, 114

Damasio, Antonio 71
Dance 41, 77, 80
Darwin, Charles 44
Davidson, Donald 131
Davies, Stephen 38–43, 55–56, 72–77, 101–102, 112–113, 117, 149, 165–166
Dennett, Daniel 135
Deonna, Julien 67–72
Determinacy 50, 107
Dewey, John 16
Diamond, Cora 155
Dorsch, Fabian 50, 58, 60, 62
Drake, Carolyn 76
Drug (counterargument) 33, 34, 99
Ducasse, Curt 16
Duck-rabbit 61, 62, 110
Duration 67, 75, 81
Dynamic properties 6, 112–118, 169, 171
Dynamism 6, 76–78, 112–115, 117, 118, 127, 151, 164, 166

Early vision 133, 134
Ekman, Paul 134
Ellsworth, Phoebe 145
Emotions
– Basic emotions 44, 135, 159, 160
– Core relational themes 72
– Emotional episodes 69, 90, 145–147, 149, 157–159, 162
– Emotional states 8, 15, 17, 18, 21, 23, 25, 26, 28, 29, 35, 51, 57, 65, 68, 71, 72, 81, 128, 139, 147
– Felt emotions 4, 18–21, 30, 32, 37, 39–42, 46, 55, 57, 65–67, 70, 73, 78, 85, 89, 102, 160, 164
– Folk notion 8, 146, 149
– Intentional mode 69
– Meta-emotions 141, 156–162
– Phenomenal skeleton 51–53, 90, 93, 94
– Somatic theories 68, 72
Emotion-characteristic-in-appearance 149, 150
Empathy 2, 63, 64
Enactivism 77, 78, 80, 115
Ernst, Marc 135
Evaluative properties 68–70, 72, 73

Evolutionary explanations 42, 43
Expression
– Emotional expressions 5–7, 18, 31, 36, 38, 43–45, 48, 74, 75, 100, 128, 132, 134, 135, 137, 138, 140, 141, 158, 160
– Expression theory 16, 17, 20
– Facial expressions 18, 41, 44, 135, 136, 138, 145, 168, 170
– Human expressions 5, 31, 34, 36, 38, 44, 45, 53, 56, 65, 101, 111, 131, 140, 171
Expressiveness
– Expressive ascriptions 15, 17, 65, 98, 117, 155, 167, 170
– Expressive behaviours 40, 42, 43, 52–54, 57, 77, 82, 91, 101, 105, 110, 112, 138, 139, 141, 142, 149
– Expressive experience 3–7, 13, 21–23, 25, 28–31, 33, 35–37, 39, 40, 42, 43, 45, 46, 48–53, 55–83, 85–123, 126, 128, 129, 132–134, 137–141, 143, 150, 156, 157, 159–164, 166–172
– Expressive perception 28, 29, 49, 58, 59, 88, 93, 159
– Expressive properties 4–6, 21, 29–32, 37, 45, 49–51, 53, 56, 59, 63, 64, 74, 80, 85–90, 94–98, 100, 107, 112, 118, 124, 127, 129, 131, 138, 140, 143, 144, 151, 159, 160, 167

Fabrice, Teroni 69
Family resemblances 146–150, 162
Fazzuoli, Giovanna 80
Feelings 4, 7, 8, 10, 12, 16, 17, 25–27, 30–35, 39–41, 45, 58, 59, 63–73, 92, 99, 101, 102, 143–145, 147, 149, 155, 157–159, 163, 165, 169
Fodor, Jerry 108, 134
Forlé, Francesca 75, 77–79, 115
Freedberg, David 80
Frijda, Nico 145

Gallagher, Shaun 136
Gallese, Vittorio 80
Gardner, Sebastian 71
Gauker, Christopher 122
Geiger, Moritz 63

Gendler, Tamar 106
Gestalt 2, 42, 114, 116, 166
Gibson, James 2
Giomo, Carla 161, 170
Goerlich, Katharina 170
Goldman, Alvin 93
Gombrich, Ernst 62
Goodman, Nelson 124–126
Gregory, Currie 2, 64
Griffero, Tonino 3
Gross, Steven 138, 139
Grouping properties 110, 115, 117

Harmonic 116, 117
Heal, Jane 93
Hearing-as 45, 46
Heaton, Pamela 170
Heresy of the separable experiences 5, 33, 85, 97–112, 118, 130, 140
Hevner, Kate 111, 166

Ichikawa, Jonathan 106
Illusions
– Hering Illusion 11
– Müller-Lyer Illusion 11–12
Imagination
– Imaginative engagement 48, 53, 55, 74, 85, 90, 139
– Imaginative project 51–53, 61, 104, 106
– Mental imagery 50, 59, 60, 106–108, 136
– Propositional imagination 46, 50, 57, 72, 139
– Sensuous Imagination 5, 50, 51, 58, 59, 88–90, 93, 94, 106, 171
Imaginative theories 44–54, 94
Immediacy 46, 50, 51, 57–60
Inanimate objects 1, 3, 7, 8, 10, 15, 18, 19, 22, 25, 26, 30–32, 37, 43, 45, 53, 63, 64, 92, 103, 123, 126, 138, 171
Ineffabilist view 124
Intentional object 34, 68–70, 72, 93, 97, 144, 145, 157
Isomorphism 104, 105, 106, 108, 110, 111, 119, 120, 129, 130, 141, 142, 159, 164, 171
Izard, Carroll 144

Jacob, Pierre 136
Jagnow, René 62, 109
James, William 67
Jastrow's figure 110
Judgement 9, 10, 12–15, 17, 26, 34, 35, 67, 71, 92, 98, 127, 128, 130, 131, 133, 136
Juslin, Patrik 118, 161
Justifications 96, 98, 103, 131, 139, 149

Kandinsky, Wassily 2, 31
Kivy, Peter 18, 20, 32, 35, 38–44, 55–57, 81, 82, 96, 99, 108, 111, 112, 118, 162
Kriegel, Uriah 22, 69
Krueger, Joel 77–79, 136
Kurt, Koffka 2, 114

Lakoff, George 130
Landscape 1, 7–9, 12–15, 21, 25, 32, 50, 59, 61, 71, 81, 91, 108, 138, 155, 171
Language games 21, 147–149, 152, 153
Late vision 134
Lazarus, Richard 72, 145
Levinson, Jerrold 44–54, 56, 57, 59, 60, 66, 74, 87, 104, 108, 137
Lindauer, Martin 142
Lipps, Theodor 2, 63, 64
Literal application 125–127, 138, 152
Loar, Brian 92, 111
Look 12–15, 18, 21, 23–25, 28–30, 33, 35, 41, 54, 56, 76, 82, 87, 89, 91, 92, 95, 98, 101, 102, 103, 107, 110, 112, 115, 118, 120, 122, 126, 146, 149, 163
Lopes, Dominc 16, 17, 47, 48, 56
Low-level features 160, 165, 166, 168, 169
Lundholm, Helge 166
Lupyan, Gary 138
Lutz, Anika 69

MacPherson, Fiona 11, 106, 133, 138
Manipulability 60, 62
Mapping 103–108, 111, 119, 125, 141
Marchi, Francesco 135, 136, 168
Marr, David 134
Martin, Michael 121
Matravers, Derek 31–38, 53, 63, 71, 97, 98
Meini, Cristina 43

Melisma 36, 38, 57, 65, 74
Melismatic gestures 36, 65, 74, 116
Meltzoff, Andrew 93, 94
Memories 27, 29, 30, 32, 53, 58, 91, 92, 99, 107, 121, 142
Memory 53, 91, 107, 121
Mendelovici, Angela 69
Mental states 21, 22, 40, 52, 60, 68, 69, 87, 93, 94, 101, 102, 105, 107, 124, 128, 130, 136, 148–150, 153, 162
Metaphors
– Metaphorical application 125, 131, 140, 154, 156
– Metaphorical concept 129, 137–140
– Metaphorical content 104, 105, 130, 131
– Metaphorical possession 124, 125
Moods 16, 23, 141, 142, 157, 158, 162
Moors, Agnes 145
Moriya, Jun 106
Morley, Iain 43, 76
Movement 5, 17, 36, 38, 39, 47, 55, 57, 59, 64, 67, 74–79, 83, 85, 93, 98, 102, 113, 115, 118, 128, 129, 168
Multi-stable figures 61
Murray, David 166
Music 1, 4, 5–7, 15, 17, 19, 21, 29, 31–53, 55–57, 59, 60, 63, 65–67, 70, 71, 73–83, 85, 88–90, 92, 93, 95–101, 103–108, 110–120, 122–124, 127–130, 132, 137–139, 141–143, 150, 155, 159, 161, 165, 166, 168–170
Musical gestures 5, 6, 36, 59, 74, 79, 80, 83, 85, 101, 103–108, 110, 111, 118, 119, 122, 137–139, 141, 142, 150, 162, 167, 169, 172
Musical pieces 36, 59, 77

Nanay, Bence 59, 62, 106, 107
Newen, Albert 68, 72, 135, 136, 144, 146–148, 168
Noë, Alva 78
Non-literal application 124, 126
Noordhof, Paul 5, 21, 40, 42–54, 58–60, 63, 64, 66, 74, 85, 87–96, 99, 100, 103, 106, 108, 137
Notes 20, 38, 39, 45, 49, 54, 72, 74–77, 82, 94, 116, 125, 127, 142, 147, 161

O'Shaughnessy, Brian 109
Osgood, Charles 166

Paintings 1, 2, 8, 9, 15, 17, 18, 32, 48, 49, 51, 52, 56, 61, 75, 79–81, 87, 91–93, 106, 108, 110, 113–115, 118, 123, 125, 127, 129
Papoušek, Harmš 43
Parovel, Giulia 2
Parsons, Kathryn 148, 149
Pathetic fallacy 3, 9–16, 21, 23, 25, 53
Pattern 18, 36, 38, 42, 43, 49, 61, 62, 65, 66, 74–78, 81, 91, 96, 101, 102, 109, 110, 113–119, 122, 129, 132, 135–140, 142–150, 162, 167–172
Pavlova, Marina 168
Peacocke, Christopher 5, 6, 103–105, 107, 108–111, 119, 120, 129, 130, 137, 140–143, 157, 159, 163, 164
Perani, Daniela 168
Perception
– Perceptual experiences 4, 5, 15, 21, 23, 28, 33, 38, 46, 50, 51, 55–62, 69, 79–81, 85, 87–89, 100, 107, 109, 113, 114, 116, 121, 133, 134, 136–138, 140, 143, 163, 167, 170
– Perceptual /perceivable features 3, 18, 24, 30, 33, 34, 36, 39, 42, 45, 46, 49–52, 57, 59, 64, 81, 87, 89, 91, 92, 94, 95, 99, 115, 117, 164–169
– Perceptual/perceivable structure of music 36, 39, 41, 57, 90, 96, 98, 104, 118, 144
– Merely perceptual properties 29, 45, 95
Pérez-Carreño, Francisca 28, 92
Perky, Cheves 107
Persona
– Persona theory 44, 46, 47, 50, 52, 71, 90
Phenomenal character 3, 4, 6, 21, 22, 25, 28, 30, 32–34, 42, 44, 46, 48, 51, 52, 55, 56–59, 62–83, 85, 87, 99, 100, 103, 105, 107, 111, 114, 119, 123, 134, 136–140, 156, 161–163, 167–169, 171
Philips, Clare 106
Physiognomy 2, 153
Piana, Giovanni 75–77, 79, 115, 116
Picasso, Pablo 106

Pitches 39, 49, 54, 62, 111, 112, 116, 117, 165
Pollock, Jackson 48, 49, 79
Pratt, Carroll 39, 143
Prinz, Jesse 67, 68, 72, 144
Profiles 38, 39, 41, 42, 56, 57, 74, 77, 90, 95, 96, 103
Projectivism
– Projection 13, 25–30, 34, 53, 64, 92, 94, 99, 143, 171
– Projective properties 25–27, 30
Putnam, Hilary 148
Pylyshyn, Zenon 133, 134

Quasi-metaphors 132, 150–156

Raftopoulos, Athanassios 109
Rationality 10–13
Ravasio, Matteo 43
Recognitional experience 80, 101, 110, 119–122, 128, 131, 132, 136, 137, 139, 140
Representationalism 5, 85, 86
Resemblances 5, 36, 38–44, 54, 56, 57, 77, 81–83, 90, 96, 98, 100–105, 111, 112, 119–144, 146–151, 154–156, 162, 164–167, 169, 172
Response-dependence 5, 87–95, 140, 169
Rhythm 29, 38, 39, 45, 49, 59, 62, 76–78, 82, 115, 140
Richardson, Alan 106
Ridley, Aaron 31–38, 56, 65–67, 71, 73, 74, 98, 143, 160
Robinson, Jenefer 8, 18–20, 22, 31–38, 41, 46, 48, 56, 65–67, 70–73, 78, 144
Roederer, Juan 43
Rothko, Mark 32, 48
Ruskin, John 9, 10, 12–14
Russell, James 135, 141, 145–147, 149, 157–160
Rythmos 6, 115–118, 166, 169

Santayana, George 9–14, 16
Sartre, Jean-Paul 4, 23–30, 171
Scherer, Klaus 144–146
Schiavio, Andrea 78
Schmitz, Hermann 3

Scruton, Roger 128–130, 155
Secondary meaning 6, 141–170
Seeing-as 5, 61, 101–104, 108–110, 115, 137
Semantic coherence 133
Sentient being 8, 31, 37, 53, 160
Shape 1, 2, 5, 12, 15, 24, 37, 49–51, 54, 56–59, 61, 62, 64, 78, 86, 90, 97, 103, 110, 112, 114, 116, 124, 129, 134, 136–140, 143, 160, 162, 165–168, 170
Sibley, Frank 132, 150–154
Siegel, Susanna 86
Simmel, Georg 2
Simple features 81, 82, 112, 113, 117, 163, 164, 166–168
Simulation 5, 63, 64, 80, 85, 90–96, 106
Smith, Craig 145
Smortchkova, Joulia 136, 168
Sounds 1, 5, 6, 8, 11, 12, 33, 36, 38, 39, 43, 45, 50–52, 55, 56, 58, 59, 62, 71, 75, 77, 81–83, 86, 92, 97, 102, 104, 105, 112, 114, 116–118, 129, 130, 137, 142, 143, 149, 150, 160, 163, 169
Spelke, Elizabeth 168
Spinicci, Paolo 160, 161
Stamatopoulou, Despina 166
Stecker, Robert 144
Stefanucci, Jeanine 23
Stokes, Dustin 133
Sub-personal level 104
Sub-personal mechanisms 82, 99

Tempo 17, 29, 77
Temporality 74–77, 80, 82, 85, 115
Tertiary qualities 10

Thesis of the Inanimate Objects' Expressiveness (IOE) 8–10, 19, 53
Time 6–10, 14, 18, 19, 23, 26, 27, 30, 35, 36, 38, 42, 47, 50, 53, 55, 62, 65, 74–77, 80, 82, 101–103, 108, 111, 116, 118, 119, 121, 122, 125, 126, 133, 140, 146, 157, 158
Tormey, Alan 3, 16–20, 41
Trivedi, Saam 39, 40, 43, 143
Tye, Michael 60, 109

Umiltà, Alessandra 80

Valence 6, 159, 161, 166
Van Gogh 17, 67
Visualisation 50
Vividness 50, 51, 58–60, 62
Voice 26, 38, 42, 102, 150
Voltolini, Alberto 62, 109, 110, 115, 133, 138
Von Ehrenfels, Christian 2

Wagner, Richard 29
Walton, Kendall 2, 46, 63, 64, 66, 80
Weeping willow 5, 85, 100–103, 105, 119
Wertheimer, Max 2, 114
Wexner, Lois 166
Wittgenstein, Ludwig 62, 109, 110, 147, 149, 152–156, 162, 164, 166
Wolfgang, Köhler 2, 114, 167
Wollheim, Richard 4, 23–30, 33, 53, 60, 62, 91–93, 95, 143, 171
Wright, Benjamin 166

Zahavi, Dan 136
Zangwill, Nick 123–126, 144
Zhok, Andrea 115, 116

www.ingramcontent.com/pod-product-compliance
Lightning Source LLC
Chambersburg PA
CBHW020331170426
43200CB00006B/344